Working Capital:
The Power of Labor's Pensions

Working Capital:
The Power of Labor's Pensions

Edited by

Archon Fung, Tessa Hebb,
and Joel Rogers

With a foreword by

Leo W. Gerard, International President,
United Steelworkers of America,
AFL-CIO • CLC

ILR Press

an imprint of

Cornell University Press

Ithaca and London

First published 2001 by Cornell University Press

Printed in the United States of America

Library of Congress Cataloging-in-Publication Data

Working capital : the power of labor's pensions / edited by Archon
Fung, Tessa Hebb, and Joel Rogers.
    p. cm.
Includes bibliographical references and index.
  ISBN 0-8014-3901-9 (cloth : alk. paper)
  1. Pension trusts--Investments--United States. 2. Labor
unions--United States. I. Fung, Archon, 1968- II. Hebb, Tessa. III.
Rogers, Joel, 1952-
    HD7105.45.U6 W67 2001
    332.67'254--dc21

        2001000197

Cornell University Press strives to use environmentally responsible suppliers and materials to the fullest extent possible in the publishing of its books. Such materials include vegetable-based, low-VOC inks and acid-free papers that are recycled, totally chlorine-free, or partly composed of non-wood fibers. Books that bear the logo of the FSC (Forest Stewardship Council) use paper taken from forests that have been inspected and certified as meeting the highest standards for environmental and social responsibility. For further information, visit our website at
www.cornellpress.cornell.edu.

Cloth printing   10 9 8 7 6 5 4 3 2 1

CONTENTS

Contents

FOREWORD

The use of workers' capital is one of the key challenges facing the labor movement today. Our deferred wages underpin capital markets in the United States
and around the world. Although we have paper ownership of $7 trillion of
deferred wages in the form of U.S. pension fund assets, this fact has not altered
financial market operations in any significant way. All too often, investments
made with our savings yield short-term gains at the expense of working
Americans and their families. Destructive investment practices that rely on
layoffs, mergers and acquisitions, plant closures, and off-shore job flight can
create quick profits and short-term stock price increases, but, over time, these
management practices erode America's wealth. The challenge for labor is to
find ways that align workers' savings with workers' values. We need to invest
our deferred wages in companies that provide good jobs in stable, strong
communities. We want to reward companies that value all the stake-holders
in the enterprise, not just their shareholders. Our capital is patient and long
term, and our challenge is to develop a capital strategy that moves our savings
beyond the quick saccharine highs of destructive corporate behavior.

In 1995, I embarked on what should have been a relatively simple task to
raise approximately $5 million for the modernization and expansion of a small
but productive steel plant in my home state of Pennsylvania. Given the billions of dollars flowing from pension funds into risky ventures in emerging
markets, I thought it would be easy to find $5 million for investment in a solid
U.S. company, generating a good rate of return. It wasn't.

I found others equally concerned that the current operation of financial
markets undermined the very workers whose savings they deploy. We met as

a "grievance committee," and our grievance was simple: financial markets are cutting our throats with our own money, and it has to stop.

We called ourselves the Heartland Labor Capital Project and began to promote an aggressive agenda to push capital strategies inside and outside the labor movement. We wanted to raise awareness with labor's pension fund trustees that there were investment options beyond those currently being offered, and we wanted to put money managers on alert that we were looking more closely at the manner in which they handled our retirement savings. We moved forward with the support of the United Steelworkers of America and the American Federation of Labor-Congress of Industrial Organizations (AFL-CIO), for whom the use of labor's capital is of paramount concern.

This research volume is drawn from the Second National Heartland Labor Capital Conference held in 1999. I congratulate the authors for their hard work, insights, and research, documenting the problems inherent in today's financial management and offering solutions to advance labor's capital strategy. This important work confronts traditional money management. It offers new and exciting models in the United States and Canada that advance not only ownership of labor's capital but also its control. The result is a set of steps that use labor's power as owners of capital to advance its goals.

Power never shifts without a struggle. This book challenges those with power by equipping those who confront the orthodoxy of today's financial markets. This volume helps define an important agenda for labor.

— *Leo W. Gerard*
International President, United Steelworkers of America

ACKNOWLEDGMENTS

In 1996, Leo W. Gerard, then Secretary-Treasurer of the United Steelworkers of America (USWA), asked a few people to join him in the USWA boardroom in Pittsburgh to discuss the pension fund investment policies of various unions and state governments, and the possible creation of an investment fund. The response to his request from individuals across the labor movement, government, and academia was immediate. This group's discussions and concerns about current money management practices gave birth to the Heartland Labor Capital Project. Its purpose was to increase the control of working people over their pension funds.

This book is the direct result of the work of the Heartland Labor Capital Project and its sponsors—the USWA and the Pittsburgh-based Steel Valley Authority. These two organizations are creating conceptual, financial, and educational tools for capital strategies that will advance labor's agenda in the twenty-first century.

Although space prohibits a comprehensive listing, the editors would like to thank many of the individuals who have contributed to this project since 1996. Most important, we thank Leo W. Gerard, International President of the USWA, for his ongoing support and encouragement of the Heartland Labor Capital Project, including the writing of this volume, and for his tireless advocacy around these critical issues.

We also want to thank Tom Croft, the Executive Director of the Steel Valley Authority and Director of the Heartland Labor Capital Project, and Kim Arthur Siegfried, Assistant to the International President of USWA, for their determination not only to advance the Heartland Labor Capital Project, but also to develop broader solutions to enable labor to control its capital.

In addition, we would like to thank the foundations and their program officers whose support of the Heartland Labor Capital Project from 1997 to 1999 made the research and writing of this volume possible: Ford Foundation and Lance Lindblom, Rockefeller Foundation and Katherine McFate, Mott Foundation and Jack Litzenburg, McKay Foundation and Rob McKay, Unitarian Universalist Veatch Fund and Victor Quintana, the United Church of Christ, and Pennsylvania State Senator Jay Costa.

We would also like to acknowledge the support of the other major sponsor of the Heartland Labor Capital Conferences, the American Federation of Labor-Congress of Industrial Organizations (AFL-CIO) and its Center for Working Capital. In particular, Monte Tarbox, Executive Director of the Center for Working Capital; Ron Blackwell, Director of the AFL-CIO Corporate Affairs Department; and Bill Patterson of the AFL-CIO Office of Investment assisted generously in the development of this volume.

The Heartland Labor Capital Project convened two major national conferences, each with a series of research papers for discussion. The first, held in 1996, focused on the issue of overcoming capital gaps and promoting "high performance" companies. Much of the work from this earlier conference provided a base of research on which this book's more detailed studies are built. Early in 1998, we held crucial colloquia to discuss the central topics that dominate labor's capital strategies and the use of economically targeted investments by pension fund fiduciaries. The themes we explored focused on capital markets, legal requirements, and responsible investing. We would like to thank all the individuals who gave freely of their time to attend these colloquia. From that rich discussion we developed the research agenda for this volume.

Working Capital: The Power of Labor's Pensions is drawn from work presented to the Second National Heartland Labor Capital Conference held in Washington, D.C., in 1999. We would like to thank all the individuals who participated in this conference as well.

We would like to thank Kate Thorne for the many hours of technical help in preparing the manuscript for publication and Fran Benson of Cornell University Press for her invaluable assistance and support of this project.

All books are labors of love, but the immeasurable contributions of those who live with us are seldom recognized. The final thanks, therefore, goes to each of our families. Their support made this work possible.

[x]

Working Capital:
The Power of Labor's Pensions

[I]

INTRODUCTION:
THE CHALLENGE OF
LABOR'S CAPITAL STRATEGY

Tessa Hebb

At $7 trillion (Anand 1998), pension funds are the primary drivers of today's financial markets in the United States and around the world. The earnings that workers defer for a secure retirement inform financial decisions that, in turn, determine the quality of employment and the character of goods and services they enjoy. Yet the institutions and individuals that manage pension funds often pursue narrow goals whose consequences undermine workers who provide the savings they tend. Can workers' long-term interests be aligned with those of financial managers, or must labor and capital oppose one another even in the use of *labor's* capital? Can workers' interests be considered on a par with the interests of those who hold financial shares in enterprises? This book presents an array of contemporary projects and promising strategies that aim toward a new financial paradigm that unleashes the power of pension fund capital and harnesses it to advance the interests of all stake-holders in the economy in equal measure.

First and foremost, this new paradigm requires widespread awareness and knowledge of the profound effects of pension funds. When these modern instruments were first bargained in the 1950s, no one foresaw the enormous influence they would yield by the beginning of the twenty-first century. In an article written in late 1999, Robert Reich examined institutions that were fading in importance versus institutions that were growing. Along with giant corporations, the federal government, and the military-industrial complex, he listed trade unions as groups in eclipse. Pension funds, however, were prominent members of the group with rising power. Although Reich's portrayal arouses controversy, it juxtaposes two forms of collective action through which workers build quality lives for themselves and their families. Whereas the successes of trade unions are a matter of historical record, the potential of pension funds remains largely untapped.

Trade unions allow workers to act in concert in the labor market, tilting the balance of power in an enterprise toward its employees and away from its owners. In the resulting bargains, workers gain, among other benefits, higher wages, a more equitable distribution of income, and better working conditions than they could have secured by acting individually. Yet what happens when workers become owners? Through the rise of institutional investment and the explosive growth of pension funds, much of the industrialized economy is, in a way, already owned by workers.

U.S. capital markets are presently financed by $7 trillion of workers' pension fund savings. This pool of assets represents the largest single source of capital in the world. We have witnessed an explosive growth in pension funds in each decade since the 1950s, when private pensions spread through many sectors of the economy. During the 1980s and 1990s alone, this capital pool has grown by 400 percent (Ghilarducci, chap. 7). Pension funds today own 45 percent of all publicly traded equity in the United States, but this fact of ownership has little impact on the practices of money managers or the operations of capital markets. By and large, the source of capital has little bearing on its deployment across investment opportunities. Thus, the fundamental shift in the ownership of capital has not resulted in a corresponding shift in the control of capital.

As early as 1978, in their book *The North Shall Rise Again*, Randy Barber and Jeremy Rifkin recognized both the danger and the opportunity that the growth of these enormous capital pools presented to working people and their representatives. Yet, instead of strategies that allow working people to take greater control of their savings to create long-term wealth, the opposite has happened. During the 1980s and 1990s, narrow and often myopic money management practices have become ascendant in the United States. These habits are fueled by rapt attention to daily valuations in stock markets. Quarterly earnings announcements that signal even fractional changes in expected profits drive large swings in share prices.

The idea that shareholders reign dominates corporate and capital market activity. According to this doctrine, short-term increases in stock valuation justify such forms of distress as closing otherwise productive facilities, shifting work to lower-wage or less regulated regions, and selling off pieces of coherent business complexes.

A capital strategy for labor aims to inject workers' welfare, broadly understood, into investment priorities. Pension fund trustees are the guardians of workers' interests, and their primary loyalty is to the beneficiaries of each fund. This text does not threaten the principle of pension fund management. Rather, it suggests that pension fund trustees and money managers should rethink how they can meaningfully pursue the long-term interest of plan beneficiaries.

Worker-Owner View

A multidimensional understanding of financial practices that advance a long-term interest constitutes a distinctive worker-owner view of investment. The chapters that follow explore components of a worker-owner view. Its most important objective is to maximize long-term market rates of return to ensure adequate retirement payments for workers. In this regard, the worker-owner view does not differ from conventional investment priorities. In particular, below-market-rate investments, sometimes called *social investments*, undermine individuals' retirement security.

Yet the worker-owner view departs from conventional investment wisdom by expanding the options, methods, and principles that guide capital allocation decisions. Capital markets are neither perfectly efficient nor value free. Therefore, those who seek to advance the long-term interest of workers inside financial markets must look beyond both the array of choices these markets presently offer and the narrow band of information they provide through price signals. Alternative investment practices and vehicles can better reward all the stake-holders in an enterprise (workers, shareholders, communities, customers, and the environment) to create wealth in the long term.

Pension funds can advance a larger social agenda reaching beyond simple individual returns. Thus, the worker-owner view is not value free, but neither are the institutions that currently control these funds. To hold, as many money managers do, that the quality of capital allocation depends solely on its risk and return profile—and thus that impacts on workers, the environment, and communities need not be directly considered—is not to be unburdened by values. Rather, it is to advance one particular value, the risk-adjusted rate of return, above all others. To claim that either this position advances no agenda, or that all parties will eventually be well served by it, simply appeals to orthodoxy that discourages debate and reduces transparency.

In chap. 2, Dean Baker and Archon Fung lay the groundwork for a worker-owner view by reviewing inefficiencies and systematic negative consequences of contemporary financial market operation. Just as carefully targeted investments can yield collateral benefits beyond monetary rates of return, contemporary financial transactions can result in collateral damage. For example, myopic choices in rapid stock turnover and leveraged buyouts can purchase short-term gains at the price of long-term losses. Other examples of collateral damage include the cost of operating financial markets, which accounts for an ever-larger share of the economy, and compensation to corporate executives that far outpaces their contributions to productivity and the wages of their workers.

Patterns of institutional investment illustrate the myopic choices pension fund managers often engage in. The share of U.S. stocks owned by institutional investors has grown dramatically, from 34 percent to 45 percent of the total equity market between 1980 and 1998. Simultaneously, these investors have increased the rate at which they trade their stocks. Known as *churning*, short-term trading has grown to the extent that 40 percent of the average institutional investor's portfolio turns over annually; these large investors account for 74 percent of all trading activity in the market. The short-term focus of investors causes some firms to attempt to increase their immediate appeal by de-emphasizing areas that enhance long-term productivity and growth, such as firm-based research and development, training and education of employees, and environmental safeguards. A preoccupation with short-term returns can also induce destructive behavior, such as corporate downsizing, overseas job flight, employee layoffs, and mergers and acquisitions. Although such practices give rise to short-term increases in stock price, some research shows that the majority of firms that undertake these activities lose value over the long run (Mercer 1998).

A worker–owner investment perspective stresses the importance of sustainable economic growth and the equitable distribution of the benefits of that growth. For example, taxes on stock churning, common in the securities regulations of many countries but not the United States, discourage speculation in favor of internal investments that contribute to long-term expansion and competitiveness.

Current Labor Capital Strategies

Whereas chap. 2 describes some of the harms arising from mainstream market operations, the next four chapters describe contemporary financial strategies within and outside the labor movement that deliberately use capital markets to secure collateral benefits for workers, communities, other stakeholders, and the environment.

In chap. 3, Eric Becker and Patrick McVeigh describe the rise of so-called institutionally responsible investing vehicles. Since the anti-Apartheid movement and even before it, arrays of mutual funds have attempted to attract ethically sensitive investors. These funds commonly offer screens, which ensure that money will not finance particular kinds of firms, such as those that produce tobacco, alcohol, or armaments; harm the environment; or have poor labor practices. Increasingly, these funds are also pursuing actions, such as proxy voting, to influence the behavior of managers. Becker and McVeigh document the explosive growth of responsible investing in the United States. According to one estimate, $1.00 in $8.00 invested in the United States in 1998—$2.2 trillion—used socially responsible vehicles.

The performance record of socially responsible funds compares favorably to other instruments in their various asset classes. The success of these screened investment funds contradicts a common contention of traditional money managers that any consideration beyond risk and return erodes wealth. As a model, socially responsible investing demonstrates success with individual and institutional investors who choose to invest their savings in a manner that reflects their values.

One criticism of socially responsible investing through screened mutual funds, however, is that concerns central to workers, such as workplace health and safety, compensation, training opportunities, and the quality of relations between labor and management, are pressed much less frequently than such issues as environmental impact or the harm caused by particular products. Consequently, many firms that do not advance worker-owner interests are included within these screens, while other "high-performance" workplaces may be excluded.

Beyond this, some contend that these screening practices have little real impact on actual firm practices. In particular cases, managers seem more sensitive to threats of divestment and negative publicity than to the actual divestment of a company's stock, which seldom lowers its price. *Screening*, which is the preemptive avoidance of particular firms, would seem weaker still in its ability to compel more socially responsible behavior. Thus, screened funds might reward "good" firms while doing little to change the behavior of "bad" ones.

Moving from avoidance to activism and from exit to voice, Marleen O'Connor in chap. 4 examines shareholder strategies, such as proxy voting, as tools for changing the behavior of large corporations (Hirschman 1970). Echoing Reich's notion of areas of institutional rise and decline, she suggests that labor's capital and "corporate governance rights will trump labor laws in importance, and shareholder rights will constitute a new focal point for labor relations in the

United States in the twenty-first century." Although its ultimate potential remains to be seen, O'Connor leaves no doubt that shareholder activism has emerged as a powerful instrument to advance the worker-owner agenda.

Increasingly, workers find that their ability to influence management comes through their position as company shareholders rather than as workers. O'Connor examines the extent to which labor-shareholder activists can further their interests within the framework of the shareholder-dominated corporation. She finds that many of the accomplishments of labor-shareholder activism are political rather than economic, and that they carry union credibility in the face of declining union membership and bargaining power. They have injected labor priorities into corporate governance agendas around issues such as training, executive compensation, and the creation of sustainable shareholder value through high-performance workplace practices. Labor's shareholder activism promotes efforts in establishing standards by which to measure and disclose corporations' human resource values. There is an implicit aligning of interest when workers become owners. The result is usually increased transparency, stronger corporate governance, and greater accountability on the part of management.

As a central worker-owner strategy, pension funds forge alliances with other shareholders to advance the long-term health and viability of enterprises. One potential pitfall of this path, however, is that it may reinforce the shareholder mantra that raises the interests of shareholders above all others.

Direct investment in the economy through fund operation and management offers a third contemporary strategy for labor's capital. In chap. 5, Michael Calabrese reviews the history of organized labor with respect to operating such funds, ranging from large commercial and residential funds that support union-built construction to more recently established funds that specialize in private equity. The chapter inventories more than two dozen funds, spanning nearly every asset class, that offer socially responsible and competitive investment opportunities for pension fund trustees.

These funds aim to generate collateral benefits and to yield market-based rates of return. Such investment approaches have a double bottom line, generating not only conventional returns but also additional benefits for stakeholders, such as more secure or better-paying jobs, increased employment, affordable housing, well-funded pension plans, and reduced environmental degradation. Collateral benefits include enhanced workplace cooperation leading to increased productivity or the delivery of products and services that might not otherwise occur without some intervention to correct a capital market failure.

Those who object to economically targeted investing argue that collateral benefits are not without cost and, in particular, that they reduce residual value that otherwise could have been claimed by shareholders. Given that shareholder value is the paramount fiduciary duty of any pension fund trustee, this view means that any investment that delivers a collateral benefit must be rejected out of hand (Langbein 1985; Romano 1993; Saxton 1995; M. Levine 1997). Calabrese's review of investment returns over time demonstrates that economically targeted investing can and does deliver competitive returns while generating a range of collateral benefits. Inefficiencies and gaps in financial markets, arising in part from costly and asymmetric information, make this combination possible. For example, research has shown that quite productive small and medium-sized private companies that provide good jobs and sustain healthy communities find it difficult to obtain capital in the United States (Carey 1993). Sometimes called the *critical middle*, these firms are typically single-plant operations that have between $5 million and $100 million in annual sales. Such firms cross every strategic manufacturing sector and employ more than half of the manufacturing workforce in the United States (Bute 1996).

The small and private nature of these firms gives rise to information asymmetries that prevent resources from being invested in the sector. Simply defined, *information asymmetry* means that one party in the exchange, either the buyer or the seller, has more information about the investment. In the case of capital gaps or capital failures in the economy, the seller knows more about the investment. As a result, this imbalance of knowledge causes the buyer to be cautious; the buyer might withdraw from the exchange if he or she is unable to verify the claims of the seller or demand a higher risk premium for the investment to offset uncertainty. This lack of knowledge on the part of potential investors raises the cost of capital for small and medium-sized enterprises. As the cost of capital determines whether the enterprise is productive, capital gaps drive many small and medium-sized firms away from competitive growth and expansion. Because investment capital is unavailable at an appropriate market price, many otherwise productive firms in the economy fail.

Privately owned small and medium-sized enterprises are more subject to this capital market failure than large public enterprises that can rely on substantial retained earnings or raise capital from selling public shares on open markets. When investors use traditional markets for equity and debt purchases, they rely on information obtained in public filings combined with due diligence of market analysts and credit/bond rating firms to provide them with adequate information by which to judge the investment. No such rating agencies exist for small and medium-sized firms seeking equity or private placement debt. Unlike public offerings, private placement debt and equity investments do not require public filings with the U.S. Securities and Exchange Commission (SEC). Thus, the need of lenders and investors to seek their own information significantly raises due diligence and monitoring costs.

The limited size of investment that small and medium-sized firms usually require further aggravates capital gaps in the economy. Traditional money managers are often uninterested in this sector, regardless of its competitive rates of return. Institutional investors look for large-scale investment to warrant the increased information and monitoring costs they face. Given that the average private placement debt investment is $32 million, whereas the average public bond issue is $150 million, firms looking for equity or debt capital under $10 million find little interest from buyers for such small-scale investments.

Two other sources of gaps in financing stem from location and labor organization. Some regions of the country, in particular venture capital-rich nodes on the East and West coasts of the United States, have large investment pools for private placements, whereas many other regions lack both the funds and the expertise to make such investments. Beyond this, some research shows that the presence of a unionized workforce can drive potential investors away, thus creating an unwarranted capital gap.

To overcome the information barriers that cause capital gaps, institutional investors must create investment vehicles with unique characteristics and expertise that allow for the reduction of risk and uncertainty. Calabrese finds that many alternative investment fund managers associated with worker-owners have access to information unavailable to mainstream investors and can better monitor these investments. This comparative advantage stems in part from the relationship between investment vehicle sponsors and workers in the enterprise. Not only do worker-owner vehicles lessen the transaction cost of the investment, but they also create a market niche by undertaking smaller-sized investments in which information costs are high. The value worker-owners place on the role of the critical-middle manufacturing and building sector of the economy adds to their willingness to make these investments.

Calabrese examines pooled economically targeted investment (ETI) vehicles that span almost every asset category in the United States. Their rates of return measure favorably against industry benchmarks, and their success suggests a few best practices and priorities for others: the commingling of funds to accumulate substantial assets; the importance of independent and professional management; and geographic diversification with reciprocal partnerships with other funds.

However, union-based investment vehicles do not automatically advance a worker-owner agenda unless they are designed or mandated to do so. In a study that offers important comparative lessons for investors in the United States and elsewhere, Hebb and Mackenzie examine the experience of several types of Canadian Labour Sponsored Investment Funds (LSIFs). LSIFs provide venture capital to the Canadian economy through pooled individual retirement savings. These funds are sponsored, and in many cases controlled, by labor bodies. The best of these funds mobilize workers' savings to invest in good jobs within local communities, basing their investment strategy on a broad social agenda that promotes worker participation, training, and respect for stakeholders beyond those holding shares. The results pay off both in returns to the funds' unit holders and within the economy as a whole.

The issue of extending the role of trade unions beyond simple ownership to one of genuine control is part of a broader legislative framework. LSIFs control more than 50 percent of the available venture capital in Canada. In a country that historically lacked sufficient venture capital, individual savers are encouraged to invest in the program through a generous government tax credit, 30 percent of annual contributions up to a maximum of $5,000. In four of the five Canadian provinces that have established funds under provincial legislation, a sole trade union body was named in each provincial act as the sponsor of the fund. In these cases, labor control of the fund, through both its board structure and its investment policies, is clearly spelled out in the legislation. In addition, the legislative framework also defines the collateral benefits to be derived from fund investment activity.

In the fifth province, Ontario, the legislation did not name the labor body that was to act as the fund sponsor, nor did it indicate a broad range of social and economic objectives for the funds beyond filling the venture capital gap within the province. As a result, fifteen of the twenty-one LSIFs in Canada are incorporated under Ontario legislation. Sponsorship ranges from small professional sports associations to large trade unions. Many of these sponsors are paid a fee by professional money managers who initiate and control the LSIF and its investment decisions with no distinctive social objectives. When the legislative framework of LSIFs lacks such goals, the funds created within it do not voluntarily adopt them.

Hebb and Mackenzie's examination of Canadian LSIFs, which are considered by many to be an international model of how labor can directly generate and use capital for regional revitalization, highlights the challenge of extending labor's capital strategy from ownership of capital to genuine control over investment decision making.

Realizing the Potential of Labor's Capital Strategies

Having explored three contemporary approaches to advancing worker-centered views of capital—screened funds, shareholder activism, and direct fund management—the following chapters examine two novel and ambitious strategies: the representation of workers in pension fund governance and making economically targeted investment a mainstream financial practice.

In chap. 7, Teresa Ghilarducci returns to the fundamental objective of pension funds—to secure comfortable retirements for workers—and examines several limitations that prevent them from fulfilling this goal. Despite an absolute growth in pension fund assets, there have been reductions in both the level of payout and coverage in the United States. She explains this erosion of pension security by identifying five major "leaks" from today's pension systems: partial coverage of the labor force, conflicting objectives in pension fund management, inefficiencies in plan management, inflation, and the failure of pension investments to sustain plans by creating new employment and wealth. Each of these erodes pension security.

Conflicts of interest for both employer representatives and money managers who dominate pension fund boards cause much of this leakage. This discord, called an *agency problem*, occurs when an individual's role requires serving two different sets of interests. In the case of pension fund representatives, these individuals serve both the plan beneficiaries and the contributing employers. Good pension management requires collective worker representation to mitigate this conflict.

Ghilarducci's research uses the health and generosity of pension programs as a function of their governance arrangements to examine this hypothesis. She finds that labor representation in pension plan governance helps to stem each of these leaks. Although a minority of plans offers such joint labor-management governance, those plans generate greater coverage and higher benefit levels than their counterparts, which lack worker representation. She argues that these governance arrangements are more crucial than the widely noted shift from defined-benefit to defined-contribution pension plans.

Yet even where there is control of pension fund investment policy, such as that found in jointly trusteed pension funds, many managers still hesitate to engage affirmatively in economically targeted investments. In chap. 8, Jayne Elizabeth Zanglein argues that ETIs should be a central element of any worker-owner strategy because of their potentially rich collateral benefits. She reviews current investment practice and regulation to determine why so many professionals are reluctant to pursue ETIs.

The chairman of the California Public Employees' Retirement System (CalPERS), one of the largest and most successful funds in the world, observes that ETIs are not by definition an asset class in and of themselves. Rather, because they offer side benefits, they form an investment perspective that allows some opportunities to be "more equal" than others. CalPERS, for example, considers investment in California to be an additional benefit. The

American Federation of Labor-Congress of Industrial Organizations (AFL-CIO), meanwhile, prioritizes the use of unionized construction labor in its Housing and Building Investment Trusts (HIT/BIT) program. For any ETI to be judged "more equal" than the next available investment opportunity, it must deliver a market rate of return with appropriate risk characteristics and be fully compatible with the fund's investment plan. ETIs usually make up no more than 5 percent of any pension plan portfolio. Consistent with the prudence of a worker-owner view, ETIs do not irresponsibly or recklessly deploy workers' retirement savings. Indeed, these investments require high levels of knowledge and extreme due diligence. Zanglein finds that these requirements of information and expertise prevent many pension funds, in particular jointly trusteed pension funds, from taking advantage of ETI opportunities.

Beyond inadequate knowledge, many trustees fear that participation in ETIs violates their legal fiduciary duties. In an earlier period, the Department of Labor actively discouraged ETIs through suits that aggressively penalized trustees who entered into poor or below-grade investments. By 1994, however, the agency clarified its position and declared that pension plan trustees could choose investments offering collateral benefits as long as they offered a prospective risk-adjusted market rate of return equal or superior to alternative investments. Thus, contemporary regulation poses no legal obstacle to ETIs; pension funds trustees may pursue them so long as they satisfy procedural requirements of prudence.

The greatest obstacle facing ETI investing today is the lack of education and expertise among pension plan trustees and their advisors. Although prudent ETIs are clearly allowed under the Employment Retirement Income Security Act (ERISA), many trustees lack the basic knowledge to make informed decisions regarding ETIs. Many find that investment professionals, attorneys, and management trustees discourage ETIs out of unfamiliarity or perceived risk aversion.

Overcoming the barriers to economically targeted investing requires expert trustee education combined with a national network of competent, educated, and willing professionals. It also requires a deeper understanding of the best practices of successful ETI investing and financial strategies and the capacity to implement the lessons of those experiences. Although $7 trillion of today's financial capital represents workers' deferred wages, workers themselves have limited ability to control or influence the investment of their capital to ensure that it works for rather than against their interests. Can this pattern be reversed? It will require a worker-owner view of capital stewardship that advances the broad interests of working people both in secure retirements and in a healthy and just economy.

Silvers, Patterson, and Mason of the AFL-CIO conclude this volume by exploring the strategies through which organized labor might advance its capital agenda. These measures include providing popular and professional education for pension beneficiaries and trustees, establishing broader and deeper representation in fund governance, fostering constructive and creative relationships between organized labor and investment professionals, expanding labor-centered shareholder activist strategies beyond U.S. borders to influence foreign-based multinationals, and advocating a more inclusive and transparent framework of corporate disclosure and securities regulation. Some tools in this mélange are already widely used, whereas others are still in development. Together, however, they offer a diversified mix of strategies for articulating and advancing a distinctive worker-owner view of how labor's capital should be deployed in financial markets.

Conclusion

Workers' capital stands on the verge of a critical threshold. Whether it gains the power to advance its aims effectively depends not on the benevolence of capital markets or corporate managers but on the ability of worker-owners and the labor movement to meet the challenge. Just as workers have organized to achieve gains in the workplace and outside of it for a range of labor regulations, they must demand changes in investment practice and its regulatory framework to promote a worker-owner investment agenda. The next step along this path is to foster a range of institutional investors and financial market professionals who will help develop and then champion a worker-owner agenda. The exercise of labor's capital requires a paradigm shift to awaken this latent force and then the expansion of new expertise to wield it deftly and powerfully, thereby making capital markets maximize long-term value for working people. We offer this volume to help develop that paradigm and build that capacity.

[11]

COLLATERAL DAMAGE:
DO PENSION FUND INVESTMENTS
HURT WORKERS?

Dean Baker and Archon Fung

As the other contributors to this volume discuss, the welfare of the United States' workers depends crucially on the operations and effects of capital markets. This reliance has grown stronger since the 1970s as both the size of pension funds and the share of workers' savings tied up in increasingly volatile capital markets have grown enormously. Because the relationship is reciprocal—capital markets are predominantly composed of workers' savings—one might expect the operations of capital markets to change to better advance the welfare and interests of the workers. One might also expect workers to demand such changes on penalty of withholding their investments. Yet, for a host of reasons that range from control to consciousness to organization, there is no such symbiotic relationship.

Instead, pension fund assets are generally invested in almost the same manner as the funds of other large institutional investors, such as life insurance companies or mutual funds. The financial managers who make investment decisions for pension funds also often invest pools of money from other sources. That the money constitutes deferred compensation for workers doesn't generally affect how it is invested. In principle, pension fund managers seek out the highest return at the least risk, just as they would with any investments. In this sense, the answer to the question of whether and how pension fund investments work for or against the interest of workers is simple: pension fund investments harm the interests of workers to the extent that capital markets in general work against their interest.

It is somewhat more difficult to determine the full impact of capital markets on workers, but there are many reasons for believing that it has not been positive in recent years. The last two decades of the twentieth century featured important economic trends that were detrimental to workers. The most important of these was an increase in wage inequality. Before the late 1970s, wages of all workers tended to move up together at approximately the same rate that productivity grew. This meant that the economy's growing prosperity was broadly shared among the workforce. This pattern reversed in the 1980s and 1990s. Wages have diverged, so that the highest-paid workers have continued to see significant wage growth, but those at the middle and the bottom of the wage distribution have experienced stagnant or declining incomes. Although wages for a worker at the ninetieth percentile (a worker who gets paid more than 90 percent of all workers) rose by 6.4 percent between 1979 and 1997, wages for a worker at the fiftieth percentile (a worker who gets paid more than 50 percent of all workers) fell by 5.5 percent. Wages for a worker at the tenth percentile (a worker who gets paid more than 10 percent of all workers) fell by 14.9 percent during the same period (Mishel, Bernstein, and Schmitt 1999). These numbers indicate that most workers did not share in the gains from the economic growth of recent decades.

Many factors contributed to this wage inequality. Foreign trade and investment have played important roles. Low-cost imports from developing nations have displaced millions of workers from relatively well-paying manufacturing jobs. Additionally, the fact that U.S. firms can threaten to move their operations to places like Indonesia, Thailand, or the Philippines, where workers often earn less than $1.00 per hour, has forced many U.S. workers to accept pay cuts. De-unionization has also been a significant factor. In the late 1970s, close to 24 percent of the workforce was covered by union contracts. At this writing, the figure has fallen to only 14 percent. This large decline in union representation has contributed to the downturn in wages for the bottom three-fourths of the workforce.

Financial markets have at least facilitated, if not actually promoted and accelerated, these trends. Funds generally flow to firms that show the greatest profit growth. Financial markets do not care whether the basis of high corporate profits is low-cost child labor in Indonesia. Nor do they care if firms use the threat of moving their operations overseas as a way to beat down wages and increase profits. Similarly, outsourcing work to nonunion firms, or any other anti-union tactic, often prompts favorable responses from financial markets, if it results in higher profits. The focus on profitability, and particularly short-term profitability, often leads financial markets to favor firms that engage in practices that are harmful to U.S. workers. Technological changes that allow increasingly rapid transactions within and across borders may intensify these proclivities. In all of these instances, workers' pension funds move alongside the money of other big investors.

Some view financial market outcomes that harm workers as the unfortunate but inevitable result of investors seeking the best return at the least risk. From this perspective, failing to exploit the availability of low-cost labor in developing nations or nonunion labor in the United States means sacrificing returns for investors. In this view, firms and their managers are virtually obliged to pursue strategies that depress wages, and investors reward those firms that pursue these strategies most effectively. To do otherwise would interfere with the natural workings of the market.

Yet the workings of the market are not quite so natural, and its consequences not so foregone. The pursuit of short-term profitability may not be the same as the pursuit of long-term profitability. This can be true in regard to both the firm's decisions about its investment strategies and the decisions that money managers make about pension portfolios. The first section of this chapter examines the extent to which markets focus on short-term profitability of companies and the short-term price movements of stock. It also examines the extent to which a short-term focus in financial markets feeds back into a short-term focus in firms' investment decisions.

The second section examines leveraged buyouts (LBOs) as an institutional structure often associated with short-term behavior. In many cases, corporate executives or investment firms have engineered leveraged buyouts that have garnered substantial profits but have devastated the firms that were taken over. The profits are obtained by selling assets, not by maintaining the firm as a profitable enterprise. This section examines the evidence that LBOs lead to cutbacks in spending on research and development (R&D) and other types of long-term investment. It also explores recent trends in LBOs to determine the extent of their impact on the overall economy.

When financial managers reach decisions as to the best available returns at the least risk, they must have some basis for determining risk. Since the 1980s, many investors have come to view investments in emerging markets as having relatively little risk. As a result, they were willing to place hundreds of billions of dollars in these markets. Recent events indicate that these investments may have been riskier than believed. Similarly, hundreds of billions of dollars have apparently moved into the hands of hedge fund managers who pursue complex investment strategies. Again, recent events suggest that these funds may not have been as safe as some investors had thought.

It is worth examining these types of derivative investments not just because they have proved to be highly volatile with their poor 1998 performance, but also because of the role that governments have played in their promotion. The International Monetary Fund (IMF) has acted repeatedly to protect U.S. investments in developing nations. Whether the actions of the IMF have benefited developing nations or the world economy is arguable, but it cannot be disputed that the IMF reduces the risk involved in investing money overseas. Similarly, the Federal Reserve Board (or simply, "the Fed") put together a consortium of banks in the late fall of 1998 (Morgenson 1998), to bail out the Long Term Capital management, the nation's largest hedge fund. Apparently, the Fed believed that the collapse of this hedge fund, and the resultant dumping of assets, would jeopardize the stability of the nation's financial system. The Fed's assessment may or may not have been correct, but by bailing out Long Term Capital's investors, the Fed reduced the risk associated with this type of investment.

Most firms are not large enough to threaten the health of the nation's financial system in this way. There is no IMF to reduce the risk associated with investing in inner city areas or in manufacturing firms that provide decent wages to their workers. By setting up institutions that support certain types of investment, the government tilts the market to favor some types of investment and disadvantage others. The third section examines patterns in investment behavior and presents a specific proposal to support investments that might better meet the needs of workers in the United States (Dymski and Veitch 1996).

It is also possible that optimal strategies from the standpoint of individual investors may not be best for the economy as a whole. For example, frequent trading of stock and other financial assets entails substantial transaction costs. Although shrewd investors may be able to profit from such transactions, the hundreds of billions of dollars spent on these financial transactions leak away. The fourth section of this chapter assesses the cost of running U.S. financial markets and describes a proposal, known as the *securities transaction tax* (STET), for reducing this expense.

It is also worth noting that financial markets do not apply the same ruthlessness in cutting all costs. Specifically, in recent years many CEOs have managed to secure compensation packages that ran into the tens or even hundreds of millions of dollars. The companies that provided these packages have not faced the same problems in financial markets that plagued many firms who paid their workers a decent wage. Cost cutting does not reach the CEO's doorstep. The lavish pay packages for CEOs and their immediate subordinates come either from firms' profits or workers' wages. For workers' pension funds, either source is bad news. The last section examines the cost of CEO compensation and its relation to job performance. It also discusses ways in which CEO compensation can be brought to more reasonable levels.

Are Capital Markets Myopic?

Although it is broadly agreed that the pace of investment transactions has dramatically increased in recent decades, experts hotly debate the effects of this capital market acceleration on the real economy—the number of jobs for workers, the quality of those jobs, and the health of firms that depend upon financial markets for their investment capital. In the conventional view, the relationship between financial markets and the real economy is a virtuous circle. Equity markets operate efficiently when investors seek out healthy firms (i.e., those that show a potential for growth and thus promise good returns to shareholders) and shun less promising businesses. Based on public information such as company product and performance announcements, news reports, regulatory filings, and, most of all, stock prices, millions of investors independently judge, bet, and thereby channel financing to the most promising firms in their attempts to reap benefits from these firms' stellar performance.

Against this view, many critics argue that financial markets in the United States are systematically biased toward short-term gains at the expense of sustained economic health. Two factors could make the circle of investment crooked and vicious. The first stems from the fact that all information is costly, and investors therefore necessarily have and use some forms of data but not others. The configuration of market institutions, furthermore, no doubt makes some types of information more available than others. In particular, widely available figures, such as earnings reports and changes in the stock price itself, are far less costly than performance information that deals with specific industries, companies, or competitive strategies. Thin information of this sort may lead investors and asset managers to divest from companies whose current activities—worker training, R&D, capital equipment, for example—pay off in the long term. They might instead favor companies that forego these types of investments for the sake of improving quarterly earnings reports. If enough investors act on this thinner, cheaper, but short-term–biased information, corporate managers will respond to the incentives they create by managing myopically, and financial markets will have induced suboptimal performance in the real economy upon which workers and their families depend.

Whether the circle of finance capital is virtuous or vicious, recent decades since the 1960s have featured two unmistakable structural transformations in

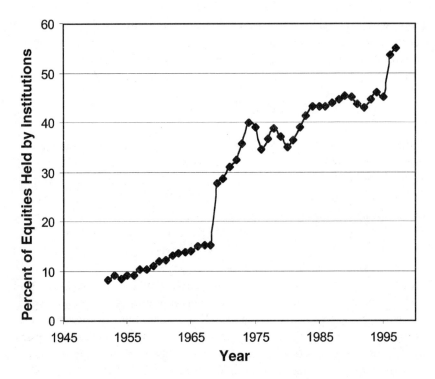

FIGURE 2.1. The growing influence of institutional shareholders.

the organization of these monetary flows. The first concerns the question of who participates in capital markets. The past four decades have seen a nearly monotonic rise in the participation and influence of institutional investors such as insurance funds, public and private pension funds, banks, and mutual funds coupled with the decline in the importance of individual household investors. In 1950, for example, institutional investors held less than 10 percent of the value of all United States equities. By 1997, this share had risen to more than half the stock (Figure 2.1).

The second major structural change concerns the speed with which these markets operate. In part as a consequence of the widespread adoption of electronic trading systems and other information technologies, the rate of transaction in capital markets has accelerated dramatically. One common measure of the speed of such transactions is annual *turnover*, which is defined as the percentage of stocks that change hands in a year compared to the basket of all available stocks. The turnover of 15 percent in equity markets in 1970 had

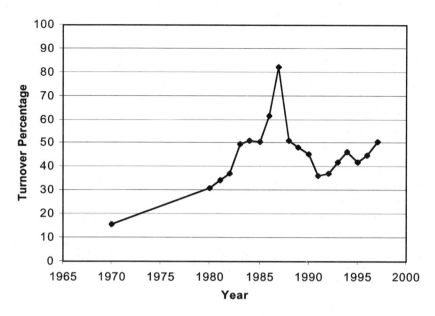

FIGURE 2.2. Historical stock turnover, 1970–1997.

tripled to 45 percent by 1996. Figure 2.2 shows the increase in annual stock turnover in U.S. equity markets since 1970.

By themselves, these two structural changes in financial markets do not necessarily indicate a change toward short-term investment behavior. Increased stock market trading activity might indicate either churning of money from one stock to another, which generates value only in the form of commissions for traders and brokers. It may, on the other hand, indicate enhanced ability for investors to detect the most promising firms and move their assets to support those firms and capture investment opportunities. Although we know of no studies that directly test this claim, Robert Shiller has demonstrated that the volatility of stock prices themselves, rather than turnover, is not subsequently justified by either price or dividend increases (Shiller 1981). To show why stock prices seem too volatile, Shiller constructed two figures—one for Standard & Poor's Composite Price Index and one for the Dow Jones Industrial Average. Each figure shows (a) the real stock price index over time and (b) the ex-post rational price, which is the present discounted value of subsequent dividends for those stocks over the period between 1870 and 1970. Although the second series—ex-post price—remains constant over the entire period on both charts, the real stock price on both fluctuates wildly. Shiller concludes that "measures of stock price volatility over the past century appear to be far too high—five to thirteen times too high—to be attributed to new information about real future dividends" (Shiller 1981, 434).

Relatedly, experts disagree on whether the concentration of stock ownership in institutional investors has made the financial markets and the "real" economy more myopic or whether institutional investors are more disposed than individual investors to consider the long-term health of the firms in which they invest. The rise of large institutions as financial market players has no doubt made the picking and selling of stocks more sophisticated in the sense that professional asset managers have more time, training, and other resources to select the most promising equity positions and monitor the progress of those positions. This professionalization of capital markets might cut two ways. One line of reasoning states that professional asset managers must compete to "beat the market" constantly, which leads them to focus on short-term stock price fluctuations.[1] A report on speculation and corporate governance put it this way:

> Portfolio managers are under great pressure to produce above average results consistently, a feat that is mathematically impossible for them as a group. So they compete feverishly, always on the lookout for a shred of information that will give them an edge. Such information may be superficial . . . As long as other traders in asset markets are playing by the same "rules," it behooves the competitive portfolio manager to see this as a signal of short-term price movement . . . Even if a market participant believes that information about a firm is of no fundamental value, he should trade on it if he believes that others will use that information to make their trades. . . .
>
> *Chief Executive Officers and their teams are paid to produce results that will raise share prices. Only if share prices accurately reflect the present value and the risk of earnings may a manager concern himself with fundamentals.* [emphasis in original] (Shiller 1992)

According to Michael Porter (1992) and many other observers, institutional investors in financial markets in America have indeed behaved this way, and managers have responded to these incentives by boosting short-term earnings at the expense of less tangible, more patient measures, such as advertising, fixed capital investment, training, and R&D of new products. McNichols and Lang (1997), for example, found that the trading behavior of institutional investors is quite sensitive to earnings news. As Michael Jacobs, the former Director of Corporate Finance at the U.S. Treasury Department, argues in his book *Short-Term America*, this problem is compounded by the structure and regulation of financial markets and corporate governance in the United States. Specifically, securities law, antitrust, the Employment Retirement Income Security Act, and common professional trading habits impose arms–length and adversarial relationships between the stockholders who formally own capital and the corporate executives who manage it. Financial relationships in Japan and Germany, by contrast, depend on closer, more communicative, and more influential relationships between bankers who make capital allocation decisions and executives in firms. This difference in capital relationships, according to Jacobs, increases the cost of capital in the United States and thereby makes it relatively more difficult for U.S. firms to take measures with longer-term anticipated payoffs.

On the other side of this argument, some observers claim that the rise of sophisticated institutional investors has brought with it longer-term investment strategies (Monks and Minnow 1995). Professional asset managers, for example, have more time and resources to obtain information beyond easily available earnings reports, and they can expend the energy necessary to monitor their investments. Beyond this, many in these institutions are sensitive to research that shows both the dim promise of "active" asset management strategies (those that involve attempts to pick winners and losers in the stock market) and the futility of trying to "beat the market." One manager of a large public pension fund commented that "we can't beat the market, because we are the market." Certain very successful institutional investors, such as the California Public Employees' Retirement System and Warren Buffet's Berkshire Hathaway, have explicitly adopted an investment philosophy that is long term and, for the latter, relationship based (Jacobs 1992). More generally, Robert Shiller (1992, 63) concludes from a survey of the literature and existing studies that

> there does not appear to be any conclusive evidence that institutional investors are in fact ignoring the long-term profitability of the companies they invest in any more than did individual investors when they dominated the market . . . the effect of the rise of institutional investors might instead be expected to encourage more careful attention to the long run by managers themselves [because professional asset managers are more trained and capable of analysis than individual investors].

The preponderance of argument and evidence is ambiguous, because there is some truth to both sides. When institutional investors engage in capital strategies that involve either passive investing (e.g., buying and holding a representative basket of stocks) or building longer-term relationships between stockholders and firm managers, they do not seem to discourage the pursuit of longer-term investments, such as R&D and worker training, to maintain the appearance of shorter-term health exhibited by quarterly earnings statements. When institutional investors engage in short-term investment strategies such as "momentum trading," in which they buy substantial shares of securities that statistically seem to be rising and sell or "short" those that seem to be falling, managers respond by reducing spending on long-term items in favor of improving earnings reports. That, at any rate, is the conclusion of Brian Bushee (1998) in his study of the relationship between institutional investors and R&D spending. As a general matter, firms are less likely to reduce R&D spending as a response to earnings declines when there is high institutional investment. However, Bushee found that firms whose share of institutional ownership is high and whose owners engage in short-term trading strategies are more likely to reverse R&D spending after earnings decline.

Capital markets as they are organized in the United States exhibit tendencies to favor short-term results over long-term benefits, which causes at least two types of collateral damage to workers and to the American economy as a whole. First, as long as the cost of capital in the United States remains higher than that of its international competitors, the innovative edge of U.S. firms will erode, taking with it the supply of jobs on which workers depend. Second, medium- and long-term investments, such as new-skills training and modern, safe, and productive workplaces, which may be foregone for the sake of immediate appearances, are often the very investments on which workers depend for sustained well-being.

We should be encouraged, however, that there is nothing inevitable about short-term investment and management. Even within the current U.S. regulatory regime, many institutional investors take the longer view in selecting and relating to firms in which they assume positions. If we look abroad, not only to Germany and Japan but also to Canada, we see many regulatory alternatives that effectively promote longer-term investment horizons. Although a discussion of measures to encourage such behavior lies beyond the scope of this chapter, part of the solution lies in creating accountable and information-rich relationships between the firm owners—the shareholders—and firm management. When these relationships provide reliable data that address companies' long-term prospects and plans, investors can discount the thinner, fickle, and noisier information about short term performance, thereby reducing the collateral damage caused by myopic investors and managers.

Market for Corporate Control: Mergers and Acquisitions

A second major feature of contemporary capital markets in the United States is the extraordinarily high level of corporate recombination via mergers or

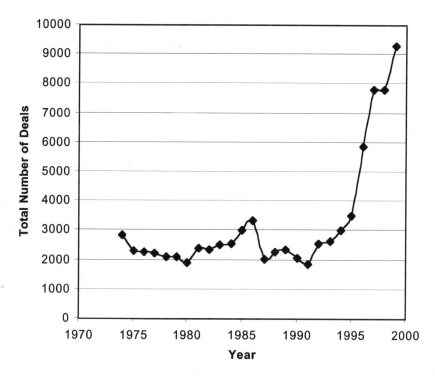

FIGURE 2.3. Mergers and acquisitions, 1974–1998.

outright purchasing of firms: mergers and acquisitions (M&A) activity. Figure 2.3 depicts the number of M&A deals in the United States between 1974 and 1998. There have been two peaks in M&A activity in the 1990s. From a low point of approximately 1,900 deals in 1980, this activity peaked first at approximately 3,300 deals in 1987. The amount of activity then slowed back to its original levels and rose again in the late 1990s to an all-time high of nearly 8,000 deals in 1997 and 1998.

Although lagging the trend somewhat, pension funds and other "tax-exempt" investment organizations are also increasing their activities in LBOs and other M&As. A 1999 study by Goldman Sachs and Frank Russell Company reports that *alternative investments*, which include venture capital funds, LBOs, and mezzanine financing, constituted 6.3 percent of the asset allocation of large pension funds and foundations in 1996, but that this figure rose to 7.3 percent in 1999 and is expected to rise again to 8 percent by 2002.

This massive activity for corporate control in the market has been both vehemently defended and criticized. Defenders such as Michael Jensen (1988) contend that these ownership changes are mechanisms to discipline poor managers, those who hold their own interests above those of shareholders and rearrange assets from relatively less to more productive uses. In some ways, changes in corporate ownership might generate more profits for shareholders or greater productivity for the firms or assets involved. Firms with bad managers—for example, those married to obsolete competitive strategies—constitute one obvious category of takeover targets; in such cases, new owners of firms can replace them with better managers who are able to generate higher profits. Beyond this, managers may have interests that diverge from those of shareholders. According to the free-cash flow theory offered by Jensen, managers generally have incentives to retain earnings and invest them to increase organizational size rather than to disburse them to shareholders. Changing the ownership of such firms can dislodge these funds from management appropriation. Even when there is competent management, some assets outside the core competencies of conglomerated firms may be underused or poorly overseen. In these cases, new owners of the firm may be able to increase the productivity of those assets by selling them to firms in related lines of business. A fourth argument in favor of ownership changes is that corporate fusion sometimes yields synergies (e.g., the linking of complementary capacities) unavailable to firms operating separately.

Skeptics of the massive increase in the tumultuousness of corporate ownership contest the alleged benefits of each of these claims. Many criticize these waves of M&As, which they claim cause enormous collateral damage by destroying much of the value-generating capacity of firms and attacking their workforces. We review four varieties of such collateral damage and the evidence supporting them: (a) the layoffs, wage reductions, and other labor cost-saving measures implemented after M&As; (b) mergers as a strategy to attack unions and otherwise replace trust between workers and managers with a more exploitative relationship; (c) the inability of some firms to sustain business after LBOs and other types of M&A activity, because they lower their investment in equipment, workforce, and especially in R&D; and (d) the failure of firms to perform better after mergers than they did before them and, therefore, the conclusion that the efficiency-enhancing claims about M&A activity should be treated with some suspicion.

The research firm of Challenger, Gray & Christmas, Inc. reported that in the first three quarters of 1998, at the peak of the most recent wave of mergers and acquisition activity, more than one of every ten jobs lost were lost as a result of a merger or acquisition (Harrison 1999). In that period, 431,456 jobs were cut in firms monitored by Challenger, Gray & Christmas, 44,742 of which could be attributed to M&A activity. This figure understates the

actual amount of job loss attributable to takeovers, because corporate restruc-
turings often shed jobs many months after a merger announcement. The
upside of this statistic is that such displaced workers typically find new
employment within a few months, although frequently at much lower wages.
A Bureau of Labor Statistics survey found that 74 percent of full-time workers who had lost their jobs between 1997 and 1999 were employed in February of 2000. However, many of these workers were forced to take part-time
work or substantial pay cuts. Fewer than one-third of these workers reported
finding new jobs at the same or higher wages.

Supplementing this finding, several quantitative researchers have examined
the degree to which M&As capture savings from these workforce reductions
and are thus motivated by them. Changes in management policy can reduce
labor costs through layoffs, wage reductions, and pension fund and benefit
reduction. In their study of large takeovers in the 1980s, Bhagat, Shleifer, and
Vishny (1990) found that an average of 6.3 percent of the labor force had been
laid off after hostile takeovers. In a study of manufacturing plants that were
taken over, Lichtenberg and Siegel (1989; Lichtenberg 1992) found that
employment growth was approximately 5 percent lower than in plants whose
owners had not changed. They found that, after takeovers, central-office,
white-collar employees experience disproportionate layoffs compared with
production workers, and that this decrease in the ratio of central-office to
production personnel increases plant productivity. In contrast to the damage
of layoffs, most studies found M&As to have little impact on wages. Neumark
(1996), for instance, found that firms with above-average industry wages (and
thus greater rents that might be appropriated by shareholders) are no more
likely to be the targets of hostile takeovers than are otherwise comparable
firms. In a study of hostile takeovers in the 1980s, Pontiff, Shleifer, and Welsbach found that new management reverted excess pension fund assets in 15
percent of hostile takeovers and that the appropriation of this wealth accounts
for a substantial amount of takeover premiums when it occurs (Pontiff et al.
1990; Shleifer and Summers 1988). Thus, many M&As cause collateral damage to workers through layoffs, pension fund reductions, and wage reductions
for more senior workers.

In addition to these effects on wages and benefits, corporate takeovers sometimes hurt the organized workforces of targeted firms. The purpose of worker
organizations is, after all, to secure such goods as higher wages, job security, pensions, and other benefits for their workers. An owner takeover that directs new
management to implement adversarial rather than cooperative relations with its
organized workforces might be able to shift these rents from workers to owners
of firms. The few empirical studies of this question lend substantial support for

the contention that shareholder gains from M&A activity often come from the pockets of unionized workers. In a study comparing the union firms that were taken over between 1973 and 1986 to those that were not targets of M&As, Joshua Rosett (1990) found that wages in firms that had been taken over grew more slowly than nontargeted firms in the years after takeover. However, this wage concession accounts for only a small amount—between 1 and 2 percent—of the takeover premiums paid by shareholders. He found, however, that the shift of rents from unionized workers to shareholders was typically much greater when the takeovers were hostile, accounting for between 3 and 10 percent of shareholder gains. In his study of the takeovers of some large union firms in the first half of the 1980s, Brian Becker (1995) offered qualified support for the hypothesis that profits for shareholders come at the expense of organized workers. He found that shareholder returns from takeovers of unionized firms were 25 percent higher than those from nonunionized firms, and that this represents a loss to employees of approximately 8 percent of annual earnings. Becker could not trace this shareholder gain, however, to direct human resource policies that, for example, reduce the wages or benefits of workers or lower employment levels.

Contesting this union-rent explanation of corporate takeovers, Fallick and Hasset (1996) examined whether union firms are more likely than nonunion firms to be takeover targets. They reason that if the transfer of rents from workers to shareholders motivates many takeovers, union firms should constitute a disproportionately large percentage of the takeovers, and similarly, more nonunion firms should initiate M&As. They find, contrary to this hypothesis, that there is an affinity in M&A activity between firms of similar union status: nonunion firms have a higher-than-expected probability of merging with nonunion firms, and unionized companies merge with one another more frequently than expected. The small amount of research into the relationship between merger activity and labor organization, then, indicates that the expropriation of rents from unionized workers does not seem to be a prime motivator of takeovers, but that unions and their members are hurt when their firms are acquired in a hostile fashion.

In addition to job loss and de-unionization, some critics contend that M&As force targeted firms to abandon long-term investments in favor of an excessive focus on short-term goals. Whereas defenders of the beneficial effects of the "market for corporate control" contend that ownership changes focus the minds of managers on improving performance (Jensen 1988), critics argue that the same factors steer managers from the kinds of decisions necessary for sustained corporate growth. Several theories explain how M&A activity induces myopic management. One common line of reasoning is that M&As often increase the debt-to-equity ratio in firms' capital structure; subsequent debt-servicing burdens might lead to reductions in capital, workforce, and research investments (Scherer 1988; Ravenscraft and Long 1993). Related to that, managers of acquired firms seem to shift their focus from "strategic" considerations that focus on long-term competitiveness to "financial control" imperatives that seek least-cost, risk-averse, and sometimes myopic solutions as a result of both debt-service pressure and the increased information costs associated with larger organizations (Hitt et al. 1996). Finally, the acquiring firms sometimes view R&D and other resources of their targets as cash cows that can be redeployed to finance more pressing needs (Hall 1988).

Most existing empirical research lends qualified support for these contentions about the various types of collateral damage caused by M&A activity. Several studies show that firm R&D expenditures drop after takeovers. Ravenscraft and Long (1993) showed that, for their sample, R&D activity dropped by an average of 40 percent in firms that were acquired through LBOs. In their study of 214 buyouts that occurred between 1986 and 1989, Phan and Hill (1995) found that short-term efficiency improvements may come at the expense of reduced investments in R&D and long-term profitability. Based on an earlier wave of takeovers in the 1960s and 1970s, Scherer found that companies reduce long-term investment in research and capital equipment as a result of debt pressure. Lichtenberg and Siegel (1989), in a study of 1,100 manufacturing plants involved in buyouts between 1981 and 1986, found that average R&D intensity was lower in the 3-year period after a buyout compared to the previous 3 years. A smaller number of studies contest this thesis, arguing that R&D levels typically do not decrease after buyouts. Using economy-wide rather than company-specific data, Jensen (1989) argues that M&A activity does not reduce research expenditures. In a study of 47 LBOs, Zahra (1995) found that corporate strategies involved more innovation—including greater product development, larger R&D staffs, and increased business creation activities—after takeovers (Zahra 1995).

Although these scholars find that LBO activity drives down R&D expenditures on a firm basis, it does not appear that LBOs drain substantial research investment from industrial sectors generally. Most observers agree that buyout targets are usually in firms and sectors with generally lower R&D intensity rather than in firms that are highly innovative or research intensive. Hall (1998), for example, found that acquisition activity was directed toward firms with relatively weak technological bases (Hall 1988). Similarly, Ravenscraft and Long (1993) found that, among the firms they studied, pre-LBO intensity was on average only two-thirds of the industry mean. Lichtenberg (1992) also found that LBO targets exhibit lower R&D levels, even before buyout, and also tend to be in less R&D-intensive industries.

Activities that cause collateral damage to workers and competitiveness are commonly justified as necessary measures to improve corporate performance and shareholder returns. A growing body of research shows, however, that ownership changes may not yield lasting increases in corporate performance or profitability. Mark Sirower (1997) debunked the notion that the recent wave of M&A activity increases shareholder value by building synergistic links between previously separate operations. In a study of one hundred large deals between 1994 and 1997, Sirower found that two-thirds of these firms remained market underperformers after a year. In the studies cited above, both Sherer and Hall found, by examining cash flows and profit levels, that operating performance does not generally yield operating improvements. Ravenscraft and Long (1993) found that performance improves after LBOs for the minority of firms that increase their R&D expenditures, whereas non–R&D-intensive firms do not generally improve in performance. Several other researchers, however, argue that takeovers sometimes result in performance improvement. Lichtenberg (1992) found that LBOs often reduce the ratio of white-collar to blue-collar workers and that this reduced ratio improves firm productivity. Salter and Weinhold (1988) and Phan and Hill (1995) found that LBOs often result in "one-shot" productivity improvements, but that these improvements diminish relatively quickly over time.

At a minimum, these studies generate some skepticism regarding claims made in defense of high levels of M&As. Importantly, they have, for the most part, failed to find the economic benefits, such as great increases in productivity and innovation, promised by the advocates of takeover as a preferred method of corporate governance. Absent these benefits, the attention of researchers and the public ought to shift to the types of collateral damage generated by mergers and buyouts. Such activity often results in direct harm to workers in the form of large-scale workforce reductions or the lowering of pensions and other benefits. Another variety of damage that is only slightly less direct occurs when buyouts install ownership that is hostile to worker organizations or seeks to shift firms from cooperative to adversarial labor-management relations. Finally, researchers have found that takeovers often harm workers by inducing myopic management priorities into firms: a focus on financial ahead of strategic goals; reductions in capital, workforce, and research investments; and the dismantling of synergistic business organizations and sale of their parts. One promising avenue of reform is to bolster methods other than acquisition for dealing with subpar management and for reconciling management and shareholder interests. Such alternatives are beyond the scope of this discussion, but Jayne Elizabeth Zanglein in chap. 8 and Damon Silvers in chap. 9 offer helpful suggestions in this direction.

Who, Where, and When of U.S. Pension Fund Asset Allocation

After discussing collateral damage from the increasing rate of stock turnover on one hand and the corporate ownership transition on the other, we examine some implications of two secular shifts in the allocation of public and private pension funds over time: the increasing involvement of pension funds in the stock market, and the even more dramatic increase of their overseas investments.

First to be considered are shifts in the allocation of (a) *private pension funds*, defined as the pension funds of corporations, nonprofit groups, unions, and multi-employer funds, and (b) pension funds of employees of state and local government. In 1997, $4.8 trillion lay in the former category, whereas the latter consisted of $2.1 trillion. The two trend lines in Figure 2.4 show the proportion of all privately held and state and local pension fund monies that were invested in corporate stocks or mutual funds—as opposed to government securities or bonds—between 1952 and 1997.

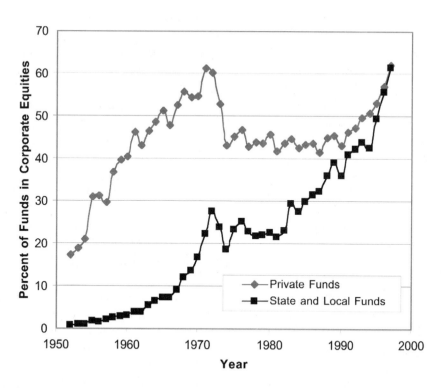

FIGURE 2.4. Pension fund equality allocation, 1952–1997.

Since 1990, both types of funds have dramatically increased the percentage of their assets under management that hold stock positions and mutual funds. Drawn by the enormous equity run-up that began in 1990, private equity funds have increased stocks as a portion of their holdings from 43 percent in 1990 to 62 percent in 1997. The trend for state and local pension funds spans a longer period and is much more dramatic. Beginning from almost no equity stakes in 1950, these public employee funds steadily increased their involvement in the stock market, with a brief stabilization from 1972 until 1983, to a point of convergence at which their percentage of equity holdings matched that of private pension funds in 1997. Between 1987 and 1997, the percentage of state and local government pension fund monies in the corporate equity market nearly doubled, from 32 percent to 62 percent of assets.

The main gain from this structural transformation toward increased equity positions is that workers in both the public and private sectors enjoy better funded, and in that respect more secure, pension plans. All other things being equal, decreasing asset allocations from very low-risk and low-return bonds and treasuries in favor of a greater and more diverse selection of equity holdings is more than justified by the greater expected long-term returns that this portfolio shift will yield.[2] Although some sort of asset shift toward equity markets—a shift that comports with the recommendations of Modern Portfolio Theory—seems incontrovertible, the move brings with it a number of risks and potential harms to workers and the economy.

The first potential source of collateral damage stems from the willingness of pension asset managers to take riskier, less certain bets in the hopes of reaping larger returns. Many unobjectionable styles of equity investment (e.g., holding diversified index funds that track market movements) do not involve undue risk. However, financial industry innovations have tempted many asset managers to take ill-understood or high-risk positions involving exotic instruments, such as various sorts of derivatives. This temptation is compounded by "agency" and "information asymmetry" problems when the interests of brokers and securities salespeople do not necessarily coincide with those of pension fund beneficiaries and trustees. The salespeople and sellers often know more than less sophisticated buyers about the benefits and risks of the products. Several well-known losses incurred by such decisions and less prominent investment histories illustrate the scale of damage that risky asset management can cause:

- At the end of 1994, Orange County, California, filed for bankruptcy after losing approximately $2 billion in derivative positions that, in effect, placed highly leveraged bets on interest rate drops. Interest rates rose, and County Treasurer Robert Citron was forced from office in shame. Citron, who claims no expertise in financial markets, blamed Merrill Lynch salesmen for persuading him to take such risky positions (*St. Louis Post-Dispatch* 1995).

- In 1995, the State of Wisconsin Investment Board (SWIB), then a $37 billion public fund, lost approximately $200 million on two derivative transactions that amounted to highly leveraged interest rate bets. Subsequent regulation imposed stricter monitoring and investment limitation controls on the SWIB (Jaresky 1995).
- In 1995, Connecticut pension funds suffered losses of $25 million on speculative derivative investments related to interest payments from mortgage-backed securities and foreign bonds. According to some in the bond-trading business, investment professionals viewed these state pension funds as a dumping ground for the least desirable bonds (Vogel 1995).
- Even when pension fund professionals are savvy in their use of sophisticated instruments, the use of these instruments may primarily benefit brokers and asset managers without yielding returns for the pension funds. Edwin Burton (1996), a trustee of the Virginia Retirement System (VRS), has recounted how a derivatives portion of the VRS program used active investment practices with very low expected rates of return—high turnover combined with haphazard "long" and "short" positions—but generated for managers fees amounting to approximately 8 percent of principal.

A second source of collateral damage from increasing equity involvement stems from a problem already discussed: the myopic equity trading and management that occur when institutional and individual investors seek high returns in information-thin environments. When these funds were invested principally in low-risk credit markets, pension funds provided long-term debt financing for public and private institutions. As they assume greater equity stakes, they tend to assume the trading strategies of other institutional investors. Often, this involves high turnover strategies of the sort described in the section Are Capital Markets Myopic? When it does, the deferred wages of workers in these public and private pension funds can be deployed to reward companies and managers that pursue short-term strategies—specifically, underinvesting in skill development, capital equipment, and R&D. This chapter and others in this book (chaps. 5 and 8) discuss strategies for developing information-rich institutions in which investors can better evaluate and incorporate long-term corporate strategies and performance into their ownership decisions. These strategies are increasingly urgent, given the dramatic migration of worker pension assets into equity markets.

In addition to investing more heavily in equities, pension funds have mimicked other institutional investors by sending a larger proportion of their money into markets abroad. The financial research and consulting firm

Greenwich Associates (1998) reports, for example, that the level of pension fund monies invested in overseas equities will have doubled in the period between 1993 and 2000. In 1993, 6.4 percent of U.S. pension fund assets lay in international equities; that figure grew to 10.7 percent—$431 billion—in 1997. By the end of 1999, Greenwich Associates expects the proportion of U.S. pension fund monies in international equities to exceed 12 percent. If we include all sorts of financing—not just equities, but also public and private debt—the trend becomes even more pronounced.

This trend toward international investment poses potential sources of collateral damage from the point of view of U.S. pension beneficiaries and for workers in general. First, one of the most popular destinations for these funds in recent years has been the "emerging markets" of Asia, Latin America, and the former Communist Bloc nations. U.S. asset managers favor investments in these areas, because they diversify the risk in their portfolios and, for a time at any rate, these international investments promised very high returns. To ease the path of these investments, the diplomatic forces of the United States and other industrialized nations urged the officials of these emerging-market nations to liberalize their financial systems by allowing foreign purchases of debt and equity and by allowing concerns in the country to seek financing from abroad (Kristof and Sanger 1999).

The standard account of recent events in these emerging markets is by now familiar and tragic. We need not embellish upon its outlines here, because the lessons seem basically correct. As a result of successful liberalization pressures from outside and desires from within, the barriers to capital flow came down in these countries, and money from the United States and Western Europe poured in. These countries lacked sophisticated financial systems to monitor and rate the quality of various securities and economic conditions generally. The information that we have criticized as being too thin—standard and reliable reports of financial performance—are lavish by the standards of emerging markets. Even the most sophisticated and respected analysts seem to have vastly overrated the potential of these economies and the firms within them, and conversely, they have underestimated the fragility of their foundations. Only in retrospect do financial professionals seem to acknowledge the deep and lasting flaws in these economies—flaws such as weak banking systems that made bad loans at artificially low interest rates. In 1997, a few U.S. hedge funds perceived this weakness and acted on it by placing highly leveraged bets against the currencies of Thailand and Malaysia. This sale set off a run on these emerging market economies, and international capital left almost as quickly as it had rushed in, with the predictable consequence of crushing the real economies there. Between June 1997 and December 1998, the stock markets of Indonesia, Malaysia, and Thailand lost, respectively, 80, 74, and 42 percent of their total value. Russia and Brazil suffered similarly. American and European investors who had taken positions in emerging markets lost dearly, but these losses were generally offset by gains in their own growing markets. The prime lesson seems to be that these emerging markets are more risky and less profitable than most professional investors thought them to be.

In addition to the direct losses that can be incurred from investing in these ill-understood markets, often with complex financial instruments, a second source of indirect collateral damage comes from the opportunity costs of moving capital off-shore. Other essays in this collection—especially those of Tessa Hebb (chap. 6) and Jayne Elizabeth Zanglein (chap. 8)—discuss the importance of investing in domestic firms with "high-road" competitive strategies and workplace practices. Sustaining these sorts of firms requires the development of financial institutions to identify and invest in them on the one hand and to move a portion of the capital that currently resides in domestic equities and international markets.

Moreover, the financial collapse in East Asia that resulted from the influx of foreign capital has had very serious consequences for hundreds of thousands of workers in the United States. Most of the nations in the region have experienced large declines in gross domestic product (GDP) since the collapse and are unlikely to return to their former growth path for many years, even in the most optimistic scenarios. The currencies of these nations have fallen between 30 and 60 percent against the dollar. As a result, U.S. exports to the region have plummeted, and the United States is being faced with a huge tide of imports, which will displace hundreds of thousands of workers. To repay their debts, as is demanded by the IMF and the international financial community, the nations of East Asia have no choice but to increase their exports drastically. The workers who lose their jobs as a result will pay a large price for the poorly planned investment strategy of money fund managers.

Worker-Centered Restructuring of Financial Markets

This section and the next offer two proposals for restructuring financial markets in ways that will make them more conducive to the interests of working people. The first proposal is for a STET. This would radically reduce the volume of short-term trading and lengthen investors' planning horizons. It could also lengthen the planning horizon of corporate managers. The other proposal is to place caps on the pay of corporate executives. In recent years, corporate CEOs have often been able to negotiate packages of stock options that have subsequently turned out to be worth tens or hundreds of millions of dollars.

There is no evidence that such huge compensation packages are necessary for good management. The excess money drains resources that could have otherwise been used to finance investment, pay out as dividends, or raise wages. There is no reason why workers, or anyone else with a stake in a corporation, should tolerate bloated executive compensation packages.

SECURITIES TRANSACTION TAX

The financial industry in the United States is often held up as a model industry. It has quickly embraced innovations in computer and information technology, allowing financial assets (e.g., stocks and bonds) to be traded ever more quickly at ever lower costs per trade. It is now possible for individuals to buy and sell stocks at home, through the Internet, at a cost of less than $8.00 per trade.[3] Not only has the financial industry used technology to facilitate trades on traditional assets, such as stocks and bonds, but it has also taken advantage of computer technology to create a vast array of "derivative" financial assets (e.g., options and index futures), which could not exist without the immediate calculations enabled by computers.[4]

Lower trading costs and the new financial instruments created since 1975 have led to an enormous increase in the volume of trades on financial markets. In 1973, $250 billion of trades took place on U.S. stock exchanges. By 1998, the volume of trades in stock was $10 trillion. In addition, more than $40 trillion in government bonds were traded. The face value of trades in futures was another $100 trillion. This vast increase in trading volume was associated with a large increase in the size of the financial sector. The number of workers employed in brokerage houses and investment banks increased from less than 300,000 in 1977 to 911,000 in 1997. The amount of output generated in this sector rose from $8.4 billion in 1977 to $108.0 billion in 1997 (*Survey of Current Business*, August 1998). Measured as a share of GDP, this is an increase from 0.4 percent to 1.3 percent.

Although Wall Street's boosters would probably cite these figures boastfully, doing so shows a misunderstanding of the purpose of financial markets. The purpose of financial markets is not to carry through trades, but rather to allocate capital from savers to investors. At any time, there are large numbers of individuals who wish to save for priorities such as their retirement or their children's education. There are also firms that wish to borrow to finance investment and individuals who wish to borrow for a home mortgage or college education. The purpose of financial markets is to act as the bridge between the people who want to save and those who wish to borrow. An efficient financial system carries through this role at the lowest possible cost.

That it has become so much more costly to run U.S. financial markets since 1975 suggests that they are not operating efficiently. The cost of carrying through individual stock trades has fallen a great deal over this period, but investors feel the need to trade so much more frequently that the net effect has been an enormous increase in the cost of running U.S. financial markets.

This point can perhaps be seen more clearly if an analogy to the trucking industry is made. The purpose of the trucking industry is to transport goods, (e.g., materials, food, and merchandise) from one place to another. If the trucking industry were like the financial industry, it would have used far more people and trucks to transport the same amount of goods in 2000 than it did in 1970. The trucking industry would have carried the goods over more miles in 2000 than in 1970, but only because it would have shipped the same items back and forth over the same distance.

In effect, this duplication of effort is what the huge increase in trading volume since 1970 implies. Stocks, bonds, and other financial instruments are traded far more frequently than in the past, but it provides no more benefit to the economy than sending the same cargo back and forth between New York and Los Angeles one hundred times. The intermediaries (i.e., brokerage houses and financial managers) profit on the trades, but from the standpoint of the economy, the growth in trading is a needless cost.

Workers feel this cost in several ways. The most immediate way in which workers are forced to bear the costs of financial markets is through paying the fees directly. A recent study indicates that pension funds have been unusually active traders, holding an average share of stock for less than 2 years (Lakonishok, Shleifer, and Vishny 1992). The study found that this trading actually caused the funds to lose money compared to the major market indexes. In addition to the fact that the trading itself lost money on average, the funds incurred costs equal to 1–2 percent annually in the form of commissions and management fees. This money was effectively taken out of workers' pockets and placed in the pockets of pension fund managers, stockbrokers, and other people involved in running the financial markets. In this way, much of the cost of running financial markets is taken directly out of workers' retirement income.

Workers may also end up paying for the cost of running financial markets when the firms for which they work incur the costs. Many corporations use part of their revenue to speculate in financial markets. Even if they break even on average in their trades (i.e., their trades are winners as often as they are losers), they still end up as losers on net, because they have to pay commissions and other fees on their trades. These costs come directly out of the company's profits. Money that otherwise might have been available to finance new investment is used instead to support financial markets.

The third way in which the cost of financial markets can impact workers is through macroeconomic policy. Although understanding how macroeconomic policy can have this impact is a bit difficult, it is extremely important. In the economic recovery of the 1990s, many politicians and economists have argued that the government should use surplus capital to eliminate the budget deficit because it was crowding out private investment. Many people making this argument were confused about the exact mechanism through which a government deficit could reduce private investment. The actual way in which a government deficit can crowd out private investment is by pulling away real resources (i.e., labor and physical capital) from private sector uses. In other words, if a worker is employed by the government or a tractor is rented by the government, the resources (i.e., the worker, the tractor) cannot simultaneously be used elsewhere in the private sector.

In the same way, the resources—the brokers, the analysts, the filing clerks, the computers, and the office space—that are used to operate financial markets cannot simultaneously be used to carry on other productive activity in the private sector. Insofar as the financial sector expands and pulls away more resources from the rest of the economy, it is diminishing the amount of resources available to produce goods and services of real value. In this way, a bloated financial sector can crowd out private investment in the same manner as can an overgrown government sector.

If the financial markets were only as costly in relation to the whole present economy as they were in 1977, it would cost $76 billion less to operate them each year. This $76 billion can be seen as a crude measure of the extent to which the financial markets have become less efficient since 1980. This additional cost should be viewed as waste in the same way that $76 billion in unnecessary government expenditures would be viewed as wasteful. Private sector waste is every bit as harmful to the economy as public sector waste.

A simple measure would go far toward curbing the waste in the financial system. A very small tax on the purchase and sale of all financial assets would greatly reduce the volume of trading. It would also raise an enormous amount of money for such uses as improving public education, providing children with health care, and supporting medical research. A recent study estimated that a 0.5-percent tax on each stock sale (0.25 percent each paid by the buyer and seller) together with comparable taxes on bonds, options, futures, and other financial assets could raise more than $100 billion per year (Pollin, Baker, and Schauberg 1999).

Although no one wants to pay higher taxes, a tax of this magnitude would have virtually no impact on anyone who intended to hold a stock for a significant period of time. A person who holds a stock for 10 years with the expectation that the price will double would get a return of 99.5 percent as a result of the tax, instead of 100 percent without the tax. On the other hand, a person who buys shares of stock in the morning, with the hope of selling them in the afternoon for a 2.0-percent gain, will see his or her expected gain fall to 1.5 percent after the tax (2.0 percent minus 0.5 percent). This fall reduces the expected profit by a full 25 percent (0.5 percent being 25 percent of 2.0 percent). Such a large reduction in expected profits would prevent many short-term trades.

A reduction in short-term trading might have other positive effects. If the average holding period of stock shares increases, then the investment horizons of corporate managers may increase as well. Long-term investors might be less concerned over quarterly profit numbers than management's long-term plans for maintaining a strong company. This could lead to increased spending on investments, such as R&D, that will only pay off in the more distant future. It may also lead firms to have a greater commitment to keeping a stable and well-trained workforce, which will also offer dividends in the long term.

Another possible benefit of a STET is reduced volatility in financial markets. The relationship between trading volume and volatility is one of the most widely debated topics in financial economics. Numerous studies have examined this relationship between trading volume and volatility, and most find that higher trading volume increases volatility.[5] Although this evidence is not conclusive, it is at least plausible that one result of the reduction in trading caused by the tax will be more stability in national and international financial markets. Because investors value security and are willing to pay a significant price to reduce risk, any reduction in volatility attributable to a STET would be one more factor arguing in its favor.

It is important to realize that STETs are not a new idea. The United States actually had a STET on stock trades until 1964. It continues to impose very small STETs on stocks to support the operations of the Security and Exchange Commission. Comparable taxes are also imposed on the trading of options and futures to finance their regulatory oversight. Virtually every nation that has financial markets imposes some sort of STET, although these taxes have been lowered in recent years to make those markets more competitive with those in the United States.

In short, many reasons exist in favor of a STET. It could raise a very significant sum of money and drastically reduce the amount of resources wasted in financial markets. It might also lead to a longer-term focus among investors and corporate managers. In addition, it could reduce volatility in financial markets. We know that it could be successfully imposed and enforced, because the United States and other world financial markets have operated with STETs for decades. The nation as a whole could likely be a big winner from such a tax; only Wall Street stands to lose.

CHIEF EXECUTIVE OFFICER COMPENSATION: TAMING AN OUT-OF-CONTROL EXPENSE

In the 1980s, major corporations were cheered on by Wall Street as they went cost cutting with a vengeance. The announcement of mass layoffs generally sent stock prices soaring. Efforts to get cheaper labor through outsourcing or moving operations to developing nations raised short-term share prices. The market's rationale was that these measures would mean higher corporate profits, and higher profits should mean higher stock prices.

Whether these moves always led to higher profits in the long term is debatable. For example, many firms lost highly productive workers in downsizing. However, firms don't apply the same meat ax to all expenses. Although the wages of workers have been stagnant or declining since the 1980s, the wages of corporate chief executive officers (CEOs) have been soaring. The average compensation of a CEO at a major corporation in 1995 was $4,367,000 (Mishel, Bernstein, and Schmitt 1996). This compares to average CEO compensation of $971,000 in 1965. (Both numbers are in 1995 dollars.) The ratio of the compensation of CEOs to that of an average worker increased from 39.5 to 1 in 1965 to 172.5 to 1 in 1995. CEOs in the United States receive far higher compensation than CEOs anywhere else in the world. Even before counting the value of stock options and bonuses, which account for the bulk of CEO pay in the United States, CEOs in the United States on average received pay that was more than twice as high as the average of other industrialized nations. Factoring stock options and bonuses would make the CEOs in the United States appear even more highly paid.

The reality that CEO compensation is much higher in the late 1990s in the United States than it was in the recent past, or in comparison to other industrialized nations at present, should raise serious questions. Have CEOs become so much more productive relative to other workers over the last quarter century? Are U.S. CEOs that much more productive than CEOs in Europe and Japan?

There is no evidence to indicate that this is the case. In fact, numerous studies have examined whether there is any link between CEO pay and corporate performance. These studies have looked at the simplest measures of success, such as the increases in share prices and the growth of profitability. Studies cited found little or no link between CEO compensation and corporate performance (Barkema and Gomez-Mejia 1998; McGuire 1997).

This remarkable finding suggests that high levels of CEO compensation cannot be justified by productivity. It would be comparable to finding that a firm paid its autoworkers 30 percent more than the standard wage although they were no more productive than the average autoworker. Overpaying autoworkers in this way would never be tolerated; management would demand pay cuts or look to outsource work. If the existing management didn't pursue this route, the stockholders would almost certainly revolt and attempt to replace it with new management that would.

Yet financial markets do not react the same way to excessive CEO pay. In fact, the markets have been willing to tolerate deliberate acts of deception to hide the true cost of CEO pay. Much of CEO compensation comes in the form of *stock options*, the right to buy shares of stock at a below-market rate. This has a clear cost to the corporation, because it involves issuing new shares of stock, thereby lowering the value of the existing shares. In 1992, the Financial Accounting Standards Board (the organization of professional accountants that determines proper accounting practices) ruled that the cost associated with these options should be treated like any other expense and be directly deducted from corporate profits. Corporate executives intensely lobbied Congress, arguing that accurate accounting of CEO stock options would significantly lower their share prices. The lobbying effort was successful: it prevented the Financial Accounting Standards Board's ruling from being implemented. Corporations can continue to hide the true cost of stock options issued to CEOs and other executives from their shareholders.[6]

The difference in the way financial markets treat the cost of CEO compensation and the wages of ordinary workers can perhaps best be explained by the human element in the working of financial markets. Corporate CEOs and the corporate boards that hire them and determine their pay are likely to have much in common. They tend to be among the richest members of society. They often interact socially and, in many cases, are personal friends. Under such circumstances, it perhaps should not be surprising that corporate boards do not attempt to cut CEO compensation with the same vigor as they would the wages of ordinary workers. The CEO is one of them, and ordinary workers are not.

It is important to realize that the sums involved are quite large. Even though the CEO is only a single individual, pay packages that run into the tens or hundreds of millions are a major expense even for large corporations. Table 2.1 shows the top twenty CEO pay packages for 1997 (*Business Week* 1998a). It also shows the number of workers at each corporation. The next column gives the "CEO tax" paid by each worker. This is the amount that annual wages could have been increased if the CEO's pay had been instead divided up equally among the companies' workers. The last column gives the "CEO and friends" tax. This is the cost to each worker based on the assumption that other top executives received a compensation package that, taken together, was equal in size to the compensation of the CEO.

TABLE 2.1. Chief Executive Officer (CEO) Pay Packages and Consequences

Corporation	CEO	Annual Pay ($)	Workers	CEO Tax: Cost per Worker ($)	CEO and Friends Tax per Worker ($)
Travelers Group	Sanford Weill	230,725,000	67,250	3,431	6,862
Coca-Cola	Roberto Goizueta	111,832,000	29,000	3,856	7,712
Healthsouth	Richard Scrusny	106,790,000	36,873	2,896	5,792
Occidental Petroleum	Ray Irani	101,505,000	12,380	8,199	16,398
Nabors Industries	Eugene Isenberg	84,547,000	N/A	N/A	N/A
Cadence Design Systems	Joseph Costello	66,842,000	N/A	N/A	N/A
Intel	Andrew Grove	52,214,000	64,000	816	1,632
HBO + Co.	Charles McCall	51,409,000	6,286	8,178	16,356
Morgan Stanley Dean Witter	Philip Purcell	50,807,000	47,277	1,075	2,150
Monsanto	Robert Shapiro	49,326,000	21,900	2,252	4,504
General Electric	John Welch	39,894,000	276,000	145	290
American Express	Harvey Golub	33,457,000	74,000	452	904
Health Management Associates	William Schoen	30,945,000	N/A	N/A	N/A
Bristol-Myers Squibb	Charles Reimbold	29,211,000	53,600	545	1,090
Providian Financial	Shailesh Mehta	28,365,000	3,884	7,303	14,606
Allied Signal	Lawrence Bossidy	28,237,000	70,500	401	802
Pfizer	William Steere	28,120,000	49,200	572	1,144
America Online	Stephen Case	26,913,000	7,371	3,651	7,302
Travelers Property Casualty	Robert Lipp	26,301,000	N/A	N/A	N/A
Colgate-Palmolive	Reuben Mark	25,390,000	37,800	672	1,344

N/A, not applicable.

The numbers in the table are quite large relative to the wages of a typical worker. At Occidental Petroleum, the company with the largest CEO tax, an average worker would have received a pay increase of $8,199 if the CEO's pay had instead been divided among the workforce. The CEO and friends column indicates that the pay increase could have been as much as $16,398, if excessive compensation going to other top executives also had been divided up among the workforce. Even General Electric's $145 CEO tax, the lowest one on the list, is noteworthy. Many political campaigns are fought over proposals for tax cuts or increases that are smaller.

To be fair, it should be noted that these are the largest CEO compensation packages for 1997. Most pay packages take a somewhat smaller bite out of workers' pay or corporate profits. Nonetheless, for most major corporations, the compensation that goes to the CEO and their top executives would be a significant sum if it were either distributed to workers or added back to profits.

Also worth noting is a pernicious side effect of excessive CEO pay. As mentioned above, the years since 1980 have seen a considerable increase in wage inequality, with those at the top gaining enormously at the expense of workers at the middle or bottom. It is likely that outlandish CEO pay encourages this trend not only because of its direct effect in shifting income upwards, but also through an indirect effect in creating new standards for corporate executives. If the CEO can make $20 million a year, then his or her assistants might believe that they should earn $1 million a year, and maybe that the employees just below them to earn $600,000 a year. High CEO pay can push up the whole pay scale at the top end of the spectrum to the detriment of ordinary workers and the long-term well-being of the company.

Fortunately, CEO pay is an area in which workers can act directly through their union pension funds. Arguably, CEO pay is a direct deduction from corporate profits. This means that, insofar as CEOs receive excessively generous pay packages, the excess comes directly out of money that should be going to shareholders. In such a situation, the fiduciary responsibility that pension fund managers have to the fund not only allows them to try to rein in CEO pay, but also legally obligates them to make such an effort. Unless it can be shown that high CEO pay has somehow led to better corporate performance (the existing research indicates the opposite), pension fund managers are obligated to bring this pay under control to increase the returns to the fund.

It is often argued that CEO pay cannot be controlled, because it comes mostly in the form of stock options. In some cases, stock prices go up enormously, and the CEO benefits along with all the other shareholders. In fact, it is a simple matter to cap the gains that a CEO can earn from rising stock prices. Contracts can be structured to ensure that CEOs have plenty of incentive to work hard to raise stock prices but prevent them from gaining unlimited wealth if they happen to get lucky and the stock price escalates. For example, the total gains from stock options could be capped within the contract at $3 million per year, with any additional gains being returned to the firm.

Proponents of the current system, in which CEOs can earn tens or hundreds of millions of dollars through stock options, often argue that these packages are necessary to tie the CEO's interests to those of the shareholders. They raise the concern that CEOs may otherwise attempt to further their own security as top managers rather than maximize the price of the company's stock. Although there is a legitimate concern here, no one has produced evidence that these sorts of packages are necessary for that purpose. Even if the potential gains were measured in the millions, instead of in the tens of millions, CEOs would still have enormous incentives to increase stock values. Furthermore, even if a CEO reached a cap on the value of options in an existing contract, he or she would still have incentive to perform well, because in most cases he or she would be in search of another contract, either from the CEO's current firm or from a new one. That firms have felt the need to evade standard accounting procedures (as determined by Financial Accounting Standards Board [FASB]) in their treatment of options points to the fact that CEOs did not get their fat packages through the natural operation of the market.

Union pension funds are large enough actors in the market that if they began to demand such caps, it would have a substantial impact. In principle, other investors could also gain from imposing such caps. Only the elite few who see the CEO as a friend rather than a cost will be bothered by this approach. If nothing else, union pension funds should be able to ensure that CEOs and other top executives are treated just like all other workers.

Conclusion

We have shown several ways in which capital markets that seem "efficient"— because they generate high returns for shareholders   cause collateral damage that harms the economy and its workers. First, quick investment decisions that occur in an environment of relatively thin information can induce myopic behavior that causes investors to discount firms with longer-term competitive strategies and encourages managers to raid long-term capacities to satisfy the demand for short-term earnings.

In addition to this high transaction rate in the market for equities, the market for corporate control—M&A activity—has been accelerating. Research cited in this chapter shows how, generally without generating greater operating efficiencies or sustained increases to shareholders, takeovers and buyouts harm workers through layoffs, reductions in benefits and wages, and underinvestment in long-term capacities such as R&D.

Third, we examined changes in the asset allocation policies of pension funds and found dramatic increases toward higher-risk equities and international investments. The former shift fuels elements of myopic investment, and the latter has turned out to be, in retrospect, much riskier abroad and at home than investors had suspected.

The fourth source of collateral damage is the exorbitant cost of operating financial markets. We offer the STET as one potential strategy for mitigating that damage.

Finally, we discussed trends and patterns around the compensation of corporate executives and found that compensation levels have been growing, far exceeding the rates at which executives from other industrialized nations are paid, and do not seem to correlate with corporate performance. Taken alone, but especially when considered together, these sources of collateral damage present challenges to our notions of what it means for capital markets to operate efficiently. Although we have, for the most part, refrained from commenting on how these sources of damage might be mitigated, other essays in this volume describe a variety of strategies that perform well for investors at the same time as they avoid creating collateral damage.

[III]

SOCIAL FUNDS IN THE UNITED STATES:
THEIR HISTORY,
FINANCIAL PERFORMANCE,
AND SOCIAL IMPACTS

Eric Becker and Patrick McVeigh

Although the roots of socially responsible investing (SRI) date 250 years, it has grown most dramatically since the 1980s. Cast into the headlines with its strategic role in the South African divestiture campaign and thrust into our collective and individual consciousnesses as institutions such as the Catholic Church call for "invested funds to be used responsibly," SRI has become a significant part of the investment universe. A 1999 study by the Social Investment Forum, a trade organization for the field, found that nearly $1.00 in every $8.00 is invested using social criteria. In recognition of this growth, both Standard & Poor's (S&P) and Dow Jones have stated that they are considering establishing socially screened stock indices (*Business Week* 1999).

What began as a fringe movement, limited largely to religious organizations and antiwar activists, has moved solidly into the investment mainstream. Its participants include the three largest pension funds in the country (Teachers' Insurance and Annuity Association–College Retirement Equities Fund [TIAA-CREF], California Public Employees' Retirement System, and New

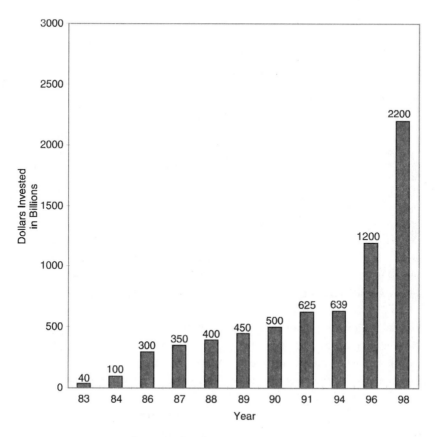

FIGURE 3.1. The growth of socially screened investing in the
United States. Source: Social Investment Forum.

York State); one out of every three investment-management firms (*Nelson's
Directory* 1997); and nearly two hundred mutual funds. Figure 3.1 depicts the
fifty-fold growth of invested assets in this field over the 14-year period from
1984 to 1998, from $40 billion to $2.2 trillion by year-end 1998.[1]

Social investing flows through three main strategies: screening, shareholder
advocacy, and direct community-based investing. *Screening* is the practice of
including or excluding publicly traded securities from investment portfolios
on social criteria. *Shareholder advocacy* describes the actions that many investors
take in their role as owners of corporations and is described in detail in chap.
4. *Community-based investment programs* provide capital to people who have difficulty attaining it through conventional channels or are underserved by conventional lending institutions. *Community-based lending institutions* include

TABLE 3.1. Social Investing by Category, 1995–1999

Category	1995 ($ billions)	1997 ($ billions)	1999 ($ billions)
Total screening	162.0	529.0	1,497.0
Total shareholder advocacy	529.0	736.0	922.0
Both screening and shareholder*	(0.0)	(84.0)	(265.0)
Community investing	4.0	4.0	5.4
Total	**695.0**	**1,185.0**	**2,159.0**

*Some social investment portfolios conduct both screening and shareholder advocacy. These assets have been subtracted out of the total to avoid double counting.
Source: Social Investment Forum, 2000.

community development banks and credit unions, as well as loan funds and venture capital funds for low-income housing and small business development. Descriptions of labor-pooled funds are found in chap. 5 by Michael Calabrese and chap. 8 by Jayne Elizabeth Zanglein. Table 3.1 gives the distribution of social investing across these categories from 1995 to 1999.

In the following section, we present a brief history of the development of SRI. We recount how it progressed from a narrowly focused agenda of religious investors to the broader social and environmental concerns of a larger audience. The campaign for a free South Africa played a key role in this emergence. In the second half of this chapter, we evaluate the financial performance of socially screened mutual funds and compare those results to the average mutual fund. We then examine the social and environmental criteria that these funds use to determine what qualifies as "socially responsible," with a focus on screens for labor and employee relations. Finally, we look at the impact of social funds on corporate behavior.

Growth of Socially Responsible Investing in the United States

INITIAL GROWTH: PROHIBITING UNETHICAL INVESTMENTS

Evidence of investors' combining ethical concerns with their investment decisions goes back several hundred years. There are many examples of investors driven by religious convictions to avoid investments in certain industries (primarily slavery, tobacco, and alcohol). Motivated by a desire to make their actions consistent with their beliefs, investors sought to shun business sectors they thought to be sinful. As a result, Christian Scientists and Methodists avoided alcohol and tobacco companies, and Quakers eschewed firms involved with the military.

So common were these beliefs, evidenced by the passage of Prohibition, that one of the first mutual funds created in the United States adopted these screens. Founded in 1928, The Pioneer Fund avoided all investments in the alcohol and tobacco industries. Pioneer, whose assets had grown to $200 billion as of December 31, 1998, continues to follow these policies today.

Although the avoidance of "sin" stocks gained little ground in the mutual fund industry over the next few decades, interest in SRI began to expand again during the 1960s. With the growth in activism against the Vietnam War, individuals in search of a consistency of actions and beliefs began to question whether their investments might be supporting what they believed to be an unjust war. Dr. Robert Schwartz, a New York City–based vice president with Shearson, became well known for helping investors avoid military-related holdings.

In 1971, a group of Methodist clergy discovered that their church regularly received letters from individuals asking how to invest in companies not manufacturing weaponry. After finding no organization that specialized in this type of investment, the ministers went to Wall Street firms asking for assistance in setting up a fund. The firms said it could not be done. On their own, this group of clergy formed the Pax World Fund. Although avoidance of military stocks was the initial concern for Pax, they were also the first mutual fund to adopt a wide range of other social screens (Domini and Kinder 1986).

EXPANSION: INVESTMENTS BECOME POLITICAL TOOLS
While the early growth in SRI was largely driven by religious belief and matters of conscience, the 1970s marked a sharp turning point. No longer just inward looking, investors began to view their investments as leverage to change the world.

University-based radicals, energized by the success of protests against the Vietnam War in shaping popular perception of this conflict, turned their sights to another great injustice: apartheid in South Africa. Even to casual observers, U.S. corporations were clearly playing a key role in supporting the racist government in South Africa. A 1978 U.S. Senate subcommittee reported, for example, that "the net effect of American investment has been to strengthen the economic and military self-sufficiency of South Africa's apartheid regime" (De Villiers 1995). The committee summarized the strategic role that U.S. corporations played by stating that ". . . South Africa would indeed be economically wounded, if not crippled, by any significant cutoff of U.S. trade or investment flows."

Given this reality, activists quickly developed new tactics to force companies to stop doing business in South Africa. Activities began in the early 1960s, with individuals selling stock in companies with South African ties and removing deposits from banks making South African loans. Soon, however, the issue became highly politicized. By the mid-1970s, activists were calling on universities, municipalities, and state governments to divest their investments from companies doing business in South Africa. SRI was growing from the realm of individual decision to a broader discussion of how institutions were investing their assets. Given the significant amount of money controlled by these institutions, social investing became a common topic in the media.

In 1976, the first divestment legislation, restricting investments in U.S. companies doing business in South Africa, became law in a state. Affecting a relatively modest amount of money by today's standards ($500 million), it nevertheless confirmed the validity of this strategy and opened the floodgates for activists to pressure other institutions.

Over the next decade, thirteen states and forty cities and counties passed binding measures to restrict investments related to South Africa. In addition, at least sixty-six colleges and universities took similar action. By this point, divestment legislation alone affected $230 billion; the investment world began to take notice.

Trillium Asset Management (formerly known as Franklin Research & Development Corporation) was created in 1982 as the first investment management company to work solely with socially concerned clients. That same year, the Calvert Social Investment Fund (SIF) was also founded and soon became known as the first of the socially screened funds to take highly publicized political stances. Calvert was the first mutual fund to advocate divestment from South Africa and to offer a South Africa–free investment option to shareholders.

Although Wall Street firms shied away from the growing political nature of SRI, many other mutual funds started up in quick succession to serve this booming marketplace. Working Assets (now known as the Citizens Funds) and New Alternatives both created new funds in late 1982. The Parnassus Fund began in 1984. The Social Investment Forum, the trade organization for this burgeoning community, was incorporated in 1985.

By 1989, divestment pressures had caused twenty-five states, nineteen counties, and eighty-three cities to pass legislation restricting investment in South Africa. One hundred and fifty-five universities joined in this movement. Responding to their own impact on hundreds of billions of dollars of investment capital and their success in inducing an exodus of U.S. corporations from South Africa, socially concerned investors broadened the scope of their activities.

Throughout the 1980s, environmental concerns began to take center stage. Joan Bavaria, president of Trillium Asset Management, created the California Environmental Resources Evaluation System (CERES) Coalition in 1989. This was a broad coalition of environmentalists, investors, and corporations seeking to create new models for environmentally sound policies. Through dialogue and occasional pressure, such large corporations as General Motors, Sunoco, Baxter, Polaroid, American Airlines (AMR), and BankAmerica have joined this process. The same year, Wall Street responded by rolling out a host of new environmental mutual funds. These included Alliance Capital's Global Environment Fund, Oppenheimer's Global Environment Fund, Schield's Progressive Environmental Fund, Fidelity's Select Environmental Fund, and John Hancock's Freedom Environmental Fund.

With institutional interest in social investing picking up, the first mutual fund designed to appeal to institutions, the Domini Social Equity Fund, was started in 1991. This 400-stock, socially screened mutual fund was designed to replicate the performance of the S&P 500 Index, the main benchmark by which most institutions measure their investment performance. The Domini Fund sought not only to eliminate investments in sin stocks and companies doing business in South Africa, but also tried to highlight firms with positive social records.

First Major Victory: An End to Apartheid

On September 24, 1993, Nelson Mandela appeared before the United Nations Special Committee on Apartheid in New York City and said, "The international community should end all sanctions against South Africa." Mandela's comments came just 2 days after South Africa's parliament approved a transitional council giving blacks their first meaningful role in controlling the affairs of the nation.

On the heels of the historic call by Mandela for an end to divestment, almost all institutional investors who had screened out corporations doing business in South Africa immediately lifted their prohibitions. This led to statements by a number of market watchers and journalists that interest in social investing would wane. Without the catalyst of South Africa divestment, they predicted, interest on the part of institutions and individuals in this field would soon dry up.

To test this hypothesis, the Social Investment Forum conducted the first comprehensive survey of the extent of social investing in the United States (Social Investment Forum 1995). This report found that the amount of money involved in social investing had not declined since the end of apartheid. Estimates from 1991, the year before Nelson Mandela called for an end to the divestment campaign, found approximately $625 billion in this field. The Social Investment Forum study found $639 billion still involved as of the end of 1994. This study also found that

- More than 90 percent of money managers surveyed reported using three or more screens with their socially invested assets. This factor largely explains why the end of the South African divestment movement did not result in a dramatic falloff in the ranks of money managers working in this field. In fact, 78 percent of money managers who handled screened assets before the end of divestment were still managing such funds after this point. The most popular screens used by investors were tobacco, alcohol, weapons, human rights, and the environment.

- Almost $1.00 out of every $10.00 under management in the United States was part of a responsibly managed portfolio. A total of 182 major investing institutions were found to be making socially responsible investments of one type or another totaling $639 billion in assets. This broad figure accounted for roughly 9 percent of the $7 trillion in funds under management in the United States, according to Nelson's 1994 Directory of Money Managers.
- An estimated $473 billion of the total was controlled by investors who sponsor shareholder resolutions on social issues. An estimated $162 billion was under management in socially screened investment portfolios.

SOCIAL INVESTING BROADENS ITS SCOPE

Strengthened by their role in helping to bring an end to apartheid (in response to a question from *Time* magazine asking if sanctions worked, Nelson Mandela answered, "Oh, there is no doubt" [De Villiers 1995, 197]), those involved in this field began looking for new targets and issues. Perhaps the most important target became tobacco.

Using the same strategies as the South African divestment campaign, activists pressured cities and states to pass legislation restricting investment in tobacco stocks. They scored victories in the states of Vermont, Florida, Pennsylvania, New York, and Maryland, along with the cities of Philadelphia and Cambridge, Massachusetts. From 1994 to 1996, tobacco-related divestment on the part of major institutions rose from approximately $7 billion to more than $157 billion. From 1996 to 1998, it increased to $523 billion.

An important event occurred in April 1996, when the American Medical Association called on all health care institutions and 1,494 mutual funds to divest of their tobacco stocks and bonds. In response to this publicity, a sizable number of mutual funds announced that they would adopt tobacco-free policies. These included the Stein Roe Young Investor and the Stralton and Thornburg families of funds. The Calvert Group now maintains a service to inform potential investors about tobacco-free funds.

In addition to tobacco, coalitions of investors also organized on issues concerning sweatshops, discrimination in the workplace, and human rights abuses in countries such as Burma and Nigeria.

Given the success of social investment activists, it was no surprise that the Social Investment Forum found a significant increase in the amount of funds involved in this field when it conducted another comprehensive survey in early 1997 (Social Investment Forum 1998). From year-end 1994 through year-end 1996, the Forum found that assets under management in the United States using social criteria grew from $639 billion to $1.2 trillion.

The highlights of this study were that

- A total of 710 major institutions (including pension funds, mutual fund families, community development funds, and foundations) were found to be involved in SRI. According to Nelson's 1997 Directory of Investment Managers, this figure of $1.185 trillion accounted for roughly 9 percent of the $13.7 trillion in investment assets under professional management in the United States.
- Although the amount of these assets involved in filing shareholder resolutions on social issues showed strong growth from 1994 (an increase from $525 billion to $736 billion), the assets in socially screened portfolios grew much faster than the overall market. Between January 1, 1995, and January 1, 1997, total assets under management in screened portfolios for socially responsible investors rose 227 percent, from $162 billion to $529 billion. Over the same period, institutional tax-exempt assets under management in the United States grew by only 84 percent (including both market appreciation and cash inflows), according to *Pensions & Investments*.[2]
- The number of mutual funds using social screens nearly tripled from 1994 to 1996. In its earlier study, the Social Investment Forum identified fifty-five mutual funds as using social criteria as part of their formal, publicly stated investment policy. By the end of 1996, this had grown to 144 funds.

INTO THE MAINSTREAM

Given the rapid growth in assets in this field, its success in bringing about corporate and social change, and the acceptable investment performance for these mutual funds (see Performance of Socially Screened Funds for this data), there are growing signs that SRI will enter the mainstream. Recently, major Wall Street firms have begun to offer products in this area.

In 1997, Smith Barney converted one of its mutual funds to a socially screened fund, with the consent of its shareholders. The Smith Barney Concert Social Awareness Fund is now one of the largest of the socially screened mutual funds. Since then, Merrill Lynch has created a closed-end fund that screens on diversity issues. In the February 22, 1999, issue of *Business Week*, S&P disclosed that it was working on a socially screened stock index. Dow Jones launched the Sustainability Group Index on September 8, 1999, and an Islamic Market Index in February 1999. The Sustainability Group Index will track the performance of leading firms worldwide who are attempting to operate in an environmentally sustainable fashion. The Islamic Market Index will track 600 companies worldwide that do not violate Shari'ah law (which requires the avoidance of alcohol, tobacco, weapons, gambling, and businesses that collect interest). *Plan Sponsor* magazine perhaps best summarizes the next chapter of the social investing story. In a 1997 editorial entitled "Social Investing—It's Everywhere," they conclude, "Social investing is an inescapable part of our world, because individuals—and institutions—can never completely compartmentalize their concerns" (July, August 1997, 2).

A 1999 study by the Social Investment Forum (Social Investment Forum 1999) of growth in this field supports these trends. Released in November 1999, it found that SRI has grown from $1.185 trillion in 1997 to $2.16 trillion in 1999. This 82-percent rate of growth compares with a 42-percent increase for all assets under professional management in the United States (as reported by *Nelson's Directory of Investment Managers* 1997). The total of $2.16 trillion accounts for roughly 13 percent of the total $16.3 trillion in investment assets under management in the United States (up from 9 percent 2 years earlier).

Labor unions emerged in the 1999 Social Investment Forum report. Although labor has long had an interest in this field since the 1978 publication of *The North Will Rise Again* by Jeremy Rifkin and Randy Barber, union participation has lagged behind other groups. This began to change in 1994, when the Department of Labor issued its Interpretative Bulletin 94-1 (see chap. 8, Overcoming Institutional Barriers on the Economically Targeted Investment Superhighway, by Jayne Elizabeth Zanglein). In 1998, labor-affiliated pension funds were, for the first time, the largest class of proponents of corporate governance shareholder resolutions (see chaps. 4 and 8 for more detailed information).

Performance of Socially Screened Funds

The historical performance of socially screened mutual funds supports the thesis that social screening does not affect the performance of stock portfolios. According to the 1996 study "Is There a Cost to Being Socially Responsible in Investing?" by John B. Guerard, Jr., "There has been no statistically significant difference between the average returns of a socially screened and unscreened universe during the 1987–1994 period. One should be attentive when selecting a socially screened mutual fund or manager. Performance can vary dramatically across managers but should not vary due to social screening over the long term."

Guerard studied a universe of stocks, not of mutual funds. Yet his conclusion suggests that social screening should not affect the performance of

TABLE 3.2. Annualized Return of Indexes and Index Funds (1994–1998)

	Standard & Poor's 500 Index (%)	Standard & Poor's 500 Index Fund Average (%)	Domini Social Index 400 (%)	Domini Social Equity Fund (%)	Citizens Index Fund (%)
1 year	28.8	28.1	34.6	33.0	42.7
3 years	28.3	27.7	32.0	30.1	33.3
5 years	24.1	23.6	26.1	24.3	N/A

N/A, not applicable.

actively or passively managed mutual funds. However, it should be noted that, just as screening does not affect the performance of the fund, it does not significantly affect the cost of capital for most firms. Neither the presence of the investment nor its withdrawal is usually significant enough in size to impact the share price, per se. Similar to shareholder action, much of the impact of screened funds occurs through the negative publicity that their withdrawal generates for the firm or industry.

As the field of socially screened mutual funds matures, we will have increased evidence with which to evaluate Guerard's contention. Today, the evidence remains limited. Just four socially screened equity funds have 10-year track records. Only nine equity funds have 5-year records. In the 3-year and 1-year time frames, the number of funds becomes more substantial and the data perhaps more meaningful.

Along with Guerard's study, the most compelling evidence yet that social screening is not detrimental to portfolio performance are the returns of the Domini Social Index (DSI) and the corresponding performance of the Domini Social Equity Fund, which tracks that index. The DSI was established in May 1990 as a socially screened alternative to the S&P 500 Index. The 400-stock socially screened index has outperformed the S&P 500 over the 1-, 3-, and 5-year periods through 1998 (Table 3.2), sometimes by substantial margins (Kinder, Lydenburg, and Domini 1998). As of December 31, 1998, the DSI recorded a beta of 1.04, demonstrating the index's close correlation with the S&P 500. We have also included the performance history of the Citizens Index Fund, a socially screened fund of three hundred stocks that was established in 1995.

The two socially screened index funds have been developing strong track records compared to both the S&P 500 Index and the funds that track it. The Domini Social Equity Fund has beaten the S&P 500 during all three periods. The Citizens Index Fund has beaten the S&P 500 by even wider margins over the 1-year and 3-year periods measured here. The table also shows that, in each period, the returns of these two funds surpassed that of the average unscreened fund with the objective of tracking the S&P 500.

We would not conclude from the data that social screening enhances portfolio returns over extended periods of time. These returns may be due to differences in sector selection and stock selection between the S&P 500 and the social index funds that are unrelated to the social screening criteria. However, this data offers evidence that social screening does not diminish returns.

Table 3.3 shows that fourteen of the twenty socially screened general equity funds that we tracked beat the 14.5-percent return of the average diversified equity fund (as measured by Lipper) in 1998.[3] The three largest socially screened equity funds (Dreyfus Third Century, Domini Social Equity, and Citizens Index), which account for 56 percent of the assets of the group, averaged a return of 35.3 percent. The dispersion of returns among the group was particularly wide in 1998, ranging from the 42.7-percent returns of the Citizens Index and Citizens Emerging Growth Funds to the 9.4-percent decline in value of the Calvert New Vision Small Cap Fund.

For the 3-year period through 1998, ten of fifteen socially screened equity funds beat the average stock mutual fund's 19.5-percent return, as measured by Lipper. Four of the five largest funds beat the average, led by the two social index funds, Citizens Index Fund (33.3 percent) and Domini Social Equity Fund (30.1 percent). Just three funds trailed the average by more than fifty basis points.

For the 5-year period through 1998, three of the nine socially screened general equity funds we tracked outperformed the 17.4-percent annual return of the average diversified equity fund. The Domini Social Equity Fund (24.3 percent) and the Dreyfus Third Century Fund (21.4 percent) both beat the average fund by handy margins, whereas the Parnassus Fund (10.6 percent) and the Calvert SIF Equity Fund (11.3 percent) severely trailed the average fund. The remaining funds were within 150 basis points of the average.

For the 10-year period through 1998, just one of the four socially screened general equity funds that existed through the period beat the 16.1-percent annual return of the average diversified equity fund. The Dreyfus Third Century Fund returned 16.8 percent annually for the period. The Calvert SIF Equity Fund was the laggard, with a 10.8-percent average annual return, whereas the Parnassus Fund (12.8 percent) and the Ariel Growth Fund (13.6 percent) were closer to the average but still substantially below it.

For 1998, three of the five socially screened balanced funds we followed beat the 13.5-percent return of the average balanced fund (Table 3.4). All three of the sector's large funds (at least $250 million in assets) beat the average, whereas the sector's two very small funds (under $30 million in assets) performed poorly. There was enormous dispersion of returns, as the Concert

TABLE 3.3. Annualized Return of Socially Screened Equity Mutual Funds

Equity Mutual Funds	Assets ($ Millions) 12/31/98	1998 Performance (%)	3-Year Annualized Performance (%)	5-Year Annualized Performance (%)	10-Year Annualized Performance (%)
Aquinas Equity Growth	42.0	22.0	24.6	N/A	N/A
Ariel Appreciation	274.0	19.6	26.8	18.3	N/A
Ariel Growth	195.0	9.9	22.8	16.0	13.6
Bridgeway Social Responsibility	2.0	37.8	26.9	N/A	N/A
Calvert Capital Accumulation	90.0	29.4	20.8	N/A	N/A
Calvert New Vision	65.0	−9.4	N/A	N/A	N/A
Calvert Social Investment Equity	147.0	10.9	17.2	11.3	10.8
Citizens Emerging Growth	93.0	42.7	24.1	N/A	N/A
Citizens Index	386.0	42.7	33.3	N/A	N/A
Delaware Group Social Awareness	39.0	15.7	N/A	N/A	N/A
Domini Social Equity	636.0	33.0	30.1	24.3	N/A
Dreyfus Third Century	973.0	30.2	27.9	21.4	16.8
Meyers Pride Value	4.0	13.6	N/A	N/A	N/A
Mennonite Mutual Aid (MMA) Praxis Growth	130.0	6.0	16.6	16.2	N/A
Neuberger & Berman Socially Responsible	100.0	15.0	19.2	N/A	N/A
Parnassus	275.0	1.4	13.7	10.6	12.6
Pax World Growth	10.0	15.2	N/A	N/A	N/A
Rightime Social Awareness	15.0	36.3	19.1	17.1	N/A
Security Social Awareness	10.0	30.4	N/A	N/A	N/A
Women's Equity	9.0	28.8	23.8	17.3	N/A
Lipper Growth Fund Average	—	22.7	19.5	17.4	16.1

N/A, not applicable.

TABLE 3.4. Annualized Return of Socially Screened Balanced Mutual Funds

Balanced Mutual Funds	Assets ($ Millions) 12/31/98	1998 Performance (%)	3-Year Annualized Performance (%)	5-Year Annualized Performance (%)	10-Year Annualized Performance (%)
Aquinas Balanced	30.0	8.5	14.5	N/A	N/A
Calvert Social Investment Managed Growth	714.0	17.5	15.1	12.8	11.5
Concert Social Awareness	252.0	27.5	N/A	N/A	N/A
Green Century Balanced	15.0	-10.1	10.2	8.7	N/A
Pax World	778.0	24.6	19.8	17.9	14.2
Lipper Balanced Fund Average	—	13.5	15.9	13.9	13.0

N/A, not applicable.

Social Awareness Fund rose 27.5 percent and the Green Century Balanced Portfolio declined 10.1 percent.

For the 3-year period through 1998, just one of the four socially screened balanced funds surpassed the 15.9-percent annualized return of the Lipper average. The Pax World Fund led the way during the period, returning 19.8 percent annually. The Calvert SI Managed Growth Fund, the only other large fund in the sector for the 3-year period, lagged by fewer than eighty basis points. The two small funds trailed further behind.

Only three socially screened balanced funds have 5-year records, and again just the Pax World Fund (17.9 percent) bested the average 13.9-percent annualized return of the sector. The Calvert SI Managed Growth Fund trailed by ninety basis points, whereas the Green Century Balanced Portfolio was far behind with an 8.7-percent annualized return.

Our data set for the 10-year period is even more scant, featuring just two socially screened funds. During that period, the Pax World Fund again beat the average (13.0 percent) with a 14.2-percent annualized return. Again, the Calvert SI Managed Growth Fund lagged, this time by 150 basis points (11.5-percent return).

In 1999 there were two socially screened international funds and one socially screened global fund (Table 3.5). International funds hold only shares

TABLE 3.5. Annualized Return of Socially Screened Global Mutual Funds

Global Mutual Funds	Assets ($ Millions) 12/31/98	1998 Performance (%)	3-Year Annualized Performance (%)	5-Year Annualized Performance (%)
Calvert World Values International Equity	222.0	16.1	11.5	8.6
Citizens Global Equity	54.0	32.3	21.5	N/A
Mennonite Mutual Aid (MMA) Praxis International	30.0	24.0	N/A	N/A
Lipper Global Fund Average	—	12.3	13.8	11.6
Lipper International Fund Average	—	12.7	10.0	7.7

N/A, not applicable.

of non-U.S. firms, whereas global funds hold shares mainly of non-U.S. firms but may own a certain percentage of U.S. stocks as well. All of the socially screened funds in this sector have bested the appropriate average in every period we measured. The best performance has been recorded by the Citizens Global Equity Fund, which handily surpassed the average global fund in both 1998 and in the 3-year performance. It returned 32.3 percent in 1998 and 21.5 percent annually for the 3-year period. That compares favorably with the 12.3- and 13.8-percent average global fund returns for the 1-year and 3-year periods, respectively.

The Calvert World Values International Equity Fund has beaten its benchmark by slimmer margins in 5-year performance. In 1998, its return was 16.1 versus the 12.7-percent average. For the 3-year period, it returned 11.5 annually versus the 10-percent average. For the 5-year period, it returned 8.6 annually versus the 7.7-percent average. The Mennonite Mutual Aid (MMA) Praxis International Fund returned 24 percent in 1998, beating the average by a wide margin. It does not have a 3- or 5-year record.

Just two social funds lie in the Equity Income category. Both are small, with less than $50 million in assets. For 1998, the Parnassus Equity Income Fund[4] returned 11.1 versus a 10.9-percent return for the average Equity Income Fund. The Aquinas Equity Income Fund returned 7.2 percent.

For the 3-year period through 1998, both funds trailed the average equity income fund's 18.9-percent annualized return by a wide margin. The Parnas-

TABLE 3.6. Annualized Return of Socially Screened
Fixed Income Mutual Funds

Fixed Income Mutual Funds	Assets ($ Millions) 12/31/98	1998 Performance (%)	3-Year Annualized Performance (%)	5-Year Annualized Performance (%)	10-Year Annualized Performance (%)
Aquinas Fixed Income	40.0	7.2	6.1	N/A	N/A
Calvert Social Investment Bond	67.0	6.1	6.3	5.9	8.5
Citizens Income	59.0	5.8	7.0	6.9	N/A
Eclipse Ultra Short Term	6.0	6.8	6.4	N/A	N/A
Mennonite Mutual Aid (MMA) Praxis Interme- diate Income	42.0	7.3	5.7	5.9	N/A
Parnassus CA Tax-Exempt	7.0	6.1	6.7	6.2	N/A
Parnassus Fixed Income	12.0	7.0	7.2	6.9	N/A
Lipper Bond Fund Average	—	5.6	6.4	6.2	8.4

N/A, not applicable.

sus Fund returned 12.6 percent annually, whereas the Aquinas Fund returned
just 6.1 percent.

The Parnassus Equity Income Fund was the only socially screened equity
income fund with a 5-year performance history. Its 12.1-percent annualized
return trailed the 16.7-percent average return.

All six of the socially screened taxable bond funds we track outperformed
the 5.6 percent return of the average U.S. bond fund during 1998 (Table 3.6).
The MMA Praxis Intermediate Income Fund led the pack with a 7.3-percent
return.

For the 3 years through 1998, returns of the six funds were tightly clustered
around the 6.4-percent average. The best return was turned in by the Parnassus Fixed Income fund, at 7.2 percent. The MMA Praxis Fund trailed with a
5.7-percent annualized return.

The four socially screened fixed income funds with 5-year histories were
evenly split around the 6.2-percent annual return of the average, with the top
funds (Citizens Income and Parnassus) returning 6.9 percent annually and the
laggards (Calvert and MMA Praxis) returning 5.9 percent annually.

Only the Calvert fund has a 10-year performance history, during which it barely bested the 8.4-percent annual return of the average bond fund. It returned 8.5 percent annually over that period.

Screening Practices of Social Funds

Most socially screened mutual funds have several exclusionary screens. They usually avoid alcohol, tobacco, and gambling firms; companies with poor environmental records; firms with very poor labor relations records; those involved in the nuclear energy industry; and those that derive significant revenues from the sale of weapons systems. Some social funds are more narrowly targeted, such as the Meyers Pride Value Fund, which focuses on gay and lesbian issues; the Cruelty Free Value Fund, which focuses on animal rights; and the Women's Equity Mutual Fund, which focuses on women's issues. These funds tend to have fewer social screens.

Furthermore, many social funds seek to invest in companies with strong records in many of these same areas, including firms with good records of charitable giving and those with diverse boards of directors and management teams. When firms do not clearly fail an exclusionary screen, social investment professionals are forced to weigh the positive and negative aspects of a company's record in making a decision about its suitability for investment.

It is important to note that socially screened funds generally do not claim to be "pure." Social investment professionals shun the terms *good company* and *bad company*, reflecting the belief that most firms are too complex to be labeled so simplistically. Social funds use exclusionary screens to avoid investments in areas with which their base of investors is uncomfortable due to a clash of values. This applies equally to institutional shareholders and individual shareholders. Labor pension funds may seek to avoid firms with egregious labor violations, whereas health care organizations may seek to avoid tobacco investments. Likewise, individuals with pacifist beliefs may seek to avoid military contractors.

A second objective of social screening is to send a message to corporations that investors are concerned about the social and environmental impacts of a company in addition to its financial performance. By questioning companies on nonfinancial matters, investors shape corporate agendas and consciousness.

For most social funds, the net result of the screening process is a portfolio that includes firms in socially and environmentally acceptable industries, while avoiding corporate "bad-actors" on a range of issues. There is certainly an element of compromise involved, as a firm's strong record in one social area may offset a poor record in another. Among the large-capitalization multinational firms that dominate the DSI and the Citizens Index, many have mixed social and environmental records. Both the DSI and the Citizens Index are topped by Microsoft and Intel, firms that have been criticized on grounds ranging from antitrust violations to environmental impact, while receiving plaudits in other areas. Meanwhile, both funds exclude top S&P 500 names such as General Electric, Exxon, IBM, and Pfizer.

The philosophy of some social investors is that it is acceptable to maintain holdings in firms with mixed records as long as they pursue shareholder advocacy in issue areas in which the firms are weak. After describing the screens themselves, we describe some of the strategies and activities that social funds use to influence corporate behavior on social and environmental issues.

COMMON SCREENS

All of the major socially screened funds avoid investments in sin stocks. Some funds, such as the Domini Social Equity Fund, the Dreyfus Third Century Fund, and the Citizens Index Fund, appear to have zero tolerance for any alcohol- or tobacco-related operations; others, such as the Calvert SIF Funds, avoid firms that are "significantly engaged in" the manufacture of alcoholic beverages or tobacco. The funds do not exclude companies in the business of selling these products, such as retailers who may sell cigarettes and restaurants that serve alcoholic beverages.

Most funds also exclude firms involved in the operation of gambling casinos, although these screens tend to be more porous. The Domini Social Equity Fund excludes firms that derive more than 2 percent of revenues from gambling operations, the Citizens Index Fund prohibits investments only in those firms whose primary business is gambling; the Dreyfus Third Century Fund and the Calvert World Values International Equity Fund, Calvert Capital Accumulation Fund, and Calvert New Vision Small Cap Fund make no mention of avoiding gambling firms.

Most social funds avoid firms that produce nuclear power. Among them are the Domini Social Equity Fund, Smith Barney Concert Social Awareness Fund, and the Calvert SIF Funds. As with alcohol and tobacco, some funds have zero tolerance, whereas others have a slightly higher threshold of acceptability. Still others do not mention nuclear power, including the Pax World Fund and Dreyfus Third Century Fund.

Although most social funds avoid investments in major military weapons systems contractors, the tolerance thresholds vary materially. For example, the Domini Social Equity Fund excludes companies that derive more than 2 percent of their revenues from military weapons sales, whereas the Citizens Index

Fund draws the line at 4 percent, the Pax World Fund at 5 percent, and the Calvert World Values International Equity Fund at 10 percent. Some of the funds also exclude any firms that appear near the top of the list of military contractors. This feature excludes conglomerates that may derive a small percentage of total revenues from military sales, but which nonetheless derive significant revenues in absolute terms.

Most social funds screen out companies that have histories of producing unsafe products or services. Although couched in various terms, these screens aim to avoid firms whose products are harmful even when used as intended. Many funds explicitly seek to invest in firms "that produce life supportive goods and services . . . In industries such as housing, food, leisure time, education, retailing, pollution control, health care, household appliances, publishing and building supplies" (Pax World Fund 1998). The preceding is an example of one of Pax World Fund's inclusive screens, which are more flexible. They allow the fund manager to purchase shares in firms that pass through all the exclusionary screens, but do not meet any of the inclusive screens. In this case, Pax owns shares in MediaOne Group, a cable television and Internet access service provider. MediaOne does not have a particularly compelling product, but it need not in order to pass these screens.

Nearly all of the socially screened mutual funds we evaluated have in place environmental screening criteria. Many funds avoid firms in environmentally challenging industries, such as natural resource extraction. Others use a "best of class" approach. For example, the Citizens Index excludes all oil companies on environmental grounds, whereas the DSI includes those oil companies that its research shows have the strongest environmental records. Among the criteria social funds use in environmental screening are a firm's history of regulatory compliance, its production of hazardous wastes, its level of toxic emissions, and its policies regarding disclosure of environmental data. The funds also evaluate eco-efficiency programs, waste reduction efforts, investment in renewable energy sources, and office recycling programs.

Human rights screening is closely tied to employee relations, as the issue is frequently defined in terms of overseas vendor standards. That is, social investors evaluate working conditions at a company's overseas plants or those of its suppliers. Some social funds exclude companies that operate in countries where human rights violations are prevalent, based on the premise that doing business in those countries may provide revenues to a ruling government that is responsible for human rights violations. For example, the Citizens Funds avoid firms that do business in Burma, where the military junta benefits from most commerce. The DSI penalizes firms that have poor treatment of workers at Maquiladora facilities in Mexico. Citizens Funds also avoid firms that do not have in place monitoring and enforcement policies to ensure responsible business practices in their overseas operations.

Few funds have strict exclusionary screens on employee or labor relations. Rather, most social funds seek to invest in firms with positive records in this area. The funds do not tend to view unionized firms more positively than nonunionized firms. They are more interested in the tone of employee/management relations. Several funds, including the Citizens Index Fund, avoid those firms on the national American Federation of Labor-Congress of Industrial Organizations (AFL-CIO) boycott list and those that have a history of labor law violations or particularly contentious labor/management relations. But more frequently, social funds evaluate a company's overall employee relations record, including worker health and safety, benefits, worker ownership, profit sharing, and layoff policies. In some cases, the funds include an evaluation of diversity programs and vendor standards in this screen, whereas in other cases the funds screen on those issues separately. We go into these screens in greater depth in the following section.

Other areas of interest to social funds include community relations, diversity initiatives, charitable contributions, and animal rights. Except for those funds that focus on a specific issue, few funds have litmus tests in these areas.

As we noted, most social funds have employee/labor relations screens that evaluate overall employee/management relations. They attempt to screen out firms with egregious labor records while supporting firms with particularly progressive initiatives. One good example is the Calvert SIF, whose prospectus states

> CSIF seeks to invest in companies that: Negotiate fairly with workers, provide an environment supportive of their wellness, do not discriminate on the basis of race, gender, religion, age, disability, ethnic origin, or sexual orientation, do not consistently violate regulations of the EEOC, and provide opportunities for women, disadvantaged minorities, and others for whom equal opportunities have often been denied. *For example, CSIF considers both unionized and non-union firms with good labor relations.*

This is not technically an exclusionary screen, but it implies that Calvert SIF is unlikely to own shares of firms that have particularly poor records of employee relations. In practice, this Calvert SIF screen uses a "best of class" approach. That is, to diversify across industry sectors, the fund invests in firms with the best labor records in industries with poor labor records, such as footwear, apparel, and toys. To invest in such a company, Calvert SIF requires that U.S. multinationals operating in such industries have in place strong programs to address labor issues in their overseas manufacturing operations. This would include supplier standards or codes of conduct, as well as procedures for monitoring compliance with such standards and codes (Calvert SIF 1998). As we will see below, Calvert has been among the leaders in the social investment field in addressing labor concerns through shareholder advocacy efforts. Only one fund is available to retail investors that focuses specifically on labor issues. The MFS Union Standard Equity Fund screens only on union issues (chap. 5, Building on Success: Labor-Friendly Investment Vehicles and the Power of Private Equity, discusses this fund in more detail).

The DSI aims to avoid firms with poor union relations, major health and safety controversies, significant workforce reductions (15 percent in the most recent year, 25 percent in the past 2 years), and severely underfunded pension plans. It seeks out firms with strong union relations, cash profit-sharing programs, considerable employee involvement through stock ownership or decision-making, and a healthy retirement benefits program. When one examines the DSI, however, it becomes apparent that even some firms with notably poor union records pass through this screen due to strengths in other social areas. An example is Dayton-Hudson, which is held in the DSI despite contentious relations with the United Auto Workers. In 1995, Dayton-Hudson lost a National Labor Relations Board ruling regarding United Auto Workers' organizing efforts, later backed up by the U.S. Sixth Circuit Court of Appeals. The company is included in the DSI in part because according to Kinder, Lydenberg, Domini & Co., it has a very strong record in the areas of community relations and diversity (Kinder, Lydenberg, Domini & Co., Nov. 1999). Dayton Hudson formally changed its name to Target in January 1999.

The largest social fund, the Dreyfus Third Century Fund, frames all of its social screening with the question of whether a company "contributes to the enhancement of the quality of life in America." The fund's prospectus states that the fund considers occupational health and safety and equal employment opportunity in its assessment. Unionization levels are not a factor. The Pax World Fund lists only "fair employment" among its social criteria in this area.

Impact of Social Funds on Corporate Behavior

We have stated that social screening accomplishes two goals. It aligns a portfolio with investor values, and it allows investors to convey their social concerns to corporate managers. This latter element may modify corporate thinking on some issues, but social investors have found that the most efficient way to promote change in corporate policies is through more aggressive shareholder advocacy, including shareholder proxy resolutions and formal dialogue with corporate managers.

Socially screened funds have joined institutional social investors, union pension funds such as the LongView Collective Investment Fund, religious institutions, and special interest groups in filing proxy resolutions on social issues. In all, 289 social policy shareholder resolutions were filed at 116 companies in the 1998 proxy season. Of that number, 120 came to a vote, 94 were omitted under SEC rules, and 72 were withdrawn by the filer (Investor Responsibility Research Center 1999). Social funds and investment managers filed or cofiled 19 of those resolutions.

The strategy behind these social resolutions is to push companies into structured dialogues with shareholders and other stakeholder groups with the hope that through substantive discussions the firms will move toward more progressive policies. Companies dread publishing shareholder resolutions on their proxies and addressing social issues at their annual meetings. Shareholder advocates have taken advantage of this corporate disinclination to address these issues publicly. Often, filers are willing to withdraw their resolutions in return for a commitment on the part of the company to either change their corporate policies or enter into a serious dialogue involving senior decision makers for the company. The shareholder campaign to encourage companies to endorse the CERES principles is an example of this approach. Other times, filers aim to bring the resolution to a vote and win a sufficient percentage of the vote to resubmit the resolution the following year. In its first year, a resolution must garner 3 percent of the vote for resubmission. This figure climbs to 6 percent in the second year and 10 percent in the third year. By attaining these thresholds, shareholders keep pressure on the company to consider addressing the underlying concern.

Just a handful of socially screened mutual funds have filed shareholder resolutions. Some funds are limited in their shareholder activism because they are part of conventional mutual fund families. For example, Dreyfus Third Century Fund, Neuberger & Berman Social Responsibility Fund, and Concert Social Awareness Fund are not able to file shareholder resolutions. They tend to focus their efforts on voting their proxies and communicating their views to corporate executives. Others do not have the resources to pursue that level of shareholder advocacy. Still others believe their social screening criteria are sufficiently tight that no firms in the portfolio warrant such resolutions. Calvert, Citizens Trust, and Domini have filed the most resolutions, with Pax World Fund, Green Century Equity Fund, and Aquinas pitching in occasionally. The index funds have an advantage in this regard because they have stable portfolios of stocks from which to make filings. In some cases, actively managed funds may not hold a stock for the 1-year period required to file a resolution.

The results from shareholder resolutions have been mixed, but clearly some firms have responded to pressure from social resolutions and dialogues. Walt Disney Corporation has been criticized for the meager wages earned by workers at the overseas plants that manufacture Disney merchandise. A 1998 resolution asking the company to report on its overseas workplace policies and monitoring programs received 8.7 percent of the vote, enough to be resubmitted in 1999. As a result, Disney agreed to audit its fifteen thousand overseas suppliers. Still, social investors are seeking independent monitoring and a commitment from Disney to ensure that its suppliers pay a sustainable living wage.

Joined by more than a dozen institutional shareholders, Trillium Asset Management filed a shareholder resolution at Home Depot for the second year in 1999, requesting disclosure of the company's equal employment opportunity data, which details the composition of the workforce by gender and race. Home Depot was hit with a $104 million settlement in 1997 due to charges of gender discrimination. Despite a 14.4-percent vote by shareholders in favor of the resolution in 1998, Home Depot's management has been unwilling to share this information.

Shareholder pressure has been critical in the movement for overseas labor standards by multinational firms. A group of social investment firms, including Citizens Trust, Trillium Asset Management, Calvert Group, Domini Social Equity Fund, Interfaith Center on Corporate Responsibility, and the Social Investment Forum have participated in the U.S. Department of Labor's No Sweat Campaign to eradicate sweatshops. Shareholder resolutions and dialogues have pushed a number of retailers and apparel firms toward instituting codes of conduct for the overseas suppliers and implementing independent monitoring programs. Among the firms to have adopted policies under shareholder pressure are Wal-Mart, Dayton-Hudson, Reebok, Nike, and Gap.

Likewise, shareholders have played an important role in convincing companies to endorse the CERES principles, a code of environmental conduct and reporting. Social investors continue to file CERES resolutions at between thirty and forty companies each year. Of those, approximately two-thirds have been withdrawn when the companies have agreed to meet with CERES representatives and consider endorsement. Resolutions at Sunoco, BankBoston, and General Motors have eventually led to endorsement of the principles and a commitment to publish an annual standardized environmental report.

It is clear to us that social funds have an impact on corporate behavior in a number of areas. In the realm of labor and employee relations, social funds have been active in pressuring firms to adopt increasingly meaningful codes of conduct for their suppliers and in calling for disclosure of equal employment opportunity data. There have also been a number of quieter successes in persuading firms to broaden their nondiscrimination statements to include sexual orientation.

Social funds and investment firms have committed greater resources to social research and advocacy. We expect that the greater experience and knowledge of social investors will lead to increasingly savvy relations with corporate managers regarding social issues.

[IV]

LABOR'S ROLE IN THE SHAREHOLDER REVOLUTION

Marleen O'Connor

Since the early 1990s, organized labor has been one of the most active players in the shareholder revolution.[1] Unions have devised innovative strategies to use shareholder rights to exercise unprecedented power over managers. Their recent victories foreshadow the potential of labor's capital. The American Federation of Labor-Congress of Industrial Organizations (AFL-CIO) has begun to coordinate the voting practices of union pension funds; if these efforts succeed, labor unions will constitute one of the largest blocks of organized shareholders in the United States (Moberg 1998). Thus, organized labor may soon wield significant political influence in the world of corporate governance.

I argue below that corporate governance will trump labor laws in importance, and shareholder rights will constitute a new focal point for labor relations in the United States in the twenty-first century (Blasi and Kruse 1991). Unions are using their rights as shareholders to influence corporate decision making outside the conventional labor law framework for two reasons. First, although the National Labor Relations Act does not adequately protect workers' rights against managers, the tables are turned as unions use their rights as shareholders to exert power over managers. Second, unions are using their shareholder rights to take advantage of the evolution in the balance of corporate power between workers and shareholders. In the 1950s, 35 percent of the private workforce was unionized and exercised substantial political power over managers, whereas shareholders faced collective action problems. By the 1990s, this situation had reversed. The institutional shareholder movement had overcome former obstacles to influence, whereas the decline of union membership and bargaining power made it more difficult for workers to protect their interests. As a result of this shift, shareholders as a class grow richer, while workers as a class grow poorer (Blair and Stout 1999). The media recognizes that the clamor for higher profits often comes from pension fund managers and suggests that they are "cannibalistically" driving the downsizing phenomenon.

This chapter examines the extent to which labor-shareholder activists can further their interests within the framework of the shareholder-dominated corporation. The following section, Labor's Shareholder Strategies Benefit Pensioners and Workers, reviews labor-shareholder activism and shows that its accomplishments are political rather than economic; unions have gained a great deal of credibility in the institutional shareholder circle. Because labor-shareholder activism provides workers with a voice in corporate governance, it has been heralded by some scholars as an alternative to the German system of codetermination. The section Stake-Holder Capitalism and Global Corporate Governance explores this notion by examining the role labor-shareholder activism plays in light of recent trends in global corporate governance standards. The section Promoting Sustainable Shareholder Value through Disclosure of Human Capital Values offers a "labor-shareholder" or "worker owner" view of the firm that focuses on creating sustainable shareholder value by using high-performance workplace practices. It examines efforts to establish standards to measure and disclose corporations' human resource values. Although unions face many barriers in their efforts to promote worker-owner interests through shareholder activism, this strategy is one of the most politically feasible and effective methods to provide workers with a voice in the new world of global corporate governance.

Labor's Shareholder Strategies Benefit Pensioners and Workers

SHAREHOLDER REVOLUTION AND UNION VOICE

Institutional investors have become the dominant owners in corporate America; the one thousand largest companies in the United States have average institutional ownership in excess of 60 percent (Coffee 1991; O'Barr and Conley 1992). However, only a small minority of institutions engage in shareholder activism (Black 1999). Unlike public funds, corporate management appoints private pension fund trustees. For this reason, private trustees typically do not challenge corporate managers (Roe 1993). The leading agents of the shareholder movement are public pension funds and union pension funds. Among public funds, those from the states of California, Florida, and Wisconsin are the most active (Romano 1993). The most active unions to use this strategy include the Teamsters; the Service Employees International Union (SEIU); the Union of Needle Trades, Industrial & Textile Employees (UNITE); and the United Brotherhood of Carpenters and Joiners of America (Carpenters).

These large pension funds have long-term investment horizons. They also hold substantial shares and so may not be able to sell their stock without depressing the market price. Rather than taking the "Wall Street Walk" of selling shares, institutional shareholders have revolutionized corporate governance by attempting to make the entire "corporate herd" focus on creating shareholder value (Zanglein 1998). They target underperforming companies with shareholder proposals to promote so-called good corporate governance practices that make managers more accountable to shareholder interests (Thomas and Dixon 1998).

For the most part, these public funds focus on process issues that apply to a broad range of corporations rather than analyzing particular business strategies on a case-by-case basis (Black 1992). Accordingly, public pension funds use voting guidelines that concentrate on the structure and competence of the board of directors. These guidelines include redeeming poison pills, limiting executive compensation, declassifying boards, and enhancing board independence. Once a company is targeted for a proposal, it is commonplace for institutional shareholders to have private meetings with corporate executives to voice their concerns about corporate governance issues (Carleton et al. 1998). During these "behind the scenes" meetings, investors can express displeasure about firm performance, and managers can provide investors with additional information about future strategies to further explain financial reports. Managers and shareholders negotiate over corporate governance issues in the shadows of the probable voting outcomes of the shareholder proposals. Some types of proposals, such as those concerning poison pills and board independence, are likely to receive majority shareholder support. Other types of proposals, such as those concerning executive compensation, are likely to receive much lower percentages (Thomas and Martin 1999).

It is clear that the institutional shareholder movement has created new norms of conduct in the boardroom by pushing directors to be more diligent in their efforts to create shareholder value. However, there is doubt as to whether those corporate governance practices have enhanced firms' financial performance. Note, however, that no study has yet examined the financial effects of union-sponsored proposals (Schwab and Thomas 1998). The existing statistical studies fail to capture the nature of the shareholder revolution on two counts. First, despite the lack of data showing that shareholder proposals alone improve the bottom line, shareholders use governance practices as important factors in evaluating the quality of management. Second, even though the actual number of successful proposals is low, managers are less likely to attempt to install entrenchment practices, because they know shareholders will veto such measures.

With this background, it is possible to see how unions use their power as shareholders to gain leverage over managers. For the most part, unions have not devised new issues for shareholder proposals because the public pension funds' proxy voting guidelines will not cover these topics. Instead, unions tend to push corporate governance practices that receive widespread support from public pension funds. By targeting a company with a proposal that will receive a high vote, unions maximize their potential to gain management's attention. Finding evidence that labor's strategy is successful, Randall Thomas and Kenneth Martin (1999) discovered that labor-shareholder proposals receive a statistically significant higher percentage of favorable votes than did similar proposals sponsored by private institutions and individuals. In addition, they found that labor-sponsored proposals obtain approximately the same percentage of votes as proposals sponsored by public institutions.

Although unions have become major players in the institutional shareholder circle, their motives for this activism may differ from those of other shareholders. Of course, labor shareholders have a general interest in promoting the long-term goals of adequate and secure workers' retirement income, and so seek corporate governance arrangements that prevent managerial self-dealing. Yet good corporate governance practices can benefit workers as well as shareholders; specifically, such practices serve as a floor that will lead to management turnover when firms perform poorly (*Director's Monthly* 1999). By monitoring managers and responding to early market signals, effective corporate boards benefit workers by avoiding major layoffs that result from long-term mismanagement.

In their path-breaking article on labor-shareholder activism, Stewart Schwab and Randall Thomas (1998, 1031) go so far as to assert: "Even if unions traditionally reduce shareholder profits, union-shareholder activism can enlarge the corporate pie without reducing the shareholding slice." Specifically, Schwab and Thomas maintain that unions are paradoxically positioned to champion shareholder value. They assert that unions have a greater incentive than most shareholders to supervise management to make sure firms stay healthy, rather than free riding on monitoring efforts by others. Firm specific human capital assets often lock workers into particular enterprises, whereas shareholders have diversified portfolios with relatively little fixed interest in any single firm (Schwab and Thomas 1998, 1037). Schwab and Thomas predict, "If unions could harness this incentive and ability to monitor and credibly relay their information to other shareholders, or to the independent directors on the board, a major role for unions could develop." Criticizing this position, Reineer Kraakman responds, "This familiar piety overlooks the obvious fact that employees as shareholders can capture only a portion of any gains that firms distribute to shareholders, while employees can capture all of the corporate revenue distributed as wages and benefits" (Kraakman 1997, 433).

In many situations, unions submit shareholder proposals to corporations that have neither unionized workers nor unionizing activity. In some cases, however, unions seek to use shareholder activism at companies where they are concurrently engaged in contract negotiations or union organizing campaigns (Schwab and Thomas 1998). By focusing on certain "wedge" issues that public funds support, unions can gain access to "behind the scenes" meetings with managers. During these meetings, it is commonly understood within the institutional investor community that unions may discuss labor issues as well as corporate governance matters (Georgeson Shareholder Communications 1998). Schwab and Thomas assert, "More tentatively, we suspect that unions are less able than other institutional shareholders to exercise influence through informal behind-the-scenes discussions" (Schwab and Thomas 1998, 1024). Although it may be true that labor-shareholders may not exercise as much political power as institutional shareholders such as the California Public Employees' Retirement System (CalPERS) or Teachers' Insurance and Annuity Association–College Retirement Equities Fund (TIAA-CREF), labor-shareholders can use their leverage to address labor topics with corporate managers who would otherwise ignore union leaders. If these negotiations proceed favorably, the notion is that the union will withdraw its shareholder proposals.

I briefly discuss three ways in which labor-shareholders have made gains for workers as well as shareholders. First, labor's use of its pension power can help to convince managers to recognize union organizing activity. For example, the Teamsters and UNITE succeeded in blocking a spin-off at Kmart and pressuring management to remove the chief executive officer (CEO). In the course of negotiations over these corporate governance matters, as a side benefit, Kmart agreed to accept a UNITE election victory in North Carolina (Moberg 1998). In a similar story, SEIU promoted a winning resolution to eliminate a poison pill at Columbia/HCA and supported two candidates for the board. In resolving the corporate governance issues, SEIU agreed to withdraw the nominations after Columbia/HCA named three new outside directors to its board. Around the same time, SEIU received an organizing agreement that recognized union representation.

Union pension power can also assist workers in strike settlement interventions. The most famous instance involves the United Steelworkers' strike at Wheeling-Pittsburgh Steel Co. in 1997, which caused the company's stock price to fall by half. The union persuaded the major shareholder of Wheeling-Pitt's parent, Dewey Square Investors Corp., to encourage management to settle the strike (Bernstein 1997b). The union was able to exert influence because Dewey Square's parent, United Asset Management Corp., manages $10 billion in union pension money.

Finally, union-shareholder activism benefits workers by ensuring that anti-union managers do not become entrenched. As an example, the Hotel Employees and Restaurant Employees International Union successfully opposed the anti-union Marriott family in preventing a dual class structure (*Labor & Corp. Gov.* 1998, Dec.). At one level, the union promoted good corporate governance. At another level, it exerted significant influence beyond collective bargaining.

For the most part, the use of shareholder activism in corporate campaigns is limited to companies embroiled in labor disputes. In a few cases, however, in which no apparent union activity was taking place, corporate managers have also accused unions of having ulterior motives. For example, one proxy statement accused a union of offering to withdraw a poison pill proposal if the company stopped dealing with an anti-union supplier (Lublin 1997). Such cases illustrate the potential conflicts between labor-shareholders and other shareholders.

However, Schwab and Thomas (1998) argue that legal restraints are not necessary to limit union's pension power in corporate campaigns, because their use of shareholder proposals is subject to significant political constraints. Foremost, unions need the support of other institutional shareholders for their proposals to pass. Furthermore, labor-shareholders are frequently checked by managers who accuse them of using shareholder proposals as a form of blackmail (Baker 1995).

For the most part, labor-shareholders have gained a great deal of credibility in the institutional shareholder circle as legitimate players; other shareholder activists do not view unions' shareholder campaigns as management-harassment tactics (Lublin 1997); they would rather focus on the merits of a proposal rather than the motives of proponents. Supporting this view, Randall Thomas and Kenneth Martin found that voting results for labor's shareholder proposals were not statistically different in cases in which unions were accused of engaging in harassment. Schwab and Thomas (1998, 1042) concluded that "union-led techniques should not be viewed as ploys to enhance labor's share of the corporate pie, but rather as techniques that generally increased incentives of management to improve firm efficiency."

Viewing the matter in a different light, Reineer Kraakman asserts that, even if unions gain a larger slice of the pie for themselves, "they are still supplying a public good—capable and innovative shareholder leadership to other institutional investors." Kraakman concluded,

> If unions gain a private advantage from their efforts, their governance role need not be less important for that reason. Because shareholders face a collective problem when ownership is splintered, they are likely to under-invest in monitoring unless they can obtain an offsetting benefit. When unions obtain such a benefit, they simply join the back of a long line headed by controlling shareholders, leverage buyout firms, and hostile acquirers—all of which can monitor on behalf of equity interests and extract private benefits for doing so. (Kraakman 1997)

With this background, we can examine in detail the ways in which labor-shareholders promote corporate governance issues. In their important work on labor-shareholder activism, Schwab and Thomas analyzed labor-shareholder proposals from 1994 to 1997. They found that since 1994, labor has consistently led the shareholder movement in submitting resolutions and winning majority support for shareholder proposals. They also found that the most frequent proposals in the 1995 and 1996 proxy seasons were those dealing with redeeming or voting on poison pills and repealing classified boards; in 1997, proposals concerning board independence and executive pay appeared more frequently. I update these results by reviewing the major proxy initiatives since 1998 and explore a new capital stewardship program that seeks to coordinate union voting strength.

SURVEY OF LABOR-SHAREHOLDER ACTIVISM

Labor fund activism usually takes the form of submitting precatory shareholder proposals. Since the late 1990s, however, labor funds have explored new methods to exercise shareholder voice, including binding bylaw amendments and written consent procedures. For example, unions have gained management attention by submitting changes in company bylaws to make their resolutions binding. These amendments respond to management tendencies to ignore precatory shareholder proposals, even when they receive majority shareholder votes (*Director's Alert* 1 1999). Managers assert that shareholders' rights to pass bylaw provisions are limited by corporate law provisions stating that the corporations' affairs shall be managed and directed by its directors, whereas shareholder activists respond that state corporate laws do not limit the substance of corporate bylaws. The courts must soon adjudicate this skirmish in the shareholder revolution.

[73]

In the first case testing the validity of binding bylaw amendments, the Oklahoma Supreme Court determined that shareholders can pursue this strategy (*International Brotherhood of Teamsters v. Fleming Cos., Okla.*, No. 90,185, Jan. 26, 1999). There, the Teamsters prevailed against the directors of Fleming Corporation to amend a bylaw to prevent the board from issuing a poison pill without shareholder approval. The Teamsters criticized the plan as a "means of entrenching" the incumbent management and submitted a proxy proposal for the 1997 Fleming annual meeting concerning an amendment to the company's bylaws to require that any rights plan implemented by the board be put to the shareholders for a majority vote. Fleming refused to include the resolution in its proxy statement and declared that the proposal was not an appropriate subject for shareholder action under Oklahoma corporate law. The Oklahoma Supreme Court ruled in favor of the Teamsters, stating that "The stock market has had a long history of shareholder passivity, but this is likely a thing of the past." It continues, "We hold under Oklahoma law there is no exclusive authority granted boards of directors to create and implement shareholder rights plans, where shareholder objection is brought and passes through official channels" (Lublin 1999, 132). Managers downplay the importance of *Flemming*, because the Delaware courts have not yet upheld binding bylaw proposals. In the meantime, shareholder use of this technique has risen dramatically, from only two bylaw amendments in 1996 to seven in 1997, twenty-two in 1998, and more than thirty in 1999 (*Labor & Corp. Gov.* 1998).

Another innovation of labor shareholders is to act by written consents without waiting for formal shareholders' meetings. This tactic was first used in early 1999, when the "Committee to Restore Shareholder Value at Oregon Steel Mills, Inc." (consisting of the AFL-CIO, the Amalgamated Bank of New York, and the Crabbe Huson Group, Inc.) filed a consent solicitation at Oregon Steel Mills that sought to declassify the board, require shareholder approval of poison pills, and establish confidential voting. A recent Steelworkers' strike had taken a substantial toll on the company's stock price. Although the consent solicitation failed, the proponents garnered more than 40 percent of the vote. The formation of this group of shareholders departed from the tendency of institutional investors to act as "lone wolves" (Coffee 1997). The willingness of a nonunion shareholder to join in this activism adds credibility to labor-shareholders' claims and may help persuade management to end the strike.

In the 1998 proxy season, labor sponsored and won more shareholder proposals than any other group (*Labor & Corp. Gov.* 1998). Specifically, labor sponsored 120 proposals, accounting for 17 percent of all resolutions. Fourteen proposals passed, with six proposals dealing with shareholder approval of poison pills and five concerning declassifying boards. Although most proposals focused on standard corporate governance issues, a few addressed corporate social responsibility issues such as calls for sourcing standards for suppliers, equal employment opportunity, and disclosure of corporate political contributions (*Labor & Corp. Gov.* 1999a). The 1999 proxy season was one of the most active for labor-shareholder activism, with unions filing more than 80 proposals. Labor unions continue to focus on eliminating antitakeover devices, such as poison pills and staggered boards, as well as limiting executive compensation and promoting board independence.

Poison pills and classified boards tend to entrench incumbent managers by making hostile takeovers more difficult. At first blush, labor-shareholder proposals to redeem poison pills and declassify boards may seem counterintuitive, because takeovers can hurt workers if they lead to layoffs. Reenier Kraakman asserts the following:

> Employees would presumably oppose destabilizing measures, such as stripping management of the power to defend against hostile takeovers that might lead to the loss of jobs. The puzzle remains as to why union funds should campaign to advance the interests of all shareholders, even to the point of advancing such seemingly anti-employee measures as proposals to dismantle poison pills. (Kraakman 1997, 434)

To understand this puzzling position, consider the history of labor's position on antitakeover devices. In the 1980s, unions allied with managers against public pension funds to pressure state legislatures to enact antitakeover legislation. Although the evidence was weak, many states responded to these charges that takeovers caused job loss by enacting statutes that permit directors to consider the interests of employees in making business decisions (O'Connor 1991). These statutes offered weak protections and did not provide workers with a right to sue directors for breach of fiduciary duty. In layoffs and plant closings unrelated to takeovers, managers often argue against any form of legislation to protect workers. Thus, in allying with managers to lobby state legislature to antitakeover statutes, unions hurt their interests as shareholders without gaining much as employees.

When the takeovers of the 1980s ended, downsizing and restructuring in the 1990s disrupted old alliances and fostered new coalitions. The tables turned as unions joined other shareholders to remove antitakeover devices. We find unions, which once pushed for antitakeover legislation, have now become leading proponents of resolutions to remove antitakeover mechanisms. Strategically, shareholder proposals dealing with poison pills and classified boards are likely to receive majority support; thus, unions can target anti-union firms with these proposals while avoiding pro-union firms. Out of the eighty proposals submitted by labor-shareholders for 1999, twenty concern poison pills—eleven in the form of binding bylaw amendments (*Labor & Corp. Gov.* 1999a)—and nineteen concern declassifying boards.

Labor unions have also devoted significant effort to combating excessive executive compensation. In the 1980s, institutional shareholders promoted the notion of paying executives in stock options as a means of aligning managers' interests with those of shareholders. At the time, however, shareholders did not realize that quantities of stock options would explode to their current levels. Until recently, most institutional shareholders did not object to the levels of executive compensation, deferring to boards' arguments that such incentive-based pay would improve firm profitability. However, a broad spectrum of institutional shareholders has started to take steps to curb recent excesses.

Union pension fund trustees and managers are concerned about the effects of excessive executive compensation on shareholders and workers (Rose 1998). The AFL-CIO has established an "Executive Paywatch" Web site to raise public awareness of some of the issues involved surrounding executive compensation. This Web site explains that, as shareholders, union pension fund trustees and managers are concerned about excessive executive compensation pay for two reasons. First, executive option grants dilute the holdings of other shareholders, representing more than 13 percent of shares outstanding for large U.S. companies, up from 5 percent in 1990 (Ferlauto 1998a). Second, boards often react to drops in the companies' stock price by lowering the exercise prices of these grants, thereby severing the link between pay and performance (McGurn 1999).

These union pension funds use executive compensation to highlight strong political and social concerns about job loss and wealth disparities.[2] Union members do not think that limiting executive compensation will save jobs or bring higher wages (McGurn 1999).[3] Rather, they focus on how excessive executive compensation may hurt firm productivity by lowering worker morale. Executive Paywatch explains, "A 1992 U.C. Berkeley Haas School of Business study found that pay inequality leads to less cooperative work environments, higher turnover, and lower product quality" (O'Reilly et al. 1996). Richard Trumka, AFL-CIO treasurer, states the case more bluntly: "CEOs get multimillion dollar sweetheart deals while working families suffer downsizing and falling wages. People want to believe in the American Dream. . . . The fact is that these exorbitant executive pay figures can put an end to that kind of hope and can devastate workers' morale" (O'Reilly et al. 1996). Executive stock options should be eliminated, because managers need to balance the interests of all the firm's stakeholders, and stock options bind them too tightly to shareholders.

In labor's campaign against excessive executive compensation, union pension funds have pushed for indexed options, increased disclosure, and greater board independence (Ferlauto 1998b). Labor has responded with two steps to curb excessive executive compensation. First, union pension funds submitted seventeen proposals in 1998 calling for more independent directors on compensation committees. For a first-time submission it received a high percentage of votes (*Labor & Corp. Gov.* 1998). Second, labor unions have been publicly calling on the U.S. Securities and Exchange Commission (SEC) to establish disclosure guidelines to publicize the ties between members of the nominating committee and the CEO (*Atlanta Journal* 1998).

These efforts are unlikely to reduce executive compensation. There is no compelling evidence that greater board independence improves overall firm performance or that a greater number of independent directors limit excessive compensation. To the contrary, some evidence suggests that inside directors may enhance firm value (*Director's Alert* 4 1999). On the other hand, a recent study by Thomas and Martin shows that target companies do not increase average total CEO compensation levels as rapidly in the year after receiving a shareholder proposal as firms not receiving such proposals (Thomas and Martin 1999).

The most promising avenue for restricting executive compensation is through the use of binding bylaw amendments. In 1998, the SEC reversed its position that treated repricing as an ordinary business matter not appropriate for shareholder Security and Exchange Commission (Securities and Exchange Commission 1998b). In this no-action letter, the State of Wisconsin Investment Board proposed a binding bylaw amendment that required shareholder approval of future repricings of stock options at General Datacomm Industries. The SEC stated that the proposal was not excludable, because it raises significant social issues because of "the widespread public debate concerning option repricing." In the future, labor-shareholders will probably enhance their submission of more binding bylaw amendments to limit executive compensation.

Grand Plan: Creating a Voting Bloc of Union Pension Funds

The AFL-CIO has taken two steps under its Capital Stewardship Program to turn the Taft-Hartley pension funds into a voting bloc. First, the AFL-CIO issued proxy voting guidelines to inform plan managers how the labor movement views important issues considered in shareholder proposals. Second, it has conducted surveys to see whether fiduciaries that manage union pension money follow these guidelines. In this way, the AFL-CIO seeks to "help fiduciaries achieve the best returns for their plans—while keeping in mind whose money it is" (Sweeney 1998). These efforts have much potential for providing union pension funds with more political leverage as shareholders in the future.

For the most part, AFL-CIO guidelines are not controversial, because they resemble guidelines established by other activist funds. For example, the guidelines recommend that independent directors make up a majority of the board and key board committees, such as the compensation, nominating, and auditing committees. In addition, they recommend separating the job of chairperson of the board from that of CEO, eliminating pensions for outside directors, and eliminating golden parachutes.

Other measures, however, clearly highlight the AFL-CIO's intention to promote worker interests through the proxy voting. Their guidelines assert that fiduciaries should not seek to maximize short-term gains if doing so conflicts "with the long-term economic best interests of the participants and beneficiaries" (AFL-CIO 1997c, 1). Examples of these long-run interests include corporate policies that affect employment security and wage levels of plan participants. To promote these long-run interests, the guidelines support proposals that promote high-performance workplace practices, such as employee training, direct employee involvement in decision making, compensation linked to performance, employment security, and a supportive environment. In addition, the guidelines also state that the corporation should not use suppliers who employ forced or child labor or otherwise violate workers' rights under international law.

One particularly sensitive area is compensation; the guidelines favor stock-based compensation if it is available to lower-level employees. In addition, the guidelines ask the plan managers to consider whether the plan "creates or exacerbates disparities in the workplace that may adversely affect employee productivity and morale" (AFL-CIO 1997c, 16).

To track the influence of these guidelines, the AFL-CIO has issued Key Votes Surveys since 1997. These surveys evaluate the voting records of investment managers in each proxy season as "litmus tests of shareholder resolutions" to assess whether union money is being voted to advance labor's interests. The surveys reveal that many firms consistently voted proxies against union positions on corporate governance matters (*Pensions & Investments* 1998). In response, the AFL-CIO encourages fund managers to consult advisors such as Proxy Voting Services (PVS) of the Institutional Shareholder Services (ISS), a private firm that provides proxy voting advice and voting services to institutional investors. The 1997 and 1998 surveys reveal that PVS has a 100-percent voting record on union positions; significantly, an ISS recommendation can make a 15- to 20-percent difference in the support that a shareholder proposal receives.

In 1997, the AFL-CIO issued a "10 Key Votes Survey" that focused on traditional corporate governance issues, such as independent directors, cumulative voting, and declassification. One vote, however, illustrates the unique worker-shareholder perspective: unions such as the Teamsters submitted a proposal to Mobil to ask the executives not to exercise stock options until 6 months after a major layoff (AFL-CIO 1997a).

Despite the fact that the survey overwhelmingly focuses on standard corporate governance issues, its use has generated significant controversy among some pension managers. Some criticize the survey for entangling them in labor disputes (*Pensions & Investments* 1998). Others worry about how the guidelines will affect investment returns and fiduciary obligations.

In 1997, the AFL-CIO surveyed 45 managers of the largest Taft-Hartley funds for the first time. They found that many of these managers voted against the AFL-CIO position on a majority of issues, and only six voted 100 percent with the AFL-CIO's recommended positions (*Labor & Corp. Gov.* 1998). The AFL-CIO publicly announced to fund managers that this first vote survey was only the beginning of their proxy monitoring, and that the 1998 survey results would be scrutinized more critically.

The AFL-CIO's approach to the 1998 survey differed in two ways: it announced the key votes before the proxy season started, and it slated forty votes for review. Again, the survey focused almost exclusively on standard corporate governance issues; the most common proposals were to create independent boards (eight proposals) and to declassify the board (seven proposals), and to rescind or obtain shareholder approval of poison pills (five proposals). Importantly, however, the AFL-CIO announced that the 1998 survey represented "a worker-owner view of value, stressing management accountability and good corporate governance. The proposals aim to create long-term value through developing the skills and human capital of their workforce, through regulatory compliance and through protecting the brand integrity." Only five resolutions, however, focused on issues that distinctively benefited workers. One resolution asked for Equal Employment Opportunity Commission disclosures. Another recommended that firms follow the MacBride principles, which seek to ensure that corporations doing business in Ireland do not discriminate against workers based on religious beliefs. Three sought to link executive compensation to employment criteria, such as avoiding mass layoffs and adhering to fair labor standards overseas. In interpreting the results of the 1998 survey,[4] 29 percent of the firms had 100-percent voting records. This percentage is somewhat misleading, because a firm could achieve a high score by only holding stock in one or two companies and voting according to the guidelines. Only four firms scored forty of the forty votes. Seven percent of the firms scored 75 percent or over; 30 percent scored 50 percent or over; 10 percent had 25 percent or over, and 12 percent had less than 25 percent.

Beyond voting recommendations, the AFL–CIO has established the Center for Working Capital, a nonprofit corporation created to promote a progressive voice in the operation of union money and to educate the public on issues pertaining to worker-owners. The Center will centralize information on union pension fund holdings, coordinate proxy voting, and foster policies and practices that promote both economic prosperity and retirement security. To begin, the AFL–CIO has established classes at the George Meaney Center in Maryland to educate pension trustees and union leaders to become activist investors.

POLITICAL GAINS OF LABOR-SHAREHOLDER ACTIVISM

For the most part, the gains of labor-shareholder activism are political rather than economic. The AFL–CIO president, John Sweeney, is seeking to revitalize the labor movement by increasing union membership and promoting corporate governance reforms (Bernstein 1997). Four political features of labor-shareholder activism facilitate union endeavors to increase membership.

First, labor-shareholders receive positive media publicity for shaking up the traditional boardroom culture to make executives more accountable to shareholders. Specifically, journalists describe unions as "rabble rousers" using "strong-arm, coercive tactics" to push corporate governance reform. From the perspective of potential members, this type of media coverage tempers the constant barrage of news items describing unions as weak and ineffective "social dinosaurs" of the industrial age. Union representatives assert that this response "acknowledges the enormous power that we have and our ability to plague corporate management" (Bernstein 1997a). Thus, one main benefit of labor-shareholder activism comes from a new public perspective that unions exercise tremendous power over managers and are "continuing to be the pioneers of social innovation" (Trumka 1996). In the last few years of the twentieth century, labor-shareholders have gained a tremendous amount of credibility within the corporate governance world. The institutional shareholder circle is a close-knit community, and opinion leaders are very influential in establishing norms for this key group. Labor leaders William Patterson, of the AFL–CIO, and Ed Durkin, of the Carpenters, served terms as president of the Council of Institutional Investors, a Washington-based group of activist funds

Second, labor-shareholder activism gains symbolic value by highlighting the fact that working people are the beneficiaries of many institutional shareholders. For the first time, labor-shareholders are recognized as a distinct category with its own political agenda. Workers own a tremendous amount of stock, but a large gap separates this ownership from effective control of capital (Blasi and Kruse 1991). Labor-shareholder activists William Patterson and Bart Naylor explain, "There's an expectation in corporate America that employee-shareholders are to be seen and not heard. But we're seeing among some employee-shareholders an awareness of who really owns the company."[5] Labor-shareholder activism can take the lead in presenting a worker-owner view of the firm by constantly reminding fiduciaries that it should matter that they are investing workers' money (*Working Capital* 5 1999).

Third, although pension power has the potential to revolutionize corporate governance, labor-shareholder activism is politically feasible. Importantly, these strategies do not require labor law reform, which is highly unlikely in the current political environment. As unions lose members, they lose political clout. Even under a democratic administration, the national political climate does not favor unions. In contrast, labor-shareholder activism receives a large degree of bipartisan political support, because it does not fundamentally challenge the basic structure of U.S. capitalism. Specifically, labor-shareholder activism accords with strong beliefs in property rights and the faith that shareholders can address policy concerns of corporations.

Finally, union efforts to make boards more accountable alter managers' perceptions of workers' interests in the enterprise. Historically, unions did not support reform proposals for German-style codetermination because labor was content to leave board decision making to managers under "job conscious unionism."[6] Unions in the United States did not focus upon challenging the "system" that established managers as "thinkers" and workers as "doers" (Taylor 1911; Braverman 1974). Managers also resisted the notion of codetermination, arguing that corporate strategy should be left to those with knowledge of finance, economics, and law. Unions' efforts to reform corporate governance institutions alters this conceptual world and transforms power relationships in U.S. corporations. Labor-shareholder activism will continue to destroy old stereotypes as organized labor further promotes the employees' role in corporate governance by pursuing more board seats.[7]

These developments have led U.S. scholars to compare U.S. unions' use of their pension power with the role of employees in the German system of codetermination.[8] The next section evaluates this notion by reviewing recent developments in *stake-holder capitalism* and the growing concept of *global corporate governance*.[9]

Stake-Holder Capitalism and Global Corporate Governance

To assess the role that labor-shareholder activism plays in promoting stake-holder capitalism, we now consider the path-dependence of U.S. corporate law and labor issues. U.S. corporate scholars predominantly view the German system of codetermination as producing weak and ineffective boards. Recent developments suggest that their shareholder-value mantra is sweeping the globe. This section highlights how new corporate governance codes dilute the influence of the workers' voice under the German system of codetermination. As the German models of codetermination give way to the U.S. model, German unions are becoming more interested in U.S. pension fund activism. U.S. unions must be careful about promoting shareholder value, as it can play into the notion that the sole function of the board is to make money for stockholders.

HISTORY OF THE STAKE-HOLDER DEBATE IN THE UNITED STATES

The United States has a long history of separating issues pertaining to workers to labor law and issues concerning shareholders to corporate law. Since 1980, however, interest in the intersection between corporate and labor law has grown. At the beginning of the 1990s, U.S. corporate governance scholars began to examine comparative corporate law as part of the policy debates about the ability of U.S. firms to compete effectively in global markets. For the most part, U.S. scholars based their analysis on how shareholders monitor managers in the European and Japanese models of corporate governance (Rock 1996). When the German economy appeared to be outstripping that of the United States in the early 1990s, corporate law scholars began to examine the German system of codetermination.[10] This comparative analysis led some to conclude that the greatest flaw of the U.S. system was its insufficient investment in human capital. Corporate law scholars saw a fundamental paradox: downsizing had weakened the traditional ties of job security and loyalty that bind employees to firms; at the same time, decentralized decision making and cross-functional teams increased the firms' dependence upon human capital. This paradox created a strong interest among U.S. corporate law and labor scholars in reshaping U.S. corporate governance structures to reallocate decision making to encourage investments in human capital (Blair 1995; Blair 1996; Blair 1997; Stone 1988). A few corporate scholars promoted labor board representation as a way to facilitate the tradeoff between commitment and adaptability in a world of rapid technological change (Gilson 1996).

However, with the improvement in the U.S. economy in the early 1990s, discussion of the merits of codetermination in the United States lost momentum. Management systems moved away from European and toward Asian models of production. From 1990 on, Charles Sabel (1996) explained: U.S. production became more Japanese, but U.S. labor relations and corporate governance became more Americanized than ever. U.S. corporate governance scholars have not made an in-depth examination of the precise role of the labor component of the supervisory board. This is a serious omission because, at this point, the most significant difference between the corporate governance systems of the United States and Germany is with respect to the role granted to labor (Gordon 1998). The prevailing view among most U.S. corporate law scholars is that the German system of codetermination produces weak boards and inefficient decision-making processes (Roe 1998). The overwhelming normative consensus among U.S. corporate law scholars is that the board should focus on shareholder interests exclusively and that workers should protect their interests through contract. Henry Hansmann and Reineer Kraakman summarize the situation, "We now have not only a common ideology supporting shareholder-oriented corporate law, but also an interest group to press that ideology"(Hansmann and Kraakman 2000, 17).

POLITICAL ECONOMY OF GLOBAL CORPORATE GOVERNANCE

Although obstacles to harmonization ensure continued diversity among national laws governing corporations, Ron Gilson explains that "convergence towards a similar set of institutions may not depend on convergence in formal rules" (Gilson 1997). Since 1998, several factors have operated to push countries toward the U.S. model of corporate governance. With CalPERS taking the lead, U.S. institutional investors have articulated global governance principles (Russell Reynolds Assoc. 1998; Lally 1997) and been joined by institutional investors from around the world (Lubin and Calian 1998). Beyond this, increasing economic globalization pushes for a universal set of business measures; cross-border deals such as Daimler-Chrysler will continue to reinforce convergence trends. Third, the 1998 global economic crisis is likely to create even greater demand for transparency and accountability, two of the central tenets of the global governance reform movement (Heard 1998). Finally, an important factor in making the U.S. model palatable to European managers is the promise of U.S.-style executive compensation.

This convergence can be seen in the voluntary corporate governance guidelines that have been adopted by several European countries. Three prominent committee reports, England's Cadbury Committee, the Netherlands' Peters Committee (Denkenberger 1998), and France's Vienot Committee, recommend boards more responsive to creating shareholder value (Breen 1996). These reports do not address concerns about creating a short-term perspective among directors and do not affirmatively encourage directors' obligations to nonshareholder constituents (Edelstein 1997). Several other organizations are in the process of drafting corporate governance guidelines, including the European Corporate Governance Network, the International Corporate Governance Network, and the Asia-Pacific Economic Corporation.

One of the most influential efforts to shape global governance norms are the recommendations of an advisory group to the Organization for Economic Cooperation and Development (OECD). The first draft of these guidelines strongly focused on protecting shareholder interests and barely mentioned the interests of workers. Responding to objections from the International Confederation of Free Trade Unions, Trade Union Advisory Council (TUAC) to the OECD, a second draft contains language emphasizing that "board members should act in the best interests of the company as a whole." The OECD guidelines (1999) go on to state, "The corporate governance framework should recognize the rights of stake-holders as established by law and encourage active cooperation between corporations and stake-holders in creating wealth, jobs, and the sustainability of financially sound enterprises." These OECD guidelines do not encourage codetermination or provide employees with rights to enforce stake-holder views of the corporation. Rather, they focus in great detail on making the board more accountable to shareholders by allowing them to vote for important decisions and voice their concerns.

The question raised by the OECD guidelines is how boards will balance the competing interests of long-term shareholders and employees to make the best decisions for the corporation when the shareholders' influence is increased and the workers' power in corporate governance is not. Because the underlying global economic environment pressures managers to side with shareholders rather than employees, the constituency language in the guidelines will not benefit the workers in OECD member countries for the same reasons that it fails to protect workers in the United States.

As corporate governance mechanisms around the world converge toward the U.S. model, the fate of existing rules governing worker voice in corporate decision making hangs in the balance. The German system of codetermination is under pressure to make boards more responsive to shareholders. When this corporate governance debate emerged in Germany in the late 1980s (Arnold 1996), participants had to use the English term *shareholder value*, because the German language lacks a translatable concept (Pistor 1998). A 1997 reform proposal sought to reduce the size of the German supervisory board from twenty to ten members to make it more efficient. The proposal failed because it was rejected by trade unions as an effort to reduce worker influence (Duskas 1997). At this point, talk of dismantling codetermination is a social taboo. Nevertheless, efforts to reduce the workers' role include manipulating appointments to committees, separating bench meetings, and restricting information to workers (Roe 1994).

Responding to these events, European unions are becoming more interested in labor-shareholder activism in the United States. U.S. unions are also looking abroad to learn from the experiences of labor unions involved in corporate governance and the investment of pension funds. For example, the Dutch pension fund ABP has adopted a governance policy that urges corporations in the Netherlands to take the high road toward long-term economic growth and shareholder value. Its message is: "ABP, as a long-term investor, will place the emphasis on the long-term objective of the company and lasting economic growth. This places demands on the company's environmental policy, the way in which the company structures its relationship with its employees, and the company's attitude to absolute human rights and fundamental freedoms" (Medina 1998).

IMPERIALISM OF U.S. MODEL
OF CORPORATE GOVERNANCE

Consider the role of labor-shareholder activism in the ideological battle over the appropriate nature of the corporation in light of these trends in global corporate governance. Labor-shareholder activism has two potential unintended negative consequences for workers. First, labor-shareholders may unwittingly hurt workers by defining the corporation solely in terms of the manager-shareholder relationship. Specifically, these labor strategies on corporate governance may simply feed into the prevailing view that the sole object of corporations is to enhance shareholder value.

Second, policy makers may use labor-shareholder activism as a means to divert attention from other methods of providing workers with voice in corporate governance, such as codetermination. For example, Schwab and Thomas have heralded labor-shareholder activism as a means to protect workers' firm-specific investments, because unions can gain access to behind-the-scenes meetings with managers to discuss corporate governance as well as labor issues. Similarly, Hansmann and Kraakman state: "In particular, the conventional conflict between the interests of labor and capital is beginning to break down. . . . Convergence of the interests of labor with those of shareholders has begun to take place on the level of ownership rather than, as earlier, via the direct participation of either workers or the state in corporate governance" (2000).

We are in a period of particularly strong tensions between workers and shareholders, yet these issues rarely surface in corporate governance debates. When they are raised, corporate governance scholars usually refer to workers as human capital and the most often heard solution is employee stock ownership. In this way, proponents of the shareholder-dominated view of the firm seek to align the interests of employees in corporate performance through stock-based incentives. Hansmann and Kraakman go so far as to assert, "Everywhere, stock ownership is becoming more pervasive in society. It is no longer so class-related as it once was." Such statements illustrate how difficult it is to try to raise issues about workers in corporate governance circles. These views simply fail to consider the demographics of stock ownership. Robert Kuttner reports the following:

> Federal Reserve data show that more than 51 million Americans owned some stock in 1992, either directly or indirectly through mutual funds and defined-contribution pension and savings plans. The wealthiest 20 percent of households own 98 percent of stock. The remaining 80 percent own only 2 percent. Thus, despite the widely publicized proliferation of mutual funds, pension plans, and the like, the distribution of financial assets remains astonishingly highly skewered. This is why people's capitalism is a convenient fiction. (Kuttner 1996, 28)

The shareholder-value mantra has taken legitimacy from stake-holder values. Nevertheless, labor-shareholders are becoming more aggressive in promoting a different ideology that suits the unique interests of worker-owners who are tired of a "part-time" United States. U.S. trade unions have begun to articulate their own view of global corporate governance practices: "The principles for a labor-oriented international governance program are rooted in the transparency of corporate financial information especially in the area of executive compensation; the creation of shareholder value through investments in human capital and partnership with labor; and, recognition of the rights of stake-holders in the governance process" (*Labor & Corp. Gov.* 1999b). The next section describes how unions can seek to promote a worker-owner vision of the firm through promoting the measurement and disclosure of human resource values.

Promoting Sustainable Shareholder Value through Disclosure of Human Capital Values

DISCLOSURE OF HUMAN RESOURCE VALUES

In the 1970s, social activists such as Ralph Nader pushed firms to disclose information about workplace practices as a means of promoting corporate social responsibility. This demand has resurfaced in the last few years through a movement referred to as the *Intellectual Capital Project* (IC Project). Using this project, "knowledge" companies, such as Skandia and Dow, are seeking new performance measures to indicate the firm's potential to innovate and improve the bot-

tom line in the future as indicators of sustainable shareholder value. The leaders
of the IC Project assert that our traditional system of disclosure does not reveal
sufficient information about firms' most important assets, the employees.
Employees show up as payroll expenses rather than being portrayed as the source
of value for firms. In addition, under the federal securities laws, firms are required
only to report number of employees. For these reasons, many companies in the
United States and abroad are moving beyond traditional financial indicators and
developing techniques to measure workplace practices along with customer sat-
isfaction, supplier relations, and product quality.[11] The IC Project focuses on
much of the same information that social activists in the past sought to disclose.
This information includes the breakdown of the number of workers who are full
time versus part-time contingent, training, turnover, diversity, compliance with
Occupational Safety & Health Administration standards, pay for performance,
and employee stock ownership. The IC Project has the capacity to promote
stake-holder interests by using the rhetoric of sustainable shareholder value. Recognizing this turn of events, Donald Langevoort explains:

> We should note first that there are two different kinds of arguments at work in
> the "stake-holder" debate. The first, and more aggressive, is that to the extent
> that corporations are simply webs of stake-holder interests mediated by company
> managers, disclosure in the interests of other stake-holders is justifiable on the
> same protective grounds as disclosure for investors. The second argument retains
> investor primacy, but argues that other stake-holder-oriented disclosure is
> needed so that investor/shareholders can evaluate properly the governance and
> financial performance of the firm. Both arguments end up in the same place,
> which can tempt those committed ideologically to the former to invoke the lat-
> ter because of its more conventional rhetoric. (Langevoort 1998, 93, 94)

In this way, the IC project could serve as a "Trojan horse" for union pension fund activism (Rutledge 1998). Specifically, disclosure of human resource
practices would be an important corporate governance tool. Under the theory that "you manage what you measure," a change in the rules concerning
financial disclosure of workplace practices could lead to different corporate
and societal perceptions about human resources invested in firm performance.
The IC Project has the potential to educate business leaders and the public
and shape the public's collective preferences in favor of human capital investments (Langevoort 1998).

Leaders of the IC project suggest that pressure for development of new
disclosure practices in the United States will likely intensify quickly, producing dramatic change during the next 10−15 years. There may be four reasons

for this optimism. First, reform of disclosure practices is more politically acceptable than substantive regulation of employment practices, because the United States has strong cultural norms that favor transparency (Lowenstein 1996). Second, the SEC sponsored a conference on the issue in 1996 that focused policy makers' attention on the possible need for new disclosure practices. Third, the Brookings Institute formed a task force to initiate a national discussion on better ways of measuring, monitoring and reporting human resource values. Fourth, and most encouraging, the Big Five accounting firms have led much of this research in an attempt to garner a larger share of the new market (Jeffers 1998).

Adoption of voluntary disclosure guidelines for workplace practices is a crucial step in the process of creating pressure for mandatory regulation. Indeed, the current global financial crisis underscores the importance of transparency and accountability to global investors; under the new world order, disclosure is preferred to substantive regulation. The environmental movement has had much success in using shareholder proposals to encourage companies to follow voluntary disclosure guidelines. Several environmental organizations track these disclosures to benchmark the quality and quantity of disclosures over time. This process encourages experimentation and publicizes examples of best practices so that generally accepted practices will evolve over time. At this point, no organization systematically tracks corporate disclosures concerning human resource values except Investor Responsibility Research Center, which tracks diversity.

Labor-shareholders' use of shareholder proposals to request information on workplace practices would attract media attention and facilitate the debate over the scope and structure of disclosure and whether it should be voluntary or mandatory. The next section explores the legal and political barriers that union pension funds must overcome to pursue this strategy.

USING SHAREHOLDER ACTIVISM TO PROMOTE HIGH-PERFORMANCE WORKPLACES

Recognizing the power of institutional investors, worker-owners have begun to encourage high-performance workplace practices through corporate governance institutions. These proposals enhance the long-range effort to establish a standardized method of reporting to publicize corporations' human resource values. Worker-owners, however, face two legal obstacles to promoting high-performance workplaces: pension fund managers' fiduciary obligations in voting proxies and the SEC's policies concerning employment-related shareholder proposals.

The Department of Labor prompted institutional investors to favor high-performance workplace practices by specifying the fiduciary duties of pension fund managers under the Employment Retirement Income Security Act. The Department of Labor encouraged fund managers to take a more active role in corporate governance matters by critically reviewing issues in voting proxies on traditional corporate governance matters, such as executive compensation and board independence. Importantly, the Department of Labor announced that pension fund managers may promote a company's "investment in training to develop its workforce, other workplace practices, and financial and non-financial measures of corporate performance" (DOL Bulletin 94-2, 7).

In the past, the SEC took the position that companies had to include in their proxy statements shareholder resolutions related to significant social policy issues implicated by a company's business operations. Since Campaign GM (Schwartz 1971), social advocacy groups have used the shareholder proposal rule to raise concerns about corporate policies involving such topics as nuclear power, the environment, and affirmative action. These groups tend to target highly visible companies to draw national attention to issues. Managers view these social proposals as involving "emotional issues" brought by "gadflies" and "crazies" seeking publicity for quixotic causes. Social activists point out that, despite the low number of votes their proposals receive, in many instances their proxy contests prompt executives to change corporate practices. For example, General Motors recently reacted to shareholder criticism of low wages paid to employees in Mexico by building homes for those workers (Graebner 1997).

Generally, the SEC allows managers to exclude proposals regarding day-to-day employment matters from a company's proxy materials as relating to ordinary business under Rule 14a-8(c)(7). The SEC routinely permits managers to omit labor-shareholder proposals that seek to pressure managers at the collective bargaining table. Such proposals include those recommending that the company (a) reach a good faith agreement in collective bargaining with its union (SEC 1983); (b) work with unions to foster cooperative relationships (SEC 1985); or (c) permit employees to retire after 30 years of service with full pension benefits (SEC 1984). However, as public opinion has evolved and issues have received national attention, the SEC changed its position and now allows shareholders to raise certain employment issues as significant social policy matters. For example, the SEC allowed shareholder proposals to raise questions concerning equal employment and affirmative action.

In recent years, controversy has surrounded the shareholder proposal rule. A 1992 SEC decision allowed Cracker Barrel Old Country Stores to exclude a proposal recommending the company change hiring practices that discriminated against homosexuals. The SEC, however, reversed this policy in 1992, indicating that it was no longer able to decide which employment matters are appropriate for shareholders to consider. In the Cracker Barrel case, the SEC reversed a long-standing policy concerning employment issues that raise social issues.[12] The SEC explained that it had "become increasingly difficult to draw the line between includable and excludable employment-related proposals based on social policy considerations." For this reason, the SEC determined that shareholder proposals focusing on employment practices that raise social policy questions will no longer be viewed as an "ordinary business exclusion."

Prompted in part by the Cracker Barrel controversy, Congress directed the SEC to study Rule 14a-8.[13] Not surprisingly, managers from major corporations have sought to maintain the Cracker Barrel policy, whereas unions and social activists support its reversal.[14] Shareholders protested the first draft of the new rules as unduly restricting shareholders' rights to bring proposals without offering much in return.[15] In the end, the SEC reversed its Cracker Barrel decision and left the system otherwise unchanged. As a result, employment-related proposals returned in the 1999 proxy season. In 1999, most employment-related proposals centered on sweatshops and international labor standards rather than workplace practices in the United States.

In the past, labor-shareholders engaged in limited experimentation with proposals requesting information on the extent to which companies engaged in high-performance workplace practices. Labor-shareholders filed seven resolutions in 1995; four came to votes, receiving an average support of 11.9 percent—a high level for a new issue. In 1996, labor-shareholders filed six high-performance workplace proposals; two came to votes, receiving an average vote of 6.9 percent. Between 1997 and 1999, shareholders did not submit any high-performance workplace resolutions. Although labor unions have not tested the limits of the new proxy rules, they will likely do so in the near future.

In response to shareholder proposals regarding high-performance workplace practices, managers provided their standard rebuttals to requests for information. Some referred to the cost of preparing the report, whereas others asserted that workplace practices are proprietary information. One firm resisted by claiming the need to maintain flexibility to decide what programs or practices are best for the company. Beyond standard rhetoric, managers criticized the Department of Labor's checklist of high-performance workplace practices as being too vague, particularly questions regarding the effectiveness of training programs. Most institutional shareholders did not have guidelines to follow when voting on the high-performance workplace shareholder resolutions. Some institutions treat the topic like other employment issues and voted against the proposals as ordinary business matters. Others, such as CalPERS and the New York City Employees Retirement System, voted in favor of the resolutions based on policies that support more corporate disclosure.

This history shows that shareholders should tailor their resolutions to request specific quantifiable measures about human resource policies, such as labor turnover and training expenses per employee. The SEC should allow shareholders to request this information, as it is not necessary to enforce paternalistic merit regulation in the current environment of sophisticated institutional investors.[16] Even if the SEC treats workplace issues such as training and downsizing as raising social issues, individual labor-shareholders will not gain management's attention unless they win the support of the public pension funds.

The topic of how institutional investors promote high-performance workplace practices remains largely unexplored. Several prominent corporate governance scholars suggest that shareholders are entering a new stage of activism (Brancato 1997; Ghilarducci 1992; Useem 1996) that focuses on these new performance measures to monitor firms' performance. These commentators emphasize that patient investors are beginning to evaluate aspects of labor relations not on social grounds but as indicators of companies' potentials to innovate in an intensely competitive environment. One of the largest institutional investors, CalPERS, has taken three steps to promote high-performance workplaces. First, in 1994, CalPERS announced that it would consider aspects of labor relations in its investment analysis (Brancato 1997; Nomani 1994). CalPERS analyzes the availability of employee training programs and the degree of responsibility given to lower-level workers. Second, in the same year, CalPERS worked with trade unions to formulate restrictions that prevent CalPERS from investing in construction projects that do not meet specific labor standards (Ghilarducci 1992). Third, in 1996, Richard Koppes of CalPERS published a widely publicized editorial that criticized firms that lay off employees to raise short-term stock prices (Koppes 1996). He said: "We will be looking for measures of performance that are based not simply on quarterly earnings and the most recent rise in the stock price. CalPERS intends to prevent such short-term vision by encouraging companies to add quality independent directors to their boards."

CalPERS justifies its concern over workplace issues as a means to measure firms' long-term economic performance. Specifically, CalPERS bases its decision on research suggesting that human resource policies improve corporate performance: "Firms with poor workplace practices have lower valuations than their peers with reputations for positive workplace practices" (Gordon et al. 1994). CalPERS' programs signal the need to rely on nontraditional measures to evaluate human resource values. Although most public pension fund trustees vote with managers on employment-related shareholder proposals, this position may change in the future. These public funds are politically sensitive to employment issues, because fund managers are elected by beneficiaries or appointed by governors (Romano 1993).

Thus far, CalPERS is the only large public fund that has taken steps to promote high-performance workplaces. Its effort may amount to little more than political posturing. In launching their program to evaluate labor practices, officials from CalPERS asserted, "With this structure in place, America will see an end to what's been called the looting of corporate America's human capital" (Koppes 1996, 36). Similar to corporate executives, public fund managers use this "statesmanlike" rhetoric as part of public relations campaigns. These efforts are significant because they indicate that public pension funds are politically receptive to new performance measures focusing on workplace practices. In time, CalPERS may take the lead in prompting other institutional investors to analyze human resource values.

Conclusion

In using labor's pension power, the AFL–CIO aims "to make worker capital serve workers, not just when they retire but on a day-to-day basis" (*Business Week* September 29, 1997). Labor-shareholder activism has much potential to realize the goals of stake-holder capitalism by promoting high-performance workplaces. Specifically, economic factors may converge with political forces to push institutional investors to promote new performance measures involving workplace practices. On the economic front, the distinctive feature of the new economy is human capital, providing labor and shareholders with more common ground than they had in the past. On the political side, organized labor is taking a leading role in educating pension fund beneficiaries on growing wage inequality, job insecurity, and pension fund governance. In these ways, labor-shareholders advance workers' goals by capitalizing on investor interest in finding new performance measures and their growing concern about the legitimacy of publicly held corporations. Using these strategies, labor-shareholder activism may become a significant countervailing force to promote stake-holder capitalism in the new world of global corporate governance.

[V]

BUILDING ON SUCCESS: LABOR-FRIENDLY INVESTMENT VEHICLES AND THE POWER OF PRIVATE EQUITY

Michael Calabrese

Although little noticed in mainstream investment discussions, union-friendly, alternative investment funds currently operate in nearly every asset category in the United States. This chapter profiles many of these vehicles to show how their strategies have generated conventional financial success and a range of collateral benefits, such as job creation, pension fund health, and economic development. Moreover, they do so while delivering very competitive returns to their investors. Pension fund trustees can thus choose from an array of alternative vehicles that satisfy the social commitments and practical retirement concerns of their members.

An informal survey of investment managers of jointly trusteed pension funds established by the Taft-Hartley Act indicates that labor-sensitive alternative investing has more than tripled since 1994 with respect to assets under management and the number of such funds in operation. The seventeen investment vehicles described in this chapter report total assets in excess of $18 billion, nearly all of which has been invested by multi-employer pension plans jointly trusteed by affiliates of the American Federation of Labor-Congress of Industrial

Organizations (AFL-CIO).[1] Real estate debt and equity funds that finance union-built construction continue to be the largest and most focused alternative investments targeted to create extra benefits for plan participants. A recent trend involves *direct* private equity investing in small, typically nonpublic companies. Private equity investing offers a surprising degree of financial and social leverage. Large corporate and public pension funds have long realized the *financial* potential of private equity and now allocate on average 5 percent of total assets to private placements. In contrast, few union-sponsored pension funds make private equity allocations at all. The track record of the Union Labor Life Insurance Company's (ULLICO's) *Separate Account P*, described in the section Profiles of Union-Oriented Alternative Investment Vehicles, provides strong evidence that investing sorely needed expansion capital in entrepreneurial young companies offers premium financial returns and social leverage.

Alternative Pooled-Investment Vehicles

The number and variety of union-friendly investment vehicles have been expanding dramatically. In 1994, more than 80 percent of all pooled alternative investments by union pension funds were dedicated to construction. No significant vehicles targeted private equity placements, direct business lending, enhanced equity, index proxy voting, or international investment.[2] Thus, both the expansion of union-built construction fund options and the creation of successful new funds in areas including private equity placements, which are described in the section Promise of Private Equity, are significant developments in the general effort to promote workers' overall interests with pension assets.

EXTRA BENEFITS GENERATED
BY UNION-BUILT CONSTRUCTION
The extra benefits delivered by most union-oriented alternative investments falsify the caricature of economically targeted investments as concessionary social investments that undermine pension security. The most clear-cut examples are the leading union-built construction funds. Most of the leading union-built real estate funds combine diversification and economies of scale, by virtue of being pooled funds, with the added advantage of recycling investments back into the jurisdictions of investing funds on a roughly proportional basis. By geographically targeting investments in new construction, the real estate debt and equity funds discussed in the section Profiles of Union-Oriented Alternative Investment Vehicles have proven they can generate several distinctive collateral benefits for plan participants.

First, to the extent that investment managers geographically target capital back into investors' jurisdictions on a reciprocal basis, union-built real estate trusts generate millions of additional hours of work for active plan participants. This not only provides an extra monetary benefit to active participants; it benefits all plan beneficiaries by increasing contributions, which are tied by formula to hours worked.

Second, union-built funds similarly strengthen the market position of employers contributing to the plan, on which participants rely to fund future obligations.

Third, enlarging the union-built share of the local market places upward pressure on plan participants' wage levels more generally. This not only provides an extra benefit to active participants, but it also translates into higher contribution levels and stability for the pension fund as an ongoing entity. As union share increases, pension plan participants become more secure.

Fourth, several of the vehicles described in this chapter also help to diversify the types of properties built by union labor in a particular jurisdiction, which benefits plan participants and beneficiaries over the long term. Because central-city commercial construction is far more cyclical than is residential construction and tends to dry up at the first sign of an economic downturn, multi-employer plans in areas where union work is concentrated in large commercial projects tend to experience greater volatility with respect to hours worked and plan contributions (Hartzell 1999). Plan income from contributions becomes more stable to the extent that the union share of local construction is diversified among residential and commercial construction (and, within the latter, among large and small projects). As described in the section Profiles of Union-Oriented Alternative Investment Vehicles, the St. Louis Council of Carpenters has successfully pursued this strategy. First it targeted the single-family residential market with the Builders Fixed Income Mutual Fund and its ProLoan organizing program, and then it focused on smaller and suburban commercial projects with the Commercial Mortgage/Plus Fund.

Finally, as union-built real estate funds reach a critical mass, they also strengthen the local labor movement and, in particular, building trades plan sponsors. These funds help to create new and, often, lasting relationships between developers, union contractors, and local unions (Butler 1999). When these funds build outside the old central cities (e.g., Boston, New York City, and Philadelphia) and begin financing the construction of residential housing, strip malls, and industrial sites in the suburbs, or even in southern and western cities, they are typically in what Landon Butler of the Multi-Employer Property Trust (MEPT) calls *battleground situations*. This phrase refers to situations in which developers or contractors have rarely used union labor. As the union-built funds grow in size, expertise, and reputation, major developers and contractors across the country come to accept the reality that the quality and reliability of union construction workers more than justify higher wages and more extensive benefits. Even in areas where 100-percent union construction is not feasible, most of the real estate funds profiled here have adopted responsible contractor policies that give preference to contractors who offer their workers a fair wage, basic benefits, and training opportunities (AFL–CIO 1999b).

PROMISE OF PRIVATE EQUITY

Although union-built real estate funds remain the largest and most developed segment of the market for nontraditional investments, private placement debt and equity are beginning to attract attention among multi-employer plans. ULLICO's stunning success with direct equity investments in nonpublic firms since 1996, which is described in the section Profiles of Union-Oriented Alternative Investment Vehicles, could provide the impetus for a number of new funds that combine private equity placements with demands that those companies agree to maintain positive labor relations. ULLICO's Separate Account P clearly shows that *direct investing* in young entrepreneurial companies, and in middle-market companies that need expansion capital, can yield premium financial returns and social leverage—that is, the ability to demand special covenants requiring union neutrality and card check recognition, union-built construction, environmental responsibility, and other collateral benefits.

Private placements are a critical source of capital for start-ups, private middle-market firms (between $5 and $100 million in sales), public firms seeking buyout financing, and those in financial distress. Despite all the publicity given to leveraged buyouts and venture capital, the broader private equity market receives relatively little attention, in large part because less information about these transactions is available. Unlike publicly traded stocks and bonds, a private equity security is exempt from registration with the Securities and Exchange Commission because it is issued in privately negotiated transactions not offered to the general public.

Until the 1980s, the private equity market was small and occupied mainly by wealthy families and financial institutions, such as insurance companies or merchant banks, that made direct investments in issuing firms. Since the mid-1980s, however, private equity has been by far the fastest growing source of corporate finance. Since 1980, it has raised more capital for companies than initial public offerings or public high-yield corporate bonds. From 1980 to 1994, total private equity capital under management grew from $5 billion to more than $100 billion. Whereas venture capital increased tenfold, from $3 billion to $30 billion between 1980 and 1994, nonventure private equity placements grew thirty-five–fold from less than $2 billion to more than $70 billion in 1994 (Fenn, Liang, and Prowse 1995).

Since 1995, private equity markets have grown at an even faster pace, with public and corporate pension funds becoming the nation's largest holders of nonpublic equity. In 1998, a record $85.3 billion in new commitments was made to private equity partnerships, a 53-percent increase over the amount in 1997 (*The Private Equity Analyst* 1999). Public and corporate pension funds supplied 43 percent of this private equity capital by 1994 and almost certainly provide a majority in 2000.[3]

By 1997, corporate and public pension plans boosted their target allocations to private equity to 7 and 4.7 percent of total assets, respectively, according to data compiled by Goldman Sachs (Hamilton Lane Advisors 1999).

Because of the extreme information asymmetries between firms and potential investors, pension funds typically participate in the private equity market as limited partners (LPs) in a partnership organized by a general partner, which is usually a professional management team.[4] As of 1994, LPs managed more than 80 percent of all private equity investments (Fenn, Liang, and Prowse 1995). For added diversification or expertise in selecting LPs, some pension funds invest in a *fund of funds*, such as the Hamilton Lane/Carpenters Union Partnership Fund (described in the section Profiles of Union-Oriented Investment Vehicles), which invests in a variety of LPs. Alternatively, pension funds can invest in a commingled fund, such as ULLICO's Separate Account P, which manages a portfolio of direct investments. In both instances, private equity managers typically take large ownership stakes and play active roles in monitoring and advising portfolio companies. These funds often exercise as much control as company insiders, particularly in venture capital or distressed company contexts. Whereas most pension funds invest through intermediaries, which are mainly LPs, some of the largest corporate pension funds "have become quite active in direct investment and co-investment," according to the Fenn, Liang, and Prowse Federal Reserve study.

Private placement debt markets are another area in which multi-employer pension plans are relatively inactive but in which intermediaries can achieve a similar combination of premium returns and collateral benefits. Privately held, medium-sized companies that earn between $5 and $100 million in annual sales find it very difficult to obtain capital to grow and expand, particularly if they are in a relatively slow-growing or "low-tech" industry. Since 1980, this capital gap between large public companies and smaller private companies has grown, in part because the traditional sources of private placement lending—commercial banks and insurance companies—are shrinking as a share of U.S. private capital markets. In 1980, U.S. commercial banks held $1.5 trillion in financial assets—more than twice the $700 billion held in total private and public pension assets. By 1997, financial assets held by pension funds exceeded total banking assets by $500 billion. Similarly, insurance company assets in 1980 were almost as large as total U.S. pension assets but by 1998 were only half as large (U.S. Department of Commerce, Bureau of the Census 1998).

Banks and insurance companies are particularly important as private placement lenders, because they have the institutional capacity to perform the in-depth due diligence required to invest prudently in nonpublic companies, as well as the long-term liability structure required to invest in illiquid private offerings. By their nature, pension funds are also ideally suited to capture the premium returns that flow on average, over time, to less liquid private placement debt and equity. Mutual funds and most individual investors put a premium on *liquidity*, or the ability to turn assets quickly into cash. Pension funds, however, aspire to eternal life; they have large reserves, and their liquidity needs are predictable and often minimal over a long-time horizon. As a result, the typical pension fund should be no more constrained to secondary public markets for stocks and bonds than the typical life insurance company. With access to appropriate intermediaries, even small pension funds can achieve the diversification and professional due diligence that enable insurance companies or hedge funds to reap premiums from private placement debt and equity investments.

Because a company that requires private equity and debt infusions expects to give up a certain degree of autonomy, conditions related to its future labor relations are negotiable if the fund manager makes them a priority (Steed 1999). By contrast, publicly traded securities, such as those traded on the New York Stock Exchange, are essentially commodities, and the transaction is impersonal. However, the management of nonpublic companies and private investors commonly negotiates a variety of covenants with respect to a large investor's participation. These can include corporate policies, such as labor union neutrality, card check recognition, union-only construction, preferences for unionized suppliers, and other collateral objectives that don't substantially diminish expected returns. Still, despite the potential to realize a financial return premium as well as the leverage to negotiate progressive corollary benefits, multi-employer pension funds have generally not joined corporate and public plans in diversifying into private equity placements (Williams 1998).

Profiles of Union-Oriented Alternative Investment Vehicles

The seventeen union-oriented investment programs profiled in this section represent virtually every traditional asset allocation category.[5] This diversity allows pension fund trustees to invest in a variety of these funds while main-taining a prudently diversified portfolio. The following funds reported total assets of $18 billion in early 1999, nearly all of which has been invested by multi-employer pension plans jointly trusteed by affiliates of the AFL-CIO. An informal survey of Taft-Hartley investment managers conducted by the author indicates that assets managed in union-oriented alternative investing has more than tripled since 1994.

UNION LABOR LIFE INSURANCE COMPANY'S SEPARATE ACCOUNT P: DIRECT PRIVATE EQUITY PLACEMENTS

When Sam Gompers persuaded the AFL to establish a union-owned life insurance company in the 1920s, he could not have foreseen that it would eventually leverage private capital to unionize workers more cost-effectively than most traditional organizing campaigns. Yet that is precisely what ULLICO and its Separate Account P are doing. "P is the only private equity fund dedicated to creating and preserving union jobs," boasted Michael Steed, ULLICO's senior vice president for investments. Its stated goals are "to achieve higher than market returns, to maintain and create union jobs, and to provide profits for unionized companies" (Steed 1999).

Large corporate and public pension funds have long realized the financial potential of private equity; they allocate an average of almost 5 percent of total assets to private placements. In contrast, few union-sponsored pension funds make private equity allocations at all. This gap may close now that ULLICO's Separate Account P has achieved success by investing in young entrepreneur-ial companies. ULLICO's Steed estimated that "for every $7 million of equity in private equity deals, a fund can influence $100 million in corporate activ-ity. Private equity should be a regular, substantial and an ongoing part of the equity allocation for Taft-Hartley pension funds," he asserted.

ULLICO's track record appears to confirm this potential. It is fair to say that creating union jobs has seldom been so profitable: Separate Account P's annual return during its first 3 years averaged 39 percent through year-end 1998, whereas ULLICO's in-house portfolio that preceded the creation of Separate Account P sports an internal rate of return in excess of 100 percent *per year* since January 1992. Steed argues that ULLICO is proving that direct private equity investing offers a surprising degree of financial *and* social leverage.

In 1992, ULLICO began direct investing, using insurance reserves, by co-investing with the Carlyle Group (a politically connected merchant banking firm) to purchase the aircraft division spun off by bankrupt defense contractor LTV Inc. As the investment bankers rushed to complete the deal,

ULLICO insisted that the buyout group ratify the existing collective bargaining agreement with the International Union, United Automobile, Aerospace and Agricultural Implement Workers of America (UAW) and agree to shore up the underfunded rank-and-file pension plan. Although ousting unions and plundering pension assets are two of the classic tactics used in leveraged buyout transactions, ULLICO's co-investors reluctantly agreed. After 2 years, ULLICO exited with a 75-percent internal rate of return.

After a period of apprenticeship as a co-investor on several deals, ULLICO added solo direct investing to its arsenal and, in December 1995, opened a group annuity account (P for *Private Capital*) aimed at multi-employer plan clients. The Separate Account P had approximately $100 million in assets by mid-1999. The following are examples of the 57 private equity deals executed by ULLICO between 1992 and early 1999. The majority of these involved financial *and* collateral benefits for investors or for organized labor more generally (ULLICO 1997b; Steed 1999):

- Super Shuttle: the bright blue vans that are rapidly taking fares from taxis at major airports across the country are part of a classic franchised service business that unions find tough to organize. Airport authorities welcome shared-ride services, because they relieve congestion and, in Super Shuttle's case, are fueled by clean-burning natural gas. In return for $3 million in expansion capital, ULLICO achieved two concessions in areas where private investors would not have bothered. First, the vans must be manufactured domestically by members of the UAW, creating five hundred jobs through 1998; and second, they require neutrality and card check recognition should a union organize the drivers or other personnel. As a result, the Teamsters (West Coast) and the Service Employees International Union (East Coast) are quickly bringing the drivers in this fast-growing and profitable company under contract.
- Global Crossing Ltd.: ULLICO's in-house portfolio increased an average 100 percent annually from 1992 through year-end 1998 (compared to a 39-percent annualized return for Separate Account P) due to one venture capital investment that made even veteran Silicon Valley investors envious. Global Crossing is building a global network of undersea fiber-optic cables with a new technology that can accommodate the explosive volume of Internet transmissions by carrying hundreds of times as much data as older cables. ULLICO invested $7.6 million in the start-up. The company went public in August 1998, after its largest cable across the Atlantic Ocean went into service, leaving ULLICO with an 8-percent ownership stake valued in excess of $1.6 *billion*—more than 200 times its cost (Lipin 1999; Mills 1999). In return, the entrepreneurs agreed to use a U.S.-based unionized company to lay the cable, to purchase most components

from union manufacturers, and to employ union seafarers and maritime officers on the construction rigs (Kennedy 1999). Steed estimates that cable construction alone employed 1,500 International Brotherhood of Electrical Workers (IBEW) and Communication Workers of America (CWA) members as of year-end 1998, with more to come as ULLICO maintained its stake in this rapidly growing company.

- Omni Facility Resources, Inc.: one of the most profitable business strategies in the 1990s was the *roll-up*, whereby holding companies consolidate fragmented industries (e.g., office supply stores, funeral homes) by buying up smaller and less efficient businesses. As both an investment and an organizing tool, there may be few opportunities as promising as a company that rolls up dozens or hundreds of small shops into one large and more profitable network. Omni rolls up small facilities maintenance firms that perform janitorial and landscaping work on a contract basis. As a term and condition of ULLICO's $7.5 million investment, Omni agreed that all of its current and acquired workforce would be unionized or covered by neutrality and card check agreements. This should facilitate efforts by the Service Employees International Union to organize thousands of maintenance workers as nonunion subsidiaries are acquired (Steed 1999).

- Newport News Shipbuilding: this deal, which was Separate Account P's first, invested in the construction of five environmentally safe, double-hulled oil tankers at a total cost of $280 million. ULLICO's $10 million equity stake gave it enough leverage to achieve an agreement in which the ships would be constructed in the United States at one of the nation's few remaining unionized shipyards, providing work for twelve thousand steel workers over a 28-month period. In addition, the firms that would operate the ships agreed to a union pre-hire agreement. Allowed under the Jones Act, which governs maritime trade, this agreement guarantees jobs for 150 members of the Seafarers International Union. ULLICO exited the investment in 1998, recovering 100 percent of invested capital plus a 20-percent internal rate of return.

- Residential Services Inc.: as of early 1999, Residential Services Inc. (RSI) had a business plan that called for the construction of seventy-five new assisted-living centers at an average cost of $7 million per location. Whereas other institutions provide mortgage financing on a building-by-building basis, ULLICO made a private equity investment of $5 million, infusing badly needed operating capital and becoming a part owner in the process. As a term and condition of this investment, RSI agreed that all seventy-five centers would be built with union labor and that all the workers at the centers would be covered by neutrality and card check recognition agreements. ULLICO projects that it will sell its 18-percent ownership stake within 5 years for an estimated annual return of 20 percent.

"That is the abject power of private equity," explained Steed, referring to the RSI deal as a particularly potent model. He said that as a part owner, "through covenants, private equity investment can control the structure of 100 deals rather than investing project by project." Steed noted that although ULLICO's "J for Jobs" program required 30 staff members in 1998 to generate $740 million in commitments for union-built construction, one staffer took just 2 months to leverage Separate Account P's $5 million equity investment in RSI into $450 million in construction. This leveraging was accomplished in addition to recognition agreements for more than 1,000 health care workers to be hired at those facilities. Ironically, Steed's biggest disappointment has been that among the companies for which ULLICO, as an investor, has negotiated neutrality and card check recognition, unions have targeted only three for organizing.

ULLICO's Separate Account P is particularly well suited for qualified pension plans subject to the Employment Retirement Income Security Act (ERISA). First, whereas LPs are usually illiquid during their typical 10-year lifespan, Separate Account P operates as an open-ended group annuity contract, which has two advantages. It allows investors to exit at any point at a unit price that is revalued monthly, and it allows the fund to operate indefinitely, freeing it from the early-cycle fundraising and late-cycle forced liquidation that burden fixed-term LPs. Second, as an open-ended fund, it can be "opportunistic" and make a wide variety of investments, including direct placements and investments in LPs, as well as investments in postventure public stock offerings.

Third, as an insurance company–pooled separate account, Separate Account P enjoys a class exemption from most ERISA-prohibited transaction constraints, similar to the exemption that applies to other qualified private asset managers (QPAMs).[6] Because fiduciary duty can be completely delegated to a qualified asset manager, the trustees need only perform due diligence in the initial hiring and monitoring of the manager; liability for specific investments made by the trust lies with the manager. Investors are sheltered from unrelated business income taxation; the trust is responsible for filing and paying taxes on any unrelated business income taxation.

Finally, direct investing puts union-oriented professionals at the table when deals are structured. In contrast, when a pension fund invests in a conventional limited partnership or in a fund of such investments (a fund of funds), discretion is delegated to the general partner, and it is difficult for the pension fund to influence the terms of individual deals. The exception might be a vehicle such as the United Brotherhood of Carpenters (UBC) new fund of funds, described next, in which the manager is acutely aware that the investors are all union affiliated and share a concern for extraportfolio outcomes.

CARPENTERS' LIMITED PARTNERSHIP
FUND OF FUNDS

Whereas ULLICO's pooled account makes *direct* private equity investments, more than 80 percent of the record $85 billion invested in the private equity market last year flowed through specialized intermediaries, nearly all of which are organized as LPs (Fenn, Liang, and Prowse 1995). As explained previously, LPs typically have a 10-year life and specialize by type of transaction (e.g., buyouts, venture capital, distressed companies), by industry, and by geographic region.

A *fund of funds*, as a limited partner, is a professionally managed pool of investments in other LPs. In 1998, commitments to funds of funds soared 138 percent, to $9.6 billion, as thirty new funds were formed (*The Private Equity Analyst* 1999). Working with Hamilton Lane Advisors of Philadelphia, which specializes in alternative investing, the UBC's Strategic Investment Council has fashioned its own fund of funds—the Hamilton Lane-Carpenters' Partnership Fund, LP. The fund's initial closing in March 1999 raised approximately $225 million in commitments from various UBC-sponsored Taft-Hartley plans.

The most obvious advantage of a fund of funds format is diversification across a number of different LPs, investment types, industries, and regions. Whereas some large pension plans achieve a similar diversification by assembling their own portfolio of LP investments, considerable in-house expertise (or a specialized advisor, such as Hamilton Lane) is needed to identify, evaluate, negotiate, and monitor LP investments on a continual basis. Obtaining this expertise may be impractical or uneconomical, particularly for a small pension fund.

In contrast, the manager of a fund of funds brings experience and economies of scale to these functions while achieving a greater degree of diversification. A fund of funds can put more assets to work quickly, because due diligence focuses on identifying proven "deal teams" rather than on the more arduous task of identifying, evaluating, and negotiating investments in individual companies. Also, just as *deal flow*, or access to nonpublic information about high-quality investment opportunities, is crucial to the success of individual LPs, an advisor such as Hamilton Lane has the extensive contacts and credibility to access exclusive partnership opportunities (Jones 1999).

A second advantage of the Carpenter LP model, compared to direct private placements, is that the fund becomes less constrained and the pension trustees more insulated under ERISA by delegating fiduciary control to a qualified plan asset manager.[7] Trustees completely delegate their fiduciary duty to the fund manager with respect to the selection and monitoring of specific LP investments (DeCarlo 1999). Of course, trustees must still perform due diligence in selecting the fund of funds manager and in monitoring the fund manager's performance from period to period.

Unlike most LPs and funds of funds, the Carpenter-sponsored pension funds banded together to select a union-friendly investment manager and to negotiate favorable terms that give the fund a risk-and-return advantage compared to comparable vehicles. For example, the Carpenter group negotiated a favorable fee structure that aligns incentives in favor of the pension investors. Hamilton Lane will receive a relatively low annual management fee of 0.5 percent of invested assets (reduced to 0.4 percent after 5 years), plus 8 percent of net profits only after the limited partners receive a 10-percent annual return (Hamilton Lane Advisors 1999). At the same time, Hamilton Lane will be at risk with a 1-percent equity investment (DeCarlo 1999).

Another advantage is that the limited partners, all of which are Carpenter pension funds, select an advisory committee to monitor the fund manager. In an extreme case, LPs who represent a majority of the assets in the fund can remove the manager. Although it is a common practice for LPs to negotiate special covenants that restrict the discretion of the general partner (Fenn, Liang, and Prowse 1995), the common collateral interests shared among the pension funds investing in this fund give the investors unusual leverage to ensure that the fund operates in a union-friendly fashion. Nevertheless, UBC General Counsel John DeCarlo notes that managers of the Carpenter plans decided not to demand any explicit conditions on the types of deals or other LPs in which Hamilton Lane can invest (DeCarlo 1999).

Although the fund of funds approach is perhaps the easiest way to persuade risk-averse trustees to join corporate and public pension funds on the new frontier of private equity investing, it also presents severe limitations compared to the ULLICO direct investing model. First, the two layers of partnerships together could consume as much as 30 percent of gross returns in fees and expenses. Second, the pension trustees' influence over the pursuit of collateral benefits is more indirect and diluted in a fund of funds. For example, an intermediary like ULLICO can negotiate *directly* with companies in which it invests to secure concessions that confer collateral benefits, such as neutrality or card check recognition. In contrast, a fund of funds takes at most a minority stake as a limited partner in funds in which *other managers* have investment discretion. Unless those other partnerships have substantial and coordinated Taft-Hartley participation, it is extremely difficult to achieve the kind of collateral benefits that could be achieved using a direct investment approach. At a bare minimum, union-oriented investors in a fund of funds should ensure that the fund manager will, before investing, insist on covenants that allow the fund to opt out of any anti-union investments made by the LPs in which it invests (Steed 1999).

KPS SPECIAL SITUATIONS FUND

KPS is an explicitly prolabor buyout fund. It invests in troubled union companies, acquiring majority control and working cooperatively with employees and their union to return the company to financial health. KPS seeks to leverage employee stock ownership plans (ESOPs) to refinance and recapitalize companies. As of 1999, the KPS Fund had a limited track record in which it had closed only one deal, an ESOP buyout of Blue Ridge Paper Products, which saved an estimated 2,200 jobs (AFL-CIO 1999b). Nevertheless, the fund's manager, Keilen and Company, is well established as a union-friendly investment boutique with a 15-year record of consulting closely with the labor movement. The firm engineered the 1983 ESOP buyout of Weirton Steel Corp., preserving more than ten thousand jobs, and played a leading role in the 1994 buyout of United Airlines, preventing the breakup of that company and creating the United States' largest employee-owned company.

Among the notable features of the KPS Fund is that it consults closely with an advisory board of worker and union representatives. The KPS Fund also relies on contacts in the labor movement for deal flow and sourcing, according to the AFL-CIO's *Investment Product Review.* The KPS Fund's investors include private financial institutions as well as Taft-Hartley pension plans. Organized as an LP, investors are able to co-invest alongside the fund, or even to opt out of individual investments.

CIGNA AMERICA FUND: PRIVATE PLACEMENT BONDS

Insurance companies historically have financed a disproportionate share of the private placement debt market. Companies that either cannot, or prefer not to, float public bond issues instead borrow directly from institutional investors such as CIGNA. CIGNA currently manages $15 billion in private placement debt, of which $250 million resides in a separately managed account for Taft-Hartley plan investors: the CIGNA America Fund. It is a fixed-income fund that targets loans to "U.S.-based operations to maintain and create jobs and provide capital to union employers" (CIGNA America Fund 1999, July). Between 1994 and 1998, the CIGNA America Fund extended loans to more than sixty companies that feature at least a 25-percent unionization rate or that borrowed to finance a union-built construction project. IBEW-sponsored funds were the initial investors and account for roughly half the CIGNA America Fund's assets.

The CIGNA America Fund seeks a balance between the higher yields generated by private placement bonds and the liquidity offered by publicly traded corporate and U.S. Treasury issues. At year-end 1998, the CIGNA America Fund had approximately two-thirds of its assets in private placement bonds and one-third in U.S. Treasuries, public, corporate, and cash equivalents. The

CIGNA America Fund's average annual return, net of expenses, over the 5 years since inception is 7.4 percent, which compares favorably with the 7.3-percent average annual return on the benchmark Lehman Brothers Government/Corporate Bond Index (CIGNA America Fund 1999, July). The fund has achieved an average 50 basis point (0.5 percent) spread over high-quality corporate bonds while limiting risk by shunning below-investment grade issues (i.e., junk bonds).

Because the CIGNA America Fund represents less than 2 percent of CIGNA's private placement debt portfolio, it is unclear whether the fund is actually increasing the capital available to good union companies or merely segregating loans it would have made in any event. CIGNA, however, insists that the fund's existence prompts the insurer's team of analysts to more aggressively seek out unionized employers who need capital. John Depenbrock, CIGNA's senior vice president for multi-employer markets, said, "We affirmatively reach out to union fund trustees and tell them to make sure their employers know that CIGNA is a potential funding source" (Depenbrock 1999). He said that CIGNA also frequently consults with union trustees at investing unions about loans on large projects in which union labor is clearly involved.

ROOFERS' LOAN FUND:
LINKED-DEPOSIT CERTIFICATES OF DEPOSIT

Linked-deposit loan programs are a very low-risk but seldom-used approach to alternative investing. Pension funds typically have a portion of their fixed-income allocation invested in very short-term bonds or cash reserves, including money market and bank certificates of deposit. Bank certificates of deposit (CDs) pay relatively low interest but are very safe, because the Federal Deposit Insurance Corporation guarantees CDs against default up to $100,000 per plan participant. In the late 1980s, two Boston-based building trade locals formed the Bricklayers and Laborers Non-Profit Housing Co. (B&L) to pioneer the concept of *development deposits*. The two multi-employer funds initially invested $6.5 million in bank CDs at the U.S. Trust of Boston, and a local public pension fund deposited $20 million. In return, the bank agreed to make reduced-rate loans to finance low-income housing projects built with union labor (*Labor & Investments* 1987; Zanglein 1995).

A new variation on this theme is the "targeted CD" program by a California multi-employer fund sponsored by the United Union of Roofers, Waterproofers, and Allied Workers (Snow Spalding and Rudd 1998). In exchange for the pension fund's $2 million deposit in a CD, the bank finances low-interest loans to consumers for the purpose of replacing or repairing their roofs, provided they hire an approved union contractor. Like the Carpenters' ProLoan mortgage program, which is described in this section, the Roofers' program benefits all parties. The pension fund receives a risk-free return at market rates. Consumers obtain a more affordable loan. The bank shoulders the risk of making home improvement loans and earns a spread between the interest rate it pays the fund and the rate it charges consumers. In addition, plan participants and signatory contractors realize extra wages, profits, and plan contributions as the fund's deposits flow back into the community to pay for the roof repair or replacement performed by union contractors.

McMorgan & Company, the Roofers' program's primary investment manager, was delegated fiduciary responsibility to structure and monitor the program. The Roofers' linked-deposit loan program is just one of a number of mechanisms by which McMorgan & Company, a union-oriented money management firm, coaxes and coordinates building trades, multi-employer plans in California to boost their plans' investment in local union-built construction. Most notably, McMorgan & Company manages a real estate investment program for its Taft-Hartley fund clients. This program makes targeted debt and equity investments in the construction of new residential and commercial properties built by union contractors.

ProLoan: Builders Fixed Income Mutual Fund

One of the most innovative and low-risk alternative investment programs is the Builders Fixed Income Fund and its ProLoan residential lending and organizing program. The Builders Fund is a publicly traded mutual fund (ticker: PRLNX) that invests at least 65 percent of its assets in investment-grade bonds, including at least 30 percent in mortgage-backed securities issued and guaranteed by Ginnie Mae, Fannie Mae, and Freddie Mac.[8] The Builders Fund's ProLoan program coordinates with participating home builders and lenders to ensure that the mortgages pooled by the fund finance primarily new-home construction and complete renovations built with 100-percent union labor (Builders Fixed Income Fund 1999).

From a fiduciary perspective, the Builders Fund is an alternative to a conventional core fixed-income allocation, because it is managed to mirror the risk and return characteristics of the Lehman Brothers Aggregate Bond Index. Although the fund places 33 percent of its assets into mortgage-backed securities that finance new-home construction, two-thirds of its assets are in U.S. corporate, Treasury, and other conventional bonds with an average credit quality of AA1. Since its inception in October 1997, the fund has almost precisely tracked the 7-percent return of the Lehman Mortgage-Backed Securities Index (Builders Fixed Income Fund 1999).

The Builders Fund had approximately $140 million in assets by mid-1999, all from Carpenter-sponsored pension funds, which generates between 500 and 600 union-built housing starts annually in St. Louis, Detroit, Chicago, and southern Illinois. The fund's goal is $1 billion in assets within 2 years, which would finance more than 2,000 new homes and more than two million hours of labor within the jurisdictions of the pension funds investing in the program (Builders Fixed Income Fund 1998). To expand its impact, the Builders Fund hopes to extend the program to additional jurisdictions and, once a track record is established, to seek investments from other building trades and public plans in those areas (Hartzell 1999).

The Builders Fund grew out of a similar program initiated by the St. Louis Council of Carpenters multi-employer pension fund in the late 1980s. At one point, the St. Louis Carpenters Fund had virtually its entire fixed-income allocation in the Builders Fund, but it has cut back to 50 percent of its bond allocation, which is a level the Builders Fund recommends to other Carpenter plans.

Both the Builders Fund and the Carpenters' union are extremely direct about their efforts to generate extra benefits for plan participants and contributing employers in addition to a market-rate core fixed income return. "It's a residential organizing tool," explained Scott Hartzell, the Builders Fund's managing director. He noted that the St. Louis Carpenters have been able to double the union-built share of the new-home construction market, pushing it up to 80 percent since the program began, compared to a 5-percent average nationwide. Once the ProLoan program becomes a critical mass in the local market for new-home lending, he said, developers and builders suddenly become very interested in participating—the price of which is union prehire agreements. ProLoan forms an ongoing partnership with selected mortgage lenders, developers, and contractors within a geographic area where Carpenter funds have made a minimum $50 million commitment. The Builders Fund guarantees participating lenders, which are typically banks, that it will buy conforming mortgages on a when-issued basis. Consumers are attracted by the unusual 6-month rate lock and *float down* feature, which protects the new-home buyer against rising interest rates even as it promises savings if rates fall during construction. Because prospective home buyers are approved only if their builder is union-approved, nonunion contractors see that the special mortgage program gives union contractors a competitive advantage. The local Carpenter Councils actively help participating developers and builders win business by making ProLoan marketing material, and even union reps, available at model-home sites to tout both the financial advantages and the quality craftsmanship associated with using union contractors. One shortcoming, according to the AFL-CIO's *Investment Product Review*, is that ProLoan "does not require the developers who participate in the program to use union labor across the board" but instead only in those crafts that invest in the program, thereby "minimizing the impact of the fund's investments" (AFL–CIO 1999b, 12).

AMERICAN FEDERATION OF LABOR– CONGRESS OF INDUSTRIAL ORGANIZATIONS HOUSING INVESTMENT TRUST: MORTGAGE-BACKED SECURITIES

Founded in 1964, the AFL–CIO's Housing Investment Trust (HIT) is the original pioneer among labor-sponsored investment vehicles. With total assets exceeding $2 billion, HIT is also the largest, most visible, and least risky of the alternative investment vehicles that generate extra benefits for pension beneficiaries and their local communities. HIT invests primarily in mortgages and mortgage-backed securities that are guaranteed by the federal government or by government-sponsored entities.[9] More than four hundred public and Taft-Hartley pension funds own unit shares. Funds typically place HIT within the fixed-income portion of their portfolio, alongside U.S. Treasury bonds or other mortgage-backed securities, because investments in HIT are fully liquid and have virtually no credit risk, because most of the highly diversified portfolio is backed by government guarantees.

Although the assets ultimately owned by HIT are similar with respect to risk and return, to the mortgage-backed securities routinely held by corporate pension funds or by individuals in Government National Mortgage Association (GNMA) fixed-income mutual funds, HIT plays a very different role. Whereas other institutions typically purchase pre-existing securities that trade on secondary markets, HIT functions as a developer in structuring deals that originate mortgages, which it then arranges to securitize through special partnerships with guarantee agencies such as Fannie Mae (Kamiat 1999).

HIT specializes in financing low-income and affordable housing built by 100-percent union labor. By playing the role of developer in the highly technical area of government-subsidized housing, HIT's deal team is able to generate both types of corollary benefits while consistently out-performing industry benchmarks.[10] The complexity and labor-intensity of packaging deals using state and federal subsidies and loan guarantees creates a niche that HIT has been able to exploit to produce market-beating low-risk yields *and* double-edged social benefits.

"There is a whole catechism you need to know in order to access public finance," explained Steve Coyle, HIT's chief executive officer. HIT's expertise in structuring projects that leverage public financing is particularly important, because it often invests in relatively high-risk inner-city and poor rural areas (Sandler 1997, 57). More than 9,200 units of low-income housing have been financed under various targeted programs structured by HIT.

In 1994, Coyle, a former official in the U.S. Department of Housing and Urban Development (HUD), engineered HUD's National Partnership for Community Investment, which used federal Section 8 rental subsidies to leverage pension and private investment. HIT made approximately $60 million in loans under the program, leveraging $240 million in total construction of affordable housing. HIT's "Urban Investment 2000" program—a partnership with HUD, Fannie Mae, foundations, cities, and state housing agencies—will target $1 billion in HIT and Building Investment Trust (BIT) investment through 2005 to promote home ownership, low-cost rental housing production, economic development, and neighborhood stabilization in fourteen or more targeted cities. In addition to generating extra wages and pension contributions for union plan participants, HIT's identification with the AFL-CIO boosts the labor movement's image and relationships with community leaders (Arnold 1999).

Like the other union-built real estate funds profiled here, HIT attempts to target much of its investment back into the jurisdictions of its multi-employer and public pension plan investors. The trust's $400 million in 1998 commitments generated approximately five million work hours for union members. In 1999, HIT's board of directors adopted an expanded union-only policy that directed the staff to demand that the owner-operators of nursing homes, hotels, and other facilities financed by HIT or BIT agree to neutrality and card check recognition with respect to future employees. HIT has also begun to offer mortgages to union members at favorable rates in selected markets, making $220 million in loans available since 1998 (AFL-CIO 1999b).

BOILERMAKERS' CO-GENERATION AND INFRASTRUCTURE FUND: PROJECT FINANCE

One of the most sophisticated and successful alternative investment programs initiated by a Taft-Hartley plan is the Boilermakers' Co-Generation and Infrastructure Fund. Managed by the Trust Company of the West (TCW), the Boilermakers' Fund uses a project finance model to co-invest in the construction of power generation plants that are then leased or sold to independent power producers, industrial companies, or the government. Over its first 12 years, the Boilermakers' Fund has invested $450 million in thirty projects, achieving a 15-percent average annual rate of return and generating an estimated 1.4 million hours of work for plan participants through year-end 1998 (Hanson 1999). Although a 15-percent internal rate of return over 12 years would be market rate for an *equity* fund, the Boilermakers' Fund takes less risk, because it provides just the senior or subordinated debt slice of each project financing. One reason the fund can take less risk—and ensure that the project employs union boilermakers—is that it usually takes the lead in structuring the deal, owing to its track record and the expertise of the management team. TCW typically syndicates the deal, investing alongside major banks, insurance companies, and other private investors (Daly 1999). By co-investing, the Boilermakers' Fund adds diversification, reduces risk, and demonstrates that the private market regards the project as a good investment regardless of covenants requiring union labor.

The $6 billion Boilermakers & Blacksmiths National Pension Trust is the sole investor in the fund. Its current investment is $200 million, approximately 4 percent of assets, with latitude to go up to 8 percent (Hanson 1999). TCW maintains that, as the fund's reputation has grown, so has its ability to put more money to work. Although the fund could be opened to other pension investors, the trustees have hesitated to do so because of potential conflicts over work rules or jurisdiction if the investments were commingled with other building trades (Daly 1999). Another option under consideration is a clone fund that could be managed by TCW with an emphasis on jobs for other trades. From a labor movement perspective, this would take greater advantage of the deal flow and expertise that the Boilermakers have built up at TCW.

Collateral benefits generated by project finance can be tightly targeted to plan participants. Because the Boilermakers and Blacksmiths National Pension Trust is a *national* fund, the fund can target projects that generate hours for members and still achieve geographic diversification. The estimated 1.4 million hours of work generated as of 1999 represent a substantial extra benefit, because the Boilermakers and Blacksmiths National Pension Trust's benefit formula is based strictly on hours worked. Thus, extra hours represent not just extra wages, but also extra current income to the pension trust and higher retiree benefits for participants in the future.

LONGVIEW ULTRA I CONSTRUCTION LOAN FUND

Amalgamated Bank of New York, the union-owned bank controlled by the Union of Needlecraft, Industrial and Textile Employees (UNITE), has begun to recruit investors for its own distinctive entry: the Longview Ultra I Construction Loan Fund. The fund will invest primarily in construction loans for new office buildings, shopping centers, hotels, industrial/warehouse properties, and multifamily residential properties. Unlike the permanent, postconstruction mortgages held by ULLICO's account J for Jobs, or the Carpenters' Mortgage-Plus Fund, which are described in this section, the Longview Ultra Fund will provide relatively short-term loans of 1 to 2 years to finance the acquisition, development, and construction of new properties built with union labor (Luraschi 1999).

In terms of collateral benefits, this model has two advantages over permanent mortgage funds. First, the Longview Ultra Fund's loans turn over far more frequently, allowing the same pension assets to finance far more new construction over a 5- or 10-year period. Second, because acquisition and construction financing carries higher risks and requires greater expertise by the lender, it is valued more highly by developers and contractors. By supplying scarce up-front financing at the "ground floor," Amalgamated Bank should have more leverage to insist on collateral benefit concessions. On the other hand, once the construction loan is repaid, the fund apparently will not be able to ensure that ongoing building service or maintenance is performed with union labor.

UNITED FOOD AND COMMERCIAL WORKERS' SHOPPING CENTER MORTGAGE LOAN PROGRAM

Despite $20 billion in jointly trusteed pension assets, the United Food and Commercial Workers (UFCW) has found it difficult to target collateral investment benefits to a membership that works primarily in the retail service sector. One innovative effort by UFCW locals in Southern California allocates $100 million to finance construction loans and first mortgages for developers (or unionized employers) who agree to include a unionized supermarket as the anchor tenant in new shopping centers or strip malls. To date, approximately $65 million has been loaned out by AMRESCO Advisers, a respected real estate investment management firm that has been delegated fiduciary duty to manage the allocation (Barry 1999).

According to an agreement reached during collective bargaining with the Food Employers Council, the purpose of the real estate allocation is to achieve a positive yield spread over comparable fixed-rate debt instruments while facilitating new shopping centers that include participating employers as tenants. The union maintains that, in addition to securing a prime location for new stores that would create jobs and pension contributions for union plan participants, the program helps to deny those locations to nonunion chains that would undercut union wage and benefit levels.

AMERICAN FEDERATION OF LABOR–CONGRESS OF INDUSTRIAL ORGANIZATIONS BUILDING INVESTMENT TRUST: REAL ESTATE DEBT AND EQUITY

HIT's companion fund, the AFL-CIO's *BIT*, is a pooled trust that invests in institutional quality commercial properties built with union labor. The fund is structured with an unusual degree of flexibility to make both debt and equity investments. Although roughly 80 percent of BIT's new commitments are equity investments that involve the ownership of real property, its $800 million portfolio also includes construction loans and permanent mortgage financing. Since its inauguration in 1988, BIT's combination of debt and equity has worked to minimize volatility while generating steady market-rate returns between 9 and 10 percent annually. Returns have remained remarkably stable at that level, despite the substantial decline in inflation and interest rates since 1994 (AFL-CIO BIT 1999). Because BIT is less profit-motivated than comparable funds, its management fees are among the lowest in the industry.

BIT's flexibility to make construction loans has proven a boon to its ability to generate and geographically target the corollary benefits that flow from union-built construction. BIT's dual role as a lender and equity investor allows it to identify more deal opportunities. Developers seek out BIT, because they can realize significant transaction savings by arranging both construction and permanent financing through a large and experienced investor such as HIT/BIT (Arnold 1999). By increasing deal flow, BIT is better able to diversify by property type (e.g., office, industrial, retail) and target high-quality projects within the jurisdictions of participating pension funds. HIT/BIT staff attribute the trusts' increasing penetration into historically nonunion cities, such as Dallas, Jacksonville, and Atlanta—sometimes working with previously nonunion contractors—to BIT's ability (unlike a mortgage fund) to become a valued partner that provides front-end construction financing.

MULTI-EMPLOYER PROPERTY TRUST: REAL ESTATE EQUITY

The MEPT is one of the largest and top-performing open-end real estate equity funds in the United States. MEPT acquires, owns, and holds income-producing commercial properties, such as office buildings; warehouse, distribution, and corporate research and development facilities; retail centers; hotels; and multifamily housing. All of its projects represent 100-percent union-built new constructions "that create economic activity and jobs in areas where beneficiaries of participating pension plans live and work" (MEPT 1998, 10).

MEPT has doubled its assets under management since 1996. As of September 30, 1999, the trust had 142 participating pension plans and $2 billion in net assets. Its investment performance has consistently exceeded industry benchmarks since 1995. In 1998, MEPT returned 13 percent (net of all fees), topping its 10.7-percent return in 1997. MEPT has also out-performed, on a risk-adjusted basis, all of the other twenty large open-end commingled funds over the 10-year period ending 1999. Riggs Bank of Washington retains fiduciary responsibility for the trust's management, which is directed by Kennedy Associates, a real estate and securities advisory firm based in Seattle.

MEPT puts a premium on targeting extra benefits to pension plan participants and their communities. In addition to union-only construction, MEPT has adopted a Responsible Contractor Policy, which requires that all building service, repair, and maintenance work on its properties use union contractors wherever available or pay prevailing wages and benefits. In 1998, it commissioned an independent study by the respected Minnesota IMPLAN Group (MIG) to measure the nonportfolio impact of 110 of its projects in 26 metropolitan areas nationwide (Minnesota IMPLAN Group 1998). The study used Commerce Department input-output data to estimate the direct and indirect effects of incremental construction activity. It concluded that, from MEPT's inception in 1982 through the first quarter of 1998, the trust's investments have generated

- 18.7 million hours of work for Building Trades members across the country;
- $390.4 million in personal income for Building Trades members;
- $58.6 million in pension contributions paid back into union-sponsored pension funds, the majority going back into Building Trades funds that invest in MEPT;
- $2.9 billion in total economic output in those 26 metropolitan areas, stimulating a total of 60 million work hours in all industries and paying total compensation of $1.1 billion.

Kennedy Associates and Landon Butler & Associates also cooperatively launched a new closed-end real estate investment trust—Multi-Employer Development Partners, LP—to make equity investments in union-built residential and commercial properties nationwide. This new fund had its first closing in February 1999 and is already investing with a target of $250 million in assets.

UNION LABOR LIFE INSURANCE COMPANY'S ACCOUNT "J FOR JOBS": COMMERCIAL MORTGAGES

ULLICO's J for Jobs mortgage account is, along with the AFL-CIO's HIT, one of the oldest and largest union-oriented alternative investment funds. *J for Jobs* is a pooled real estate debt fund designed to provide multi-employer pension funds with a nationally diversified portfolio of high-quality mortgage loans secured by income-producing properties. The fund yields the added benefit of financing new construction or renovation projects that are 100-percent union built, which generates substantial jobs and hours targeted to benefit investing plan beneficiaries on a "best efforts" basis (Kennedy 1999).

At year-end 1998, J for Jobs had a total market value of $1.1 billion. Most of the fund's more than 110 holdings are first mortgages against income-producing commercial and multifamily properties. According to the fund's most recent audit, 45 percent of the mortgage portfolio is secured by office buildings, 31 percent by shopping centers, 10 percent by industrial buildings, and approximately 10 percent by apartment buildings (ULLICO 1997a).

Net assets increased by 21 percent in 1998 alone, half of which came from new investors attracted by the fund's market-beating income yield, which has averaged approximately 2 percent greater than alternative fixed-income vehicles.[11] The J for Jobs account posted a gross return of 11.6 percent in 1998, outpacing the Lehman Aggregate Mortgage Index by 2.9 percent (ULLICO 1999). The fund's total return consisted of a 9-percent income yield plus capital appreciation of 2.5 percent (due primarily to falling interest rates). Over the 1999 3-year period, the J for Jobs account returned an average 8.6 percent annually, compared to an average 6.8 percent on the benchmark Lehman Brothers Aggregate Bond Index.[12]

Although J for Jobs takes the relatively conservative approach of holding permanent (long-term) mortgages, it nonetheless ensures a substantial flow of new union-built construction. ULLICO implements its union construction policy by requiring borrowers to sign a "certification of union construction" that covers all contractors and subcontractors. ULLICO then contacts the local building trades council and verifies that the builders are signatory to collective bargaining agreements before locking in its forward commitment to provide permanent mortgage financing.

During the first 9 months of 1999, J for Jobs issued 24 new loan commitments, representing $790 million in project financing, 5.5 million square feet of development, and twelve thousand union jobs. ULLICO estimates that these new commitments alone will generate an additional fifteen million hours of union construction work (Steed 1999). ULLICO estimates that between 1995 and 1999, J for Jobs generated more than $2 billion in new construction, creating twenty-one thousand construction jobs. Because ULLICO seeks to make mortgage loans on new construction within the geographic jurisdiction where pension investor participants are actually employed, a high proportion of J for Job's activity confers extra benefits directly on plan participants, while strengthening plan sponsors (Kennedy 1999).

In 1999, ULLICO launched a real estate equity fund that takes a full- or partial-ownership position in a wide range of commercial and multifamily residential properties. The majority of the new equity fund's investments are in new construction or in properties with favorable potential for redevelopment. Like J for Jobs, all construction is union built, and ULLICO's ownership position ensures that, going forward, building service and maintenance, improvements, renovations, and repairs are performed by union labor wherever feasible.

The equity fund will also leverage its ownership, by bringing in co-investors and third-party debt, to create more union jobs than it would otherwise. For example, the equity fund's first commitment consisted of a $3.6 million equity stake in a $37 million, 288-unit multifamily residential project in Seattle. "Bottom line, we will be able to use a small investment, control the project, create an estimated 375 union construction jobs, and provide opportunities for unionized employees," explained Ken Hartman, ULLICO regional vice president (Kennedy 1999, 1).

CARPENTERS' COMMERCIAL MORTGAGE/PLUS FUND

The St. Louis-based Commercial Mortgage/Plus Fund is similar to ULLICO's J for Jobs account, except that it targets smaller commercial projects, such as strip malls, office buildings, and industrial sites. In 1997, at approximately the same time that the St. Louis Council of Carpenters allowed ProLoan to expand into a geographically diverse mutual fund, the union decided to target a new market segment that tends to be less unionized.

In heavily unionized towns, such as St. Louis, Chicago, and Detroit, the big downtown projects in the $30–$100 million range tend to use union labor, no matter how the financing occurs. Yet small retail and industrial construction in the $1–$5 million range frequently is built by nonunion workers (Tocco 1999). As the Carpenters financially have colonized the St. Louis residential market with ProLoan, they are beginning to influence the small-commercial-construction market with Mortgage/Plus.

Mortgage/Plus opened in 1997 and had $35 million invested in commercial first mortgages by early 1999. It is managed by the General American Mortgage Company, the mortgage investment specialist that managed ProLoan during its first decade as a private pooled fund. The fund's gross return in its first full year was 9.2 percent (8.4-percent net of expenses). The Laborers Fund for central Illinois also became an investor. The fund hopes to track the geographical expansion of the ProLoan fund, which would improve diversification and liquidity as the fund grows larger.

AMALGAMATED BANK'S LONGVIEW INDEX FUNDS: ACTIVE PROXY STRATEGIES

It should not be surprising that a union-owned bank created the first stock index fund that achieves all the advantages of a "passive" index while adding extra value through active ownership strategies. Taft-Hartley plan trustees, along with several public pension funds, have led a virtual shareholder rights revolution since the 1990s that is widely credited with making corporate executives and boards more accountable and focused on adding value for the benefit of shareholders (see chap. 4, Labor's Role in the Shareholder Revolution). Since 1994, the Amalgamated Bank of New York, founded in 1923 by the Amalgamated Clothing and Textile Workers Union (and now owned by UNITE), has harnessed this new "enhanced indexing" strategy to attract more than $5 billion into its series of five "actively governed" index funds (Luraschi 1999).

The Amalgamated Bank's original Longview Fund, which is designed to replicate the investment performance and low costs of a conventional Standard & Poor's (S&P) 500 composite index, exceeded $3 billion in assets by early 1999. Over the 5-year period through December 31, 1998, this LongView 500 LargeCap Index Fund returned 24.2 percent annually, a bit better than the 24.1-percent return on the nearly identical S&P 500 Composite Index. The Amalgamated Bank has added three additional equity index funds that permit greater diversification by company size: the LongView 400 MidCap Index, the LongView 600 SmallCap Index, and the LongView 1500 Total Market Index, which is a composite index based on the other three. According to the Bank, the gross returns on all four equity index funds slightly exceed the return on the corresponding S&P composite index over the 1999 3-year period.

By taking full advantage of the valuable ownership rights attached to public stock, Longview Fund managers attempt to add extra value over the inter-mediate-to-long-term time horizon that corresponds to a pension fund's position in a passive index trust.[13] The Department of Labor has repeatedly stated that ERISA requires pension fiduciaries to regard shareholder voting rights as plan assets and manage them accordingly.[14] Indeed, because an indexing strategy forecloses the option of *exiting* (selling) indexed stocks that perform poorly due to faulty governance, there is a strong argument to be made that active ownership strategies are a fiduciary obligation when they can be performed cost effectively.

Unlike many passive index funds, the LongView funds monitor both corporate performance and corporate policies to identify companies that underperform compared to other firms in their industries due to a lack of management accountability or other governance failings. Strategies to enhance long-term shareholder value include active voting of proxies; initiating shareholder proposals; organizing coalitions of other institutional investors; and communicating, by letter or in meetings, with company officials about problems the funds have identified using fundamental analysis.

These strategies have been shown to increase returns to large public plans that pursued it on a targeted basis. A Wilshire Associates 1994 study of the so-called California Public Employees' Retirement System (CalPERS) effect of corporate governance activism examined the performance of 62 companies targeted by CalPERS over a 5-year period. Although the stock of these companies trailed the S&P 500 Index by 85 percent over the 5-year period before CalPERS initiated shareholder activism, the same stocks outperformed the index by 54 percent over the following 5 years. This added $150 million annually in additional returns to the fund—a return on investment far greater than the market's return on purely passive stock holdings.[15] Although it is far more difficult to quantify the value added to an index fund by active governance strategies, the LongView approach will likely benefit pension investors, because overall costs are no higher than other investors pay for a purely passive index.

In 1999, LongView targeted between twenty and twenty-five companies for shareholder resolutions on issues ranging from poison pills, golden parachutes, equal employment opportunity, board independence, high performance workplace practices, and age discrimination. Although majority votes for shareholder proposals opposed by management remain fairly rare, in 1997, Longview, working with UNITE and other Taft-Hartley activists, won clear majorities at four companies—Columbia/Health Corporation of America (HCA), J.C. Penney, Rite-Aid, and Consolidated Natural Gas— and demanded that companies either redeem or allow shareholder votes on poison pill antitakeover provisions (Investor Responsibility Research Center 1997).

INTERNATIONAL BROTHERHOOD OF ELECTRICAL
WORKERS–NATIONAL ELECTRICAL CONTRACTORS
ASSOCIATION (NECA) EQUITY INDEX FUND:
FOCUSED PROXY VOTING

In 1997, the IBEW established its own S&P 500 Index trust exclusively for electrical industry multi-employer pension funds. The fund, which invests more than $4 billion in assets for 37 plans, is primarily focused on minimizing costs. Whereas even the largest institutional investors pay between 4 and 8 basis points for passive indexing, the IBEW NECA Equity Index Fund charges just 1.5 basis points (0.015 percent), or $150 per $1 million under management. It is managed by the First National Bank of Maryland, which concedes that the fund is priced at cost because it provides a business development opportunity for the bank and its investment advisory subsidiary, Allied Investment Advisers (Perrone 1999). The fund has outperformed the S&P 500 by 10 basis points (0.1 percent) since its inception in April 1997, primarily because of the lower fees (IBEW-NECA Equity Index Fund 1999).

Although the IBEW index fund does not use the full range of active governance strategies to enhance value, it does generate a collateral benefit by delegating proxy voting authority to the Marco Consulting Group of Chicago. Marco has developed an in-house capacity to track and analyze the impact of corporate proxy issues and generally follows the AFL-CIO's Proxy Voting Guidelines.[16]

MASSACHUSETTS FINANCIAL SERVICES (MFS) UNION STANDARD EQUITY FUND: SCREENED MUTUAL STOCK FUND

In 1993, Bob Eason, a longshoreman and trustee of his union's pension fund, decided to find an investment company that would, for the first time, create a "socially responsible" mutual fund that screened out companies with poor labor relations. As it turned out, he became an architect and marketer of the fund. The fund—the MFS Union Standard Equity Fund—seeks long-term capital appreciation by selecting from among a screened universe of more than 500 large-cap companies judged to be "labor sensitive." MFS, one of the nation's oldest and largest mutual fund companies, actively manages the portfolio, no less than 65 percent of which must be selected from companies approved by a labor advisory board that includes twenty Taft-Hartley trustees and labor-friendly academics. In 1997, MFS opened the fund to individuals as well as institutions and pushed net assets above $100 million by the end of 1998 (MFS Union Standard Equity Fund 1999b).

The Union Standard Equity Fund's performance puts it in the top quartile of domestic stock funds over the 3-year period ending December 31, 1998. Because of its focus on large unionized companies, the fund's sector weightings are heavily skewed toward industrial goods, consumer staples, utilities, and communications and away from technology and financial services companies. This weighting has also given the fund a lower risk rating (beta), because basic industry stocks are less volatile. Its largest holdings at year-end 1998 included Bristol Meyers Squibb, Phillip Morris, General Electric, Exxon, BellSouth, and Johnson & Johnson.

"I invest in a list of companies that meet certain criteria that are labor-friendly," explained portfolio manager Mitchell Dynan (Gilpin 1998). The fund's labor advisory board applies guidelines or screens that apply the following criteria to determine whether a company is sufficiently labor sensitive to be included in the universe of eligible investments. If a company meets the criteria, it is added to the universe of approximately 530 companies from which Dynan selects the best potential financial performers. The fund's labor criteria require that companies have

- At least 5-percent unionization of the company's workers;
- No current labor strife, such as strikes or lockouts;
- No pattern of outsourcing or unjustified plant closings;
- Compliance with labor and occupational health and safety laws;
- No products on AFL–CIO boycott list;
- A degree of foreign ownership or control.

The value of steering union-influenced investment toward large, publicly traded companies with good labor relations—and away from other public companies with negative labor policies—may be less controversial as an investment strategy than as a labor strategy. First, modest additional demand for a large-cap stock, such as General Motors or Phillip Morris, is unlikely to lower the firm's cost of capital or otherwise promote an expansion of its domestic workforce. Likewise, shunning the stock of companies such as Wal-mart is unlikely to have a tangible impact on the operations of bad companies.

Second, to the extent that a fractional share of a company's widely traded public stock gives an investor any leverage at all, it is a *negative* power that is typically exercised via shareholder activism. As a result, screened funds have no ownership rights at the companies they most want to change.

Finally, although from a labor perspective a high-performance screen may be preferable to giving money managers complete discretion, union trustees could achieve a far greater impact by focusing their demands for alternative investing on *private placements* in smaller, nonpublic companies. By doing so, they can own sizable stakes and negotiate union-sensitive covenants that shape a growing company's policies into the future.

Strategies to Expand Union-Led Alternative Investing

As the profiles above suggest, labor-oriented investment programs expanded rapidly since 1994 and offer options in every asset allocation category—from real estate and core fixed-income to stock index funds and private placement equity. The leading union-led alternative investing programs demonstrate a remarkable ability to match, and in some cases to substantially exceed, their benchmarks on conventional measures of financial return in relation to risk. The three largest union-built construction trusts, for example, have adopted very different investment models that have consistently delivered market-rate returns at relatively low risk for periods exceeding 10 years. Although union-oriented funds are relatively new to private equity, ULLICO's track record (4 years for Separate Account P, 7 years in its general account) has outperformed

all but a handful of U.S. investment funds of any type, simultaneously achieving covenants concerning the fair treatment of workers at the rapidly expanding young companies in which it invests.

How can these union-initiated intermediaries be replicated and expanded?
Could there be five more funds like ULLICO's Separate Account P, financing the expansion of middle-market companies and seeding positive labor
relations in a raft of entrepreneurial "new economy" enterprises? After all,
despite these sparkling track records, less than 5 percent of multi-employer
plan assets are committed to union-friendly investment programs—and virtually no public or single-employer plans do so, despite their far greater size,
with the notable exception of public employee funds invested in HIT. What
affirmative steps by the labor movement could increase the number of fund
options and assets committed—particularly in the potentially potent category
of private equity and debt placements?

SOME COMMON CHARACTERISTICS OF SUCCESSFUL UNION-FRIENDLY INVESTMENT FUNDS

To determine whether the labor movement could take any further affirmative
steps to expand on the most successful of these labor-friendly investment
models, it may be helpful to summarize some of the characteristics that many
of these funds have in common.

Commingled Funds with Professional Management

Very few pension funds are large enough to support an in-house staff with
enough skill, experience, and contacts to identify, analyze, and monitor alternative investments. Pooled funds can provide resources and incentives necessary to attract top talent. Second, a commingled fund run by a qualified plan
asset manager has advantages under ERISA; as noted above, individual fund
investments are not treated as plan assets, allowing the fund far more latitude
and insulating trustees. Third, the professionals who manage a pooled fund
acquire a degree of independence that helps to avoid the sort of bias, conflicts
of interest, or wishful thinking that might influence a fund making direct
investments in its own industry. The trustees' role is limited to a procedural
due diligence to assure that fund managers have the qualifications to deliver
market-rate returns and agreed-upon collateral benefits.

Geographic Diversification with Reciprocal Targeting

One reason the St. Louis Council of Carpenters has expanded its ProLoan residential mortgage program into a multistate vehicle is to reduce risk, because
entire real estate markets tend to rise or fall with variations in local or regional

economic conditions. This makes national pools like HIT, ULLICO's J for Jobs, and MEPT more attractive, particularly because they target an equivalent amount of investment back into the jurisdiction of the pension funds investing in their pool. A targeted or strategic fund may nevertheless find it more practical, as the St. Louis Carpenters did, to begin with a local fund and broaden its focus as assets grow and a favorable track record is documented.

Other Risk Reduction Strategies

Union-oriented funds tend to be, within their asset class, on the lower end of the risk spectrum. This probably reflects the reality of marketing to less sophisticated and more risk-averse multi-employer plan trustees, but it also reflects concerns that critics, with 20/20 hindsight, will claim that the secondary objectives (e.g., union-built construction) led to unexpected losses. A good example of a union-led fund structured to minimize risk is the AFL-CIO's HIT, which has attracted a very large asset base by holding almost exclusively mortgage-backed securities that are guaranteed against default by government-sponsored entities. The Carpenters' ProLoan core fixed-income mutual fund is similarly "risk neutral," despite its aggressive organizing profile. Even ULLICO's Separate Account P avoids entry-level venture capital and is quite diversified for a fund of its type.

Economies of Scale, Reducing Costs

Cost concerns also motivate pension funds to pool assets through intermediaries. Because alternative investing tends to be information- and labor-intensive, the relative cost of top talent and other overhead tends to decline as assets rise. For example, HIT/BIT has been able to reduce steadily its fee schedule as assets increase, even though it has expanded its staff overall, in part because of the non-profit ethic that comes along with sponsorship and control by the AFL-CIO.

Partnering with Private Investors

Most union-oriented funds—in real estate, private equity, and project finance—frequently co-invest alongside other investors, preferably for-profit private investors, for several reasons. First, it confirms that the fund's due diligence is solid, because other professional investors are analyzing the same information. Second, it provides further evidence that the expected return on investment meets market standards irrespective of collateral benefits, which presumably would not be factored in by the private investors. In this respect, ULLICO's Separate Account P keeps itself in good company by investing alongside wealthy individuals, hedge funds, insurance companies, and others who have independently judged the company a good risk purely on its financial merits. The Boilermakers' Infrastructure Fund uses this same strategy, which has the additional benefit of leveraging scarce assets into a larger number of projects through which the fund can influence the choice of union versus nonunion contractors.

Comparability to Benchmarks

Many union-friendly funds have structured their investments so that pension consultants can compare their performance very directly with standard benchmarks. For example, the ProLoan/Builders Fixed Income Fund mirrors the risk and return characteristics of the Lehman Aggregate Bond Index, so that trustees can easily justify using it as part of their core fixed-income allocation. Similarly, HIT can be compared directly to a GNMA bond index, because it holds primarily mortgage-backed securities with a similar risk and return profile, whereas MEPT can be compared directly to real estate equity indexes. Rough benchmarks also exist for the different slices of the more volatile private equity market (i.e., venture capital, mezzanine financing) and are useful to the degree that a fund specializes in a particular style.

Collateral Benefits

Finally, all the union-sensitive funds are either structured to generate collateral benefits with every investment (the union-built construction trusts) or are dedicated to generating social benefits on an opportunistic basis (e.g., the private equity funds) depending on the company and their degree of financial leverage.

Negative Characteristics Investment Funds Should Avoid

The flip side of these common positive characteristics are negative features that typically should be avoided. These include the following:

- *Insufficient diversification,* both geographically and with respect to the number of investment situations underlying the allocation;
- *Real or apparent self-dealing,* which is far more worrisome and difficult to defend when trustees have direct control over investments benefitting or harming companies or unions in the same industry or geographic area;
- *Lack of adequate in-house expertise or oversight,* or, at the opposite extreme, unnecessarily high overhead or consulting costs when a similar investment is available on a commingled basis at a far lower cost;
- *Large commitments to investments that are "opaque,"* because risk and projected returns are unusually difficult to quantify or assess.

OTHER STRATEGIES TO EXPAND LABOR-FRIENDLY PENSION INVESTING

Although the AFL-CIO and a number of national unions have devoted considerable staff time and resources to promoting shareholder activism, relatively little was done until the mid 1990s to encourage more options and assets for progressive pension investing. Because multi-employer–defined benefit plans are steadily shrinking as a share of U.S. pension assets, an assertive and well-coordinated program with support across a range of unions is needed to ensure that labor's expanding "pension power" does not rely on market forces alone. The 1999 publication of the AFL-CIO's *Investment Product Review*, which evaluates and grades investment funds claiming to create labor-friendly collateral benefits, is an important part of this process. In addition to its value as a sort of "consumer guide" to responsible investing, the *Investment Product Review* also serves the critical purpose of signaling both the investment community and Taft-Hartley pension plan trustees that the impact of investment products on organized labor's interests is important and is being monitored.

The following affirmative strategies could also increase the share of pension investments generating collateral benefit.

Educating Trustees and Other "Gatekeepers"

When the Carpenters union decided in 1998 to launch its private equity fund of funds, members knew they needed to make sure the concept would not be nixed by the consultants and attorneys relied on by local Carpenter plan trustees. So, in January 1999, the Carpenters hosted a conference to discuss private equity investing and their new fund with leading Taft-Hartley pension consultants (DeCarlo 1999). Much of the reluctance of multi-employer plans to make alternative investments (regardless of whether they yield extra non-portfolio benefits) is thought to stem from a lack of understanding that alternative investments are well established among a wide range of institutional investors, including corporate and public pension funds. Plan attorneys, administrators, and management-side trustees are other critical groups that could be targeted for education and discussion of union-friendly investments.

Establishing New Intermediaries

Today's labor leaders look back approvingly on the foresight of Gompers and the AFL-CIO leadership that created ULLICO in the 1920s and HIT in the 1960s. Yet no comparable new investment model has been spurred by the labor movement itself in recent years. For example, with the recent explosion of opportunities to perform direct private equity and debt investments, it seems a particularly good time to grant or lend the resources necessary to create one or more new vehicles to expand the sort of dual-purpose private placement strategy being pursued by ULLICO. The Union Privilege Benefits program is another potential vehicle by which the voluntary investments of millions of union members could be rechanneled into more labor-friendly mutual funds that mirror the pension-oriented products described previously.

Nurturing a Cadre of Alternative Investment Professionals
Since 1990, a group of rookie investment managers has become the proven stars running multibillion-dollar, union-led vehicles such as HIT and ULLICO's Separate Account P. Yet there is apparently no conscious effort by the labor movement to develop the pro-union investment managers for the future. Although there is no easy way to do this, two small steps come to mind. First, union staff and multi-employer plan trustees with the skills and inclination could be offered "scholarships" to learn investing skills (e.g., part-time master's of business administration programs). Second, investment firms that rely on unions as clients, including the existing union-led investment programs, could be urged to hire these recruits and others known to be sympathetic to labor's agenda.

Encouraging New Programs That Leverage Pension Capital
During President Clinton's first term, HIT/BIT's Coyle played a major role in persuading HUD Secretary Henry Cisneros to structure Section 8 public housing subsidies to leverage far larger amounts of private pension capital that would be guaranteed against default. A similar Cisneros initiative leveraged Section 108 community-development block grants with pension funds. In both programs, HIT was a major investor and able to condition its participation on union-built construction. Various proposals have also been floated to finance public investment in infrastructure by issuing *taxable* bonds, which would appeal to tax-exempt pension funds and would also be guaranteed against default and securitized by future streams of user fee revenue.[17] On a national level, such schemes will likely require a favorable political climate.

Expanding Worker Choice in Defined-Contribution Plans
Union members increasingly control some of their own investment allocations through 401(k) and other defined-contribution accounts. Unions and workers themselves could push to have the typically plain-vanilla mutual fund choices expanded to include one or two more socially responsible options, such as the Builders Fixed-Income Fund or the MFS Union Standard Equity Fund. Since defined-contribution plans represent a growing majority of new private pension savings, it is important to find ways to give individual workers a choice to participate in funds that achieve targeted economic or social benefits.

Expanding Worker Voice in Single-Employer–Defined Benefit Plans

Finally, unions face the challenge of addressing a goal dating back to the newly merged AFL-CIO's original ten-point pension benefit bargaining guide of 1956, which is joint trusteeship (or at least some participation) in the management of single-employer pension plans (Ghilarducci 1995). It remains unclear whether in the 1990s any union in a strong bargaining position has seriously tested management's likely opposition to even a single union trustee on the company plan for rank-and-file workers. Given the evolution of ERISA and the track record of jointly trusteed multi-employer plans, it seems at least possible that unions at some firms would not need to give up too much to win some voice. Legislatively, the issue could be revisited, at least incrementally. In 1990, Rep. Peter Visclosky (D-IN) introduced legislation that would have required an equal number of elected worker trustees on all private single-employer plan boards. Although the legislation failed, it did receive the vote of most Democrats.

Conclusion

Private pension assets allocated to union-friendly alternative investing programs have more than tripled since 1994. The number of competing alternative investing vehicles is increasing at a rapid pace and now provides an option in every asset allocation category. The largest and best-established examples of alternative investments targeted to create extra benefits for plan participants are the leading union-built construction financing funds.

A recent, but potentially more powerful trend, involves *direct* private equity investing in smaller, typically nonpublic companies. Large corporate and public pension funds have long realized the *financial* potential of private equity and now allocate an average of almost 5 percent of total assets to private placements. In contrast, few union-sponsored pension funds make private equity allocations at all. This gap should narrow now that ULLICO's Separate Account P has demonstrated that the direct investment of sorely needed expansion capital in young entrepreneurial companies—and in middle-market companies needing expansion capital—can yield both premium financial returns and social leverage. Unlike investments in public equity markets, private equity investors have the ability to demand special covenants requiring union neutrality and card check recognition, union-built construction, environmentally sound policies, and other corollary benefits. Although private equity investing offers a surprising degree of financial *and* social leverage, as is the case with union-built real estate and other offerings, the ability of pension fund investors to generate valuable extra benefits on top of a market rate of return depends in large part on how quickly highly qualified and trusted intermediaries can be created and successfully linked to progressive, savvy, and aggressive multi-employer and public plan trustees.

More needs to be done, on a coordinated basis, to encourage new, high-quality union-friendly investment products and increase the allocations by union-influenced pension funds to these alternative investment vehicles.

[VI]

CANADIAN LABOUR-SPONSORED
INVESTMENT FUNDS:
A MODEL FOR U.S. ECONOMICALLY
TARGETED INVESTMENTS

Tessa Hebb and David Mackenzie

Canadian innovations in labor-friendly asset management offer rich lessons for those in the United States who seek new ways to organize and control capital. The Canadian trade union movement currently controls much of its nation's venture capital through Labour-Sponsored Investment Funds (LSIFs), which account for 50 percent of the available venture capital in Canada. The best of the LSIFs mobilize workers' savings to invest in good jobs within local communities. The investment strategies of these LSIFs are rooted in a broader social agenda that promotes worker participation, training, and respect for stake-holders.

Yet the creation of these funds has not been without tension inside and outside the labor movement. For instance, in Canada's largest province of Ontario, founding legislation left open the issue of sponsorship. The result has been a group of funds that are labor sponsored in name but hold little if any of the social values and objectives of the labor movement. The so-called rent-a-union funds pay willing unions and associations to act as sponsors with only nominal involvement in the funds' activities. This type of fund holds roughly one-third of the assets currently invested in LSIFs. Rent-a-union funds use the generous tax credits and other benefits offered by government but manage their capital without the explicit objectives of creating and saving jobs or promoting worker empowerment. Fortunately, the provincial legislation that establishes LSIFs usually mandates a particular labor body, most often the provincial federation of labor, to act as sponsor.

In the following sections, we describe the structure and diversity of LSIFs and their role in provincial economies, and we evaluate their efforts to reap social benefits that extend beyond monetary rates of return.

Defining Canadian Labour-Sponsored Investment Funds

HISTORY OF CANADIAN LABOUR-SPONSORED INVESTMENT FUNDS

Quebec, perhaps due to its unique communitarian tradition, was the first Canadian province to establish an LSIF. During the severe economic downturn in the early 1980s, the trade union movement identified the failure to invest in small- and medium-sized firms as a major capital gap that exacerbated a severe employment crisis in the province. Members of the Quebec Federation of Labour (FTQ) realized that their retirement savings could be pooled and invested in Quebec to generate jobs in local communities. They convinced the center-left Parti Quebecois government of Premier Rene Levesque to support legislation that created an investment pool that would use workers' savings, directed by workers' representatives, to invest in small- and medium-sized enterprises. The primary purpose of the fund is to create, save, and maintain jobs within the province. Giving labor the power to control a pool of capital was a tough sell; many business elites and the opposition Liberal Party bitterly opposed the proposed legislation.

The act to establish the Solidarity Fund (FTQ) was the last order of business to be taken up by the government in the spring legislative session of 1983. A grueling all-night debate forced the legislature beyond the allotted time and into the morning hours of Quebec's national holiday on June 24. But the Parti Quebecois and the supporters of the Solidarity Fund (FTQ) were determined to see the legislation enacted. They settled all outstanding issues, and the bill passed. By that time, however, it was very late, beyond the official close of the legislative session. The members of the Quebec Legislature agreed to turn the clocks back to midnight to establish the Solidarity Fund (FTQ). Solidarity (FTQ) has since become the model for LSIFs in Canada and around the world.

The legislation creating Solidarity (FTQ) established several defining characteristics. First, the named labor body, the *Federation de Travailleurs et Tra-*

vailleuses du Quebec (FTQ), is the sole sponsor of the fund within provincial jurisdiction. This legislation ensures fund control by organized labor through a board of directors in which the FTQ appoints ten of the sixteen members and has input on the appointment of the other six board members, including the chief executive officer.

The second defining characteristic within the legislation is a statement of the objectives of the fund. The stated goals for the fund signal the intended collateral benefits generated from its activities. The act states that the purpose of Solidarity is to

- Invest in firms within Quebec whose total assets are less than $50 million, or whose net assets are not greater than $20 million, to create, maintain, and protect jobs;
- Promote the training of workers in economic matters and enable them to increase their influence on Quebec's economic development;
- Stimulate the Quebec economy;
- Invite workers to subscribe to the fund.

The invitation for workers' participation is facilitated by a tax credit that can be used within each worker's individual Registered Retirement Savings Plan (RRSP), which is the Canadian equivalent of an Individual Retirement Account (IRA). The LSIF tax credit allows a maximum of $5,000 to be invested each year and receives a 15-percent federal tax credit and a 15-percent provincial credit for a maximum rebate of $1,500. Initially, this tax credit was 40 percent and was split between the two levels of government, but in 1996 the credit was reduced. This investment can be made within a tax-deferred RRSP deduction. For the average earner, the RRSP tax deferral is worth a further 30 percent of the contribution. The LSIF tax credit is an incentive for individual investors to display the patience and risk tolerance required in all venture capital investing. The Quebec legislation defines long-term investment in the Solidarity Fund (FTQ) as no withdrawal until retirement. Early withdrawals, except in exceptional circumstances, incur tax penalties. By contrast, most other provinces allow for withdrawal from the fund without penalty after 8 years.

With the model of Quebec's Solidarity Fund (FTQ) in place, it did not take long for other jurisdictions in Canada to recognize the value of pooling workers' savings to create more available venture capital for investment in local communities. The success of the Solidarity Fund (FTQ) attracted attention across the political spectrum. Every political party in Canada has supported LSIF legislation. The Canadian federal government first implemented national legislation in 1988, followed by British Columbia, Manitoba, Ontario, and New

Brunswick. The naming of the sole labor sponsor within the legislation occurred in four of the five provinces where LSIFs have been established provincially. All provinces, with the exception of Ontario, named the provincial Federation of Labour as the designated trade union body to deliver LSIFs.[1]

Ontario, and in particular its capital, Toronto, is Canada's economic driver and financial center. In 1990, much to the surprise of many, the New Democratic Party (NDP), Canada's left-of-center party affiliated with labor, came to power in Ontario. Among the array of progressive changes that followed the NDP victory—a strengthened labor code, employment equity laws, and worker-ownership legislation—was a proposal to establish an LSIF in Canada's financial heartland. Toronto's Bay Street financiers fought the creation of a labor-controlled fund. However, the proposal also drew bitter criticism from within the labor movement.

The success of LSIFs in other jurisdictions has thus far failed to generate a philosophical consensus in Ontario's labor movement regarding this model of worker-controlled venture capital. The leadership of the Canadian Auto Workers, for example, continues to express vocal opposition to LSIFs on two major grounds.

First, the fact that LSIFs offer tax credits for retirement savings held in individual retirement savings accounts runs counter to the traditional labor view that workers' retirements should be secured only in pooled pension funds. Almost 30 years after the introduction of RRSPs, this individual retirement savings program remains one of the few deductions from income that has not been reformed as a tax credit. The result is that deductions generated from RRSP annual contributions are more valuable to high-income earners than low-income earners. For many trade union activists, the entire RRSP retirement program is just another example of regressive tax laws and the skewed distribution of wealth in Canada. For many, labor control of these funds and the participation of many thousands of union members fail to offset these concerns about solidarity.

The second major objection to LSIFs, more frankly ideological, is that they turn many workers into capitalists. This perspective is part of the long divide within labor and the left between pragmatic reformists (e.g., this chapter's authors) and adherents of a harder line. Internal differences among unions affiliated with the Ontario Federation of Labour meant that the provincial NDP Government could not legitimately name the Ontario Federation of Labour as the sole sponsor of the LSIF when legislation was introduced. As a result, Ontario alone has no restrictions on the number of funds within its jurisdiction that can be sponsored by trade unions or associations. Fifteen of Canada's twenty-one LSIFs exist under Ontario legislation.

The outcome of this debate is a group of LSIFs that have, at best, a loose affiliation with labor and no commitment to collateral social benefits beyond rate of return. Many of these funds have been set up simply to capture the available tax credits offered by the government. They became known as *rent-a-union funds*, because they are run by professional money managers and have only the loosest affiliation with the labor organization they pay to act as their sponsor. Their management consists typically of Bay Street financiers, many of whom oppose labor movement agendas. Some funds are sponsored by such groups as professional athletes' associations.

The rent-a-union funds, therefore, provide ammunition to the part of the left that opposes any attempt to fashion worker-friendly investment instruments, redirect pension-fund monies, experiment with worker-ownership, or do anything else that might be tagged as a form of "workers'" capitalism. They also challenge those in labor and the left on the other side of the debate: unionists and community activists seeking innovative ways to ensure that control of capital is not left in the hands of professional money managers alone.

To define and deepen the LSIF social vision more explicitly, Canadian funds that take their lead from Quebec's Solidarity Fund (FTQ) have formed an alliance with an agreed set of progressive principles to ensure not just labor sponsorship of the capital pool, but also labor control. It is control, rather than nominal sponsorship, that enables LSIFs to fulfill their legislated aim of generating collateral benefits and to advance wider trade union goals.

LABOUR-SPONSORED INVESTMENT FUND ALLIANCE
Five Canadian funds explicitly advance a progressive investment policy and have formed a coalition called the *LSIF Alliance*, and are all signatories of the following Defining Statement of Principles:

1. Solidarity Fund (FTQ): established in 1983 under the sponsorship and control of the Federation de Travailleurs et Travailleuses du Quebec;
2. Working Opportunity Fund (WOF): established in 1991 under the sponsorship and control of the British Columbia Federation of Labour;
3. Crocus Investment Fund: established in 1992, sponsored and controlled by the Manitoba Federation of Labour;
4. Workers Investment Fund: established in 1994, sponsored and controlled by the New Brunswick Federation of Labour;
5. First Ontario Fund: established in 1995, sponsored and controlled by the United Steelworkers of America; the Communications, Energy, and Paperworkers Union; the Service Employees International Union; the Power Workers Union; and the Ontario Worker Co-op Federation.

CANADIAN LABOUR-SPONSORED INVESTMENT FUNDS

Labour-Sponsored Investment Fund Defining Statement
ORGANIZATION AND DIRECTION BY A LABOR BODY

- Organization: the initiative for the creation of the fund comes from a defined labor body, which serves as its sponsor and promoter.
- Direction: the board of directors is controlled by the labor body, and the governance of the funds requires that major decisions, including but not limited to targeted investments, be made by the board of directors.
- Labor body: a labor body is a federation, trade union, or group of unions whose membership equals or exceeds one hundred thousand. It might also be a provincial labor body chartered by the Canadian Labour Congress.

COMMITMENT TO MEETING ECONOMIC AND SOCIAL GOALS. These economic and social goals extend beyond the provision of equity capital. Common goals include

- A commitment to job retention and job creation;
- A commitment to regional economic development;
- The use of a social audit during the investment analysis of a potential investee company in areas of health and safety, environment and employment practices;
- The willingness of investee companies to improve labor-management relations.

Funds may also have unique economic and social goals. These economic and social goals should be reflected

- In the mandate of the Fund;
- In mechanisms created as part of the investment analysis;
- As part of the Fund's post-investment activity.

COMMITMENT TO PROVIDE AN EQUITABLE RATE OF RETURN TO SHAREHOLDERS, RISK CAPITAL IN A DIVERSIFIED PORTFOLIO, AND PARTICIPATION BY A BROAD BASE OF AVERAGE WORKING PEOPLE

- Distinct structures or marketing initiatives aimed at working people;
- Access and direct marketing to members of unions;
- Composition of the fund's investor group such that a significant number are members of legitimate labor bodies;
- Educational programs providing economic education to working people.

[133]

FACILITATION OF COOPERATION BETWEEN LABOR AND BUSINESS

- Business and labor representation on an investment advisory committee;
- Institutional investment by business groups;
- Promotion of participative management practices at investee companies.

Categories of Labour-Sponsored Investment Funds

Forming the Alliance has created two categories of funds within the Canadian LSIF asset class. Alliance funds adhere to a set of defining characteristics that include both a broad social and economic agenda combined with control of the board by a recognized trade union body.

The non-Alliance funds discussed previously are not signatories to the Alliance principles and do not have genuine labor control of the board and investment policy of the fund or a strong commitment to providing collateral benefits, beyond filling a capital gap in the Canadian venture capital market.

Table 6.1 demonstrates the results of a 1997 survey of the LSIF industry's (Falconer 1997) management and investment policies, as well as its collateral objectives. This table shows that LSIFs can be divided into two categories: those that adhere either explicitly or implicitly to Alliance principles, and those that lack labor control and social commitment. Majority control by a trade union body of the board of directors has a substantial impact on fund investment decisions and direction. Six of the twenty-one funds have labor majority control of the board. Of that group, five are Alliance members. Only Alliance funds have a strategic investment program that includes a strong commitment to collateral benefits.

As discussed in the section Creating Regional Networks for Investment, alliance funds build community and regional investment networks. These funds also perform social and environmental audits before investing in companies. Their social audits screen potential investments for ethical practices around environmental responsibility, product safety standards, positive employee relations, and corporate citizenship. Moreover, these funds have greater involvement and participation by trade unions, and that in turn generates trust with workers inside the enterprise and facilitates their contribution to social audits. Workers, for example, can inform Alliance LSIFs of any major discrepancies that may exist between the company's balance sheets and the actual running of the firm. Impact of the social audit on fund performance is examined in the section Collateral Benefits Gained from Labor-Controlled Labour-Sponsored Investment Funds.

Alliance LSIFs offer worker training and education as part of their mandate. There is also an emerging component of worker ownership for employees

TABLE 6.1. Survey of Labour-Sponsored Investment Funds (LSIFs) in Canada

Fund	Board Control	Community Regional Investment	Worker Education	Social Responsibility	Worker Ownership	Labour-Management Corporation	Fund Economic Benefits
Crocus Investment Fund	Majority	Yes	Yes	Yes	Yes	Yes	Yes
First Ontario LSIF, Ltd.	Majority	Yes	Yes	Yes	Yes	Yes	N/A
Quebec Solidarity Fund (FTQ)	Majority	Yes	Yes	Yes	Yes	Yes	Yes
Retrocom Growth	Majority	No	No	Yes	No	Limited industrial relations	Yes
Workers Investment Fund	Majority	Yes	Yes	Yes	Yes	Yes	N/A
Working Opportunity	Majority	Yes	Yes	Yes	Yes	Yes	Yes
Active Communications	Mix	No	N/A	N/A	N/A	N/A	N/A
Canadian Medical Discoveries	Mix	No	No	No	No	No	Yes
Canadian Venture Opportunities	Mix	No	No	No	No	Not specifically	N/A
DGC Entertainment Ventures	Mix	No	No	No	No	No	N/A
Working Ventures	Mix	Yes	No	No	Yes	Yes	Yes
B.E.S.T. Discoveries	Mix/fee	No	No	No	No	No	N/A
C.I. Covington	Mix/fee	No	No	No	No	No	N/A
Canadian Science and Technology Growth	Mix/fee	No	No	No	No	No	N/A
Capital Alliance Ventures	Mix/fee	No	No	No	Yes	No	N/A
Centerfire Growth Fund Incorporated	Mix/fee	No	No	No	No	No	N/A
FESA Enterprise Venture	Mix/fee	No	No	Limited environmental relations	No	Limited industrial relations	N/A

TABLE 6.1. *Continued*

Fund	Board Control	Community Regional Investment	Worker Education	Social Responsibility	Worker Ownership	Labour-Management Corporation	Fund Economic Benefits
Sportfund	Mix/fee	No	No	No	No	Limited industrial relations	N/A
Triax Growth	Mix/fee	No	No	No	No	No	N/A
Trillium Growth Capital, Inc.	Mix/fee	No	No	Compliance with	No	Limited industrial relations	N/A
VenGrowth Investment	Mix/fee	No	No	Compliance with	No	Limited industrial relations	N/A

Fund	Alliance Member	Sponsor	Board Control	Union Participation	Strategic Investment
Crocus Investment Fund	Yes	Manitoba Federation of Labour	Majority	Yes	Yes
First Ontario LSIF, Ltd.	Yes	CEP, Power Workers, SEIU, USWA	Majority	Yes	Yes
Quebec Solidarity Fund (FTQ)	Yes	FTQ	Majority	Yes	Yes
Rectrocom Growth	No	Electrical Workers/ Construction	Majority	Yes	Yes
Workers Investment Fund	Yes	New Brunswick Federation of Labour	Majority	Yes	Yes
Working Opportunity	Yes	British Columbia Federation of Labour	Majority	Yes	Yes
Active Communications*	No	A.C.T.R.A.	Mix	No	Limited
Canadian Medical Discoveries	No	P.I.P.S.	Mix	No	Early stage management
Canadian Venture Opportunities	No	UFCW, The Labourers International Union of North America, UNITE, United Brotherhood of Carpenters	Mix	No	No
DGC Entertainment Ventures	No	Director's Guild	Mix	No	Limited

Fund		Sponsor			
Working Ventures	No	CFL[1]	Mix	Limited	No
B.E.S.T. Discoveries	No	Federation of Professional and Technical Engineers	Mix/fee	No	Technology sector
C.I. Covington	No	Canadian Police Association	Mix/fee	No	No
Canadian Science and Technology Growth	No	Air Traffic Control Association	Mix/fee	No	Early-stage technology
Capital Alliance Ventures	No	Association of Foreign Service Officers	Mix/fee	No	Technology sector
Centerfire Growth Fund Incorporated	No	International Brotherhood of Painter and Allied Trades	Mix/fee	No	No
ENSIS Growth Fund Incorporated[2]	No	BPI Mutual Fund	Mix/fee	No	
FESA Enterprise Venture	No	The Federation of Engineering & Scientific Associations	Mix/fee	No	Technology sector
Sportfund	No	Canadian Football Players League Association	Mix/fee	No	Sports/entertainment
Triax Growth	No	TCU	Mix/fee	No	Publicly traded
Trillium Growth Capital, Inc.	No	Brewery, General & Professional Workers Union	Mix/fee	No	No
VenGrowth Investment	No	Association of Public Service Financial Administrators	Mix/fee	No	No

A.C.T.R.A., Alliance of Canadian Cinema, Television, and Radio Artists; B.E.S.T., Business Engineering Science and Technology; CEP, Communication, Energy, and Paperworkers Union; CFL, Canadian Federation of Labour; DGC, Directors Guild of Carpenters; FESA, Federation of Engineering and Scientific Associations; FTQ, Fédération de Travailleurs et Travailleuses du Québec; N/A, not applicable; P.I.P.S., Professional Institute of Public Service of Canada; SEIU, Service Employees International Union; TCU, Transportation-Communications International Union; UFCW, United Food and Commercial Workers International Union; UNITE, Union of Needletrades, Industrial, and Textile Employees; USWA, United Steelworkers of America.

[1] No longer available.
[2] Newly created fund in Manitoba.

through direct Employee Stock Ownership Plan (ESOP) investment in the case of the Crocus Fund and indirect investment in the firm through the mandatory purchase of Solidarity's shares by investee firms. Participative management is also encouraged for firms that receive Alliance fund investments. We argue that these characteristics result in strong fund performance, because they enhance firm productivity.

Both types of LSIFs, Alliance and rent-a-union, fill capital gaps within the Canadian economy. But Table 6.1 indicates the progressive Alliance funds have a broader social and economic agenda. Critics of economically targeted investments (ETIs) claim that the dual mandates—seeking investments with a market rate of return and delivering collateral benefits—are mutually exclusive. Investing is assumed to be a zero-sum game, and any benefits that occur beyond those to shareholders must come at a cost to the investor. However, the Canadian experience of these two types of ETI funds within a single asset class demonstrates that funds with investment policies that seek collateral benefits often outperform funds that do not. Furthermore, examining the management of these two types of funds within the LSIF asset class shows that trade union control has a positive effect on the performance of the funds, both in increased market rates of return and in additional collateral benefits gained.

FILLING A CAPITAL GAP

The tax incentive for labor-sponsored funds was created to encourage a new capital supply into venture capital investing that would otherwise not exist. This policy has been successful in addressing a chronic capital gap for small- and medium-sized companies in Canada (Laliberte 1999). In 1990, when LSIF vehicles were not fully developed, the venture capital industry in Canada stood at $3 billion, with new money invested at the rate of $200–$300 million annually. By early 1998, the total sector stood at $8.4 billion (Macdonald and Assoc. 1998). In 2000, LSIFs accounted for 50 percent of venture capital in Canada and are the fastest-growing segment of the market. Their impact is particularly visible in provinces that are historically undersupplied by venture capital, such as Quebec and Manitoba.

The venture capital market in Canada is defined in much broader terms than that of the United States. In Canada, the investment class is measured by the size of the company rather than by sector or type of investment. It applies to firms with assets of less than $50 million and fewer than five hundred employees. Venture capital in the United States generally refers to equity investing in emerging sectors of the economy. These sectors often include companies in such fields as high tech or bioengineering. In Canada, venture capital is a broader basket that includes much of what is referred to as *mezza-*

TABLE 6.2. Venture-Backed Companies—Engines of Growth

1991–1996	Average Annual Growth Rate (%)
Jobs created	26
Sales	14
Exports generated	34
Research and development invested	40
Taxes paid	17

nine financing in the United States. Canadian venture capital includes older, more established industries; company turnarounds; succession plans; and subordinated debt structures, as well as emerging sectors and equity positions.

Filling the venture capital gap in Canada has been critical in terms of increased productivity and employment. Table 6.2 details a 1997 study by Macdonald and Associates for the Business Development Bank of Canada that examined the impact of the venture capital pool on the Canadian economy (Business Development Bank of Canada 1997). It found that, on average, the surveyed investee firms increased their employment base by 26 percent per year. "Venture-backed companies have continued to create new jobs in recent years at a rate that has far outstripped that achieved by the economy as a whole or by large companies" (Business Development Bank of Canada 1997, 8). By contrast, employment increased in the Canadian economy as a whole by only 1.2 percent annually from 1992 to the end of 1996, whereas Canada's largest one hundred companies increased employment by an annual rate of only 8.8 percent.

With LSIFs attracting more money into the venture capital sector of the economy, the dollar value of the deals in Canada has tripled since the early 1990s. In 1995, the industry invested a then-record-breaking $669 million in 364 companies. By 1996, this amount had increased to $1.1 billion invested in 525 companies in Canada. In 1997, an unprecedented $1.8 billion was invested in 794 companies. LSIFs led the investments, disbursing $671 million in 1997, up by more than 66 percent from $403 million in 1996 (Macdonald and Assoc. 1998). In fiscal 1997–1998, Solidarity (FTQ) alone invested $614 million.

Levels of venture capital have increased dramatically in Quebec since the inception of the Solidarity Fund (FTQ).

Thanks to the presence of the Fund, Quebec as a region went from being a region with limited sources of venture capital to one gathering the largest share of overall venture capital in the country. While the province's economy represents 21 percent of Canada's GDP, it had some 52 percent of the country's venture capital under management in 1995. Today the province has levels of capital per capita that compare favorably with areas like California and New York known for their availability of venture capital. (Laliberte 1999, 41)

Of the 1,366 Canadian venture capital investments in 1997, 38 percent were made in Quebec. The amount invested in each deal was lower than in Ontario, where only 30 percent of the total investments were made, but, when measured in dollar terms, it represented 39 percent of the $1.8 billion of capital placed.

In his early study of the Solidarity Fund (FTQ), Jean Marc Suret (1994) criticized the use of a tax credit structure to supply capital to the venture capital market. His work is predicated on the opportunity cost to government that is borne when it crowds out private investors through subsidized investments. Marc Levine (1997) of the University of Wisconsin echoed this criticism. Yet the Canadian case demonstrates that intervening to correct a capital gap has not displaced private investors in the market, particularly in regions of this country that are not money centers and historically have been unable to access capital for small- and medium-sized companies. There are no other sources for the close to $700 million LSIFs invested in 1997. Ted Anderson of Ventures West Management, a private venture capitalist, is also president of the Canadian Venture Capital Association. He said,

> Whether or not we're going to have enough money for the future to continue the pace of investment is an issue. To be honest, the labour-sponsored venture capital program has been a source of capital for the industry. . . . That is really the critical component of capital we have available at the moment. (Heinzl 1998)

The growth of venture capital in Manitoba is particularly striking. The labor-controlled Crocus Fund fills a capital gap in a predominantly rural province with a limited manufacturing base. The growth of investments in this province is 60 percent greater than in the venture capital industry as a whole.

It should be noted, however, that Table 6.3 reflects a relatively new phenomenon, an increase in venture capital investing in foreign markets. In 1997, the rate of increase for such investment was 190 percent. This investment pattern reflects the private component of the venture capital industry in Canada. The trend toward investment of venture capital beyond Canadian borders makes domestic pools of venture capital and the LSIF intermediary vehicles even more critical for filling Canadian capital gaps.

Clearly, all LSIFs, regardless of their board and management structure, fill a role in venture capital investing. As indicated in Table 6.1, six of the twenty-

TABLE 6.3. Venture Capital in Canada

Venture Capital Investment by Sector in Canada (% of dollar amount)

Sector	1997	1996
Traditional	34	31
Biotechnology	11	15
Medical/health	10	10
Computer related	26	20
Other technology	20	24

Venture Capital Investment by Region in Canada

Region	1997 ($ million)	1996 ($ million)	Change (%)
British Columbia	207	103	101
Alberta	61	42	45
Saskatchewan	51	42	21
Manitoba	88	39	126
Ontario	704	467	51
Quebec	546	325	68
Atlantic Canada	22	27	-19
Foreign countries	142	49	190
Total	**1,821**	**1,094**	**66**

one funds have a broader strategic agenda in determining their investments. Two other funds with mixed-board control make limited investments in sports and entertainment sectors. For the most part, funds with mixed-board control and no social or economic agenda tend to seek out large deals for investment, often in the technology sector. By contrast, trade union–controlled funds emphasize investment in small- and medium-sized companies, many of which are in more traditional manufacturing and labor-intensive sectors of the economy. Labor-controlled funds are also more likely to pursue a community and regional focus (see Table 6.1), which contributes to their ability to deliver a greater range of collateral benefits across their jurisdictions. Regional networks are discussed in the section Collateral Benefits Gained from Labor-Controlled LSIFs. The LSIFs controlled by labor with collateral benefits of increased employment, greater productivity, worker education, and labor-management relations perform in sharp contrast to the rent-a-union funds in Canada.

RATE OF RETURN
Central to the argument against ETI is the belief that collateral benefits of investments must come at the expense of shareholder return. For critics of

ETIs, investing is a zero-sum game. Any attention paid to other stake-holders in the enterprise—workers, families, and communities—means the needs of plan participants are being sacrificed. But an examination of projects with comparable market-based returns shows that this argument is false.

When selecting an investment, pension plan trustees seek returns commensurate with the risk they assume. By using social audits, investors screen out attributes that can be associated with bad management; these attributes include poor labor relations, dangerous environmental practices, and disregard for consumers and communities. ETI opponents see these screens as distractions from securing the best possible return for plan beneficiaries. Yet funds with social and economic agendas seek firms that value their stake-holders as well as their shareholders. A company should be a good place to work, and it should create safe and purposeful products. In our view, the contention that all or most social performance improvements require the sacrifice of profitability is simply inaccurate. For example, when irresponsible companies are held accountable for poor practices, the short-term profits associated with unsustainable practices disappear. Evidence from the track record of social investing, which is presented in chap. 3, suggests the opposite: firms with good social practices often outperform firms that lack them. This result seems to hold true when comparing the rates of return within the Canadian LSIF asset class. At the close of 1998, labor-controlled funds, operating with a broad social and economic agenda, had solidly outperformed mixed-board LSIFs, small-cap funds, and the Toronto Stock Exchange total return for that year.

Labor-controlled funds post above-average returns, because a progressive social and economic agenda can add additional value for the firm as well as for investors, workers, governments, and the wider economy. The labor-controlled Crocus Fund was the top-performing LSIF in 1997; in 1998, its return was 10.8 percent, the second highest in its class. Due to the tax credit, the individual investor receives an even higher adjusted return; for the Crocus Fund, this amounted to 19.9 percent in 1998.

The figures in Table 6.4 demonstrate that the principles that distinguish labor-controlled funds from their counterparts also deliver an increase in market share and, on average, higher rates of return to investors during this period. The Alliance group consistently outperformed rent-a-union funds on all counts.

Rather than detracting from the rate of return, social audits provide accurate information on which to base investment decisions. Because Solidarity (FTQ), as a vehicle controlled by the Quebec Federation of Labour, enjoys trust and credibility among working people, it receives honest appraisals from employees. Discrepancies between financial balance sheets and shop floor perceptions quickly surface. This is especially important around issues of inven-

TABLE 6.4. One-, 3-, and 5-Year Returns for Labour-Sponsored Investment Funds (LSIFs) to December 31, 1998

Fund	1-Year Return (%)	3-Year Return (%)	5-Year Return (%)
Quebec Solidarity Fund (FTQ)★	8.10	8.70	8.00
Working Opportunity	0.78	5.82	4.67
Crocus Investment Fund	10.58	9.40	8.36
First Ontario LSIF, Ltd.	5.61	3.84	—
Workers Investment Fund	N/A	—	—
Averages	**6.27**	**6.94**	**7.01**
B.E.S.T. Discoveries	-1.95	—	—
C.I. Covington	0.66	6.20	—
Canadian Medical Discoveries	-9.57	-1.73	—
Canadian Science and Technology Growth	3.97	—	—
Canadian Venture Opportunities	-19.64	-8.44	—
Capital Alliance Ventures	-12.81	-0.45	—
Centerfire Growth Fund, Inc.	-10.44	—	—
DGC Entertainment Ventures	0.78	3.64	—
ENSIS Growth Fund, Incorporated	N/A	—	—
FESA Enterprise Venture	-14.91	-3.92	—
Retrocom Growth	4.11	3.54	—
Sportfund	-29.45	-3.55	—
Triax Growth	-0.89	—	—
Trillium Growth Capital, Inc.	-5.64	-5.83	—
VenGrowth Investment	15.01	11.23	—
Working Ventures	0.87	1.07	2.11
Averages	**-5.33**	**0.16**	**2.11**
LSIF Group Benchmark	**-2.76**	**1.86**	**5.49**
TSE Total Return	**-1.58**	**13.25**	**10.67**

B.E.S.T., Business, Engineering, Science, and Technology; DGC, Directors Guild of Canada; FESA, Federation of Engineering and Scientific Association; N/A = not applicable; TSE, Toronto Stock Exchange.
★ Solidarity (FTQ) returns from its annual report, 1998.
Source: The Globe and Mail Fund Report, February 1999.

tory, equipment, suppliers, and labor-management relations. Solidarity (FTQ) officials doubt that workers would be as forthcoming with investment vehicles not controlled by labor (Laliberte 1999).

WOF of British Columbia has screened and subsequently turned down more than one thousand firms for investment since its inception in 1992. By 1999, it had chosen to invest in forty-one high-performance firms in British Columbia. The presence of a social audit increases rather than decreases the due diligence required for the investment.

TABLE 6.5. Three-Year Beta Ratings of Canadian Labour-Sponsored Investment Funds (LSIFs)*

Fund	3-Year Beta as of February 1999
Crocus Investment Fund	0.03
First Ontario LSIF, Ltd.	0.01
Quebec Solidarity Fund (FTQ)	0.00
Retrocom Growth	-0.01
Working Opportunity	0.13
Canadian Medical Discoveries	0.17
Canadian Venture Opportunities	0.62
DGC Entertainment Ventures	0.13
Working Ventures	0.09
C.I. Covington	-0.06
Capital Alliance Ventures	-0.05
FESA Enterprise Venture	0.21
Sportfund	0.05
Triax Growth	0.39
Trillium Growth Capital, Inc.	0.02
VenGrowth Investment	0.11
Group Average	**0.12**
Toronto Stock Exchange 300 Total Return	**1.00**

DGC, Directors Guild of Canada; FESA, Federation of Engineering and Scientific Association.
*All LSIFs with 3-year history as of February 1999.
Source: The Globe and Mail Fund Report, February 1999.

FUND DIVERSIFICATION

Diversification is a critical component of pension plan investment decisions for ETIs. Again, the Canadian LSIFs illustrate the impact of ETIs on portfolio diversification. As a proportion of total equity holdings, LSIFs invest in private equity placements rather than in the domestic stock markets. The 3-year betas of the LSIF industry measured against the Toronto Stock Exchange 300 total return show that the performance of these ETIs remarkably does not correlate to that of the Canadian domestic public stock exchange (Table 6.5).

Because LSIFs invest in small, privately held companies,[2] they are able to buffer the effects of stock market volatility within the portfolio effectively. In the 1980s, the argument has been made for international investing by pension funds as a means to offset the impact of domestic stock market swings. However, studies indicate that, since 1994, international stock markets have become more closely correlated to U.S. stock market activity due to global financial market integration. As an additional advantage, Canadian LSIFs and perhaps ETIs generally provide substantial diversification to pension plan portfolios.

Collateral Benefits Gained from Labor-Controlled
Labour-Sponsored Investment Funds

LSIFs can advance labor's larger agenda by generating collateral social benefits. LSIFs bring a social and economic mandate to their investment policies, one that fosters a climate for a fundamental and positive expansion of investor goals beyond the mantra of shareholder value. Absent that purpose, LSIFs are no more than investment pools in which trade union leaders play at capitalism.

The general challenge to labor is articulated in articles from two divergent perspectives within the progressive community — one, a sophisticated British Marxist; the other, a liberal Democrat from the United States. Robin Blackburn (1999) and Robert Reich (1999) examine the impact of the growing pool of workers' savings that underlies financial markets. They suggest that the trade union movement should harness pension power. Taking control of these vehicles is not an end in itself but rather a critical first step toward a democratic investment agenda based on the premise that workers generate capital and should also direct its uses.

If labor-controlled LSIF vehicles did not deliver on the promise of collateral benefits, then criticism of the vehicle within the labor movement would be justified. But vehicles such as Solidarity (FTQ) see collateral benefits of job creation, local investment, worker participation, and education as the primary purpose of the fund. Labor-controlled funds work for fundamental changes in investment criteria that, in the long-term, challenge firms to value all their stake-holders, not solely their shareholders. Beyond collateral benefits, LSIFs increase the financial judgment and capacity of workers through worker participation and education. This virtuous cycle adds value to the firm, which in turn creates strong shareholder returns.

SAVING, MAINTAINING, AND CREATING JOBS

Whereas all LSIFs target the venture capital market in Canada, only labor-controlled funds focus on employment maintenance and creation (see Table 6.1). These funds thus target the traditional labor-intensive manufacturing sector in addition to the high-tech and biotech sectors. As a group, industries supported by venture capital tend to have higher employment rates than large companies or the economy as a whole (see Table 6.2).

Making this priority explicit, the 1983 act that established the Solidarity Fund (FTQ) (the Act to Establish the *Fonds De Solidarité des Travailleurs du Quebec*) states, "The main functions of the Fund are: (1) To invest in qualified undertakings and provide them with services in order to create, maintain and protect jobs; . . ." Making employment the primary goal within the legislation keeps this collateral benefit in the forefront of Solidarity's objectives. The same approach was taken in the establishment of the WOF in British Columbia, the Crocus Fund in Manitoba, and the newly established Workers Investment Fund in New Brunswick, all part of the LSIF Alliance.

The legislative framework in Ontario did not make an employment mandate explicit in the act. Each fund incorporated in Ontario has been free to establish its own mission within the framework of investing in small- and medium-sized enterprises, with the majority of investment in privately held companies in Ontario (85 percent). Only First Ontario, the sole Ontario-based LSIF to join the Alliance, has explicitly defined its commitment to employment within the statement of intent.

Because rent-a-union funds do not have an explicit mandate for job creation, they do not track the employment impact of their investments. We can assume that their employment averages would be similar to the venture capital industry figures as a whole (see Table 6.2).

Alliance LSIFs maintain records of their employment impacts on investee firms. Independent studies show that labor-controlled funds have had a dramatic impact on job creation and retention (Perrin, Thorau and Assoc. 1998; SECOR 1996). Crocus Fund management estimates that the cost for each job they create is on average $23,000, far less than the $40,000 average for most venture capital investments. Table 6.6 shows the employment impact of these funds since their inception through 1998. Although all venture capital investing by LSIF vehicles yields the collateral benefit of job creation, union-controlled Alliance LSIFs attempt to create and maintain more jobs with better working conditions and higher wages.

A 1999 study by Jim Stanford, of the Canadian Auto Workers, titled *Labour Sponsored Funds: Examining the Evidence*, was highly critical of LSIFs in gen-

TABLE 6.6. Total Jobs Saved, Retained, and Created by Alliance Labour-Sponsored Investment Funds (LSIFs) to December 1998

Fund	Total Jobs Saved/Retained/Created
Quebec Solidarity Fund (FTQ)*	65,534
Working Opportunity	1,348
Crocus Investment Fund	4,051
First Ontario LSIF, Ltd.	1,230
Workers Investment Fund	N/A
Total	**72,163**

N/A, not applicable.
*SECOR study.
Source: LSIF annual reports, 1998.

eral and the employment creation aspects of these funds in particular. Stanford's examination concluded that LSIFs were only responsible for fifteen thousand to twenty-five thousand jobs created through direct investment of the funds. However, both Quebec's Solidarity Fund (FTQ) and British Columbia's WOF have challenged this finding by using third-party independent assessments to verify the impact of LSIFs on job creation.

Stanford's critique misinterprets the percentages of each fund directly invested in small- and medium-sized enterprises. He also charges that LSIFs place large amounts of their assets in bonds as opposed to venture capital investing. He claims that government-subsidized dollars intended for venture capital investing instead sit idly in safe government Treasury bills. Stanford argues that this practice weakens the LSIFs' ability to impact employment significantly.

LSIFs offer three reasons to justify their bond holdings. First, a portion of the bond portfolio acts as a temporary parking place for newly accepted contributions before appropriate venture investments can be made. Although LSIFs do hold larger bond portfolios in the early years after their inception, we find that, as LSIFs mature, there is a rapid decline in assets held in the bond portion of their portfolios. Second, bond holding balances the high risk of venture capital pools within the portfolio. Finally, short-term bonds are required to have sufficient assets to meet annual redemption requirements from LSIF fund holders without requiring liquidation of venture capital holdings. Roughly 15 percent of each LSIF pool is redeemed annually by investors. For these three reasons, LSIFs allocate approximately 30 –40 percent of assets to bonds.

UNION PARTICIPATION

The 1997 survey of LSIFs (see Table 6.1) raised the question of union participation as the primary investor within the fund. Only union-controlled funds identified the participation of union members and average workers as a primary objective.[3]

By establishing sales structures and marketing initiatives aimed at working people, union-controlled funds broaden participation in investment across a larger segment of the economy. Through the active participation of workers, LSIFs become a tool for broader popular intervention in economic life rather than simply a pool of capital governed by conventional understandings.

Alliance Funds have documented the characteristics of their subscribers extensively: to date, there are more than four hundred thousand subscribers to Alliance LSIFs in Canada. More than 60 percent of those subscribers are union members (Solidarity Fund 1998). A significant portion of Alliance LSIF investors has annual incomes that fall below $60,000 Cdn. (Perrin, Thorau and Assoc. 1998). For many individuals, their Alliance LSIF investment marks their first contribution to a retirement savings plan of any kind.

Workplace participation in LSIFs is another point of tension in the labor movement between those who support the LSIF capital strategy and those who believe it undermines worker solidarity. Critics fear that promoting among workers the use of an RRSP program, which is a system of individualized retirement savings accounts, allows employers to escape the responsibility of providing appropriate workplace pension plans. Furthermore, they dispute the extent of worker participation in LSIFs, as statistically the RRSP program is primarily used by the highest-income earners in Canada, who use the tax deduction to reduce their annual taxes.

This criticism has validity for the so-called rent-a-union funds. As one professional money manager put it, "When I saw what the labour-sponsored vehicle offered with the tax breaks, I thought, 'Geez, if I can structure it in a way that I could get my investors those tax breaks, then why not?' It would be sort of negligent not to as a corporate finance person . . . To qualify, I needed a union" (Freeman 1995).[4]

Rent-a-union funds make no effort to encourage worker participation in their objectives, nor are there any collateral benefits associated with their investments beyond filling venture capital gaps. It is fair to characterize these funds as taking full advantage of tax credits for wealthy individual investors, many of whom philosophically oppose the values of the labor movement and even work to undermine labor's place in civil society. Although critics of LSIFs paint all funds with the same brush, it is crucial to distinguish, as we have done, those that genuinely advance a social agenda from those run by money managers who exploit LSIFs for their own purposes.

Only the funds controlled by trade union bodies actively seek to increase labor participation by recruiting workers as their primary subscribers. First Ontario, for example, raises 60 percent of its new capital through union activists who sell shares to other union members in their workplaces and communities. A further 30 percent is raised through local credit unions in Ontario. Crocus Fund similarly uses a combination of workplace and broker sales. New Brunswick's small Workers Investment Fund, created through a minimal $1 million investment by the Atlantic Canada Opportunities Agency, was unable to increase its asset base until 1998, when it began to offer its fund through a workplace campaign with automatic payroll deductions. The fund has now doubled its assets.

The Solidarity Fund (FTQ) uses only unionized workers as sales agents who sell shares to their coworkers in their own workplaces. This mechanism establishes a level of comfort and trust among working people. As a condition of investment,

TABLE 6.7. Total Alliance and Non-Alliance Fund Assets, 1998

Fund Category	Number of Funds	Total Assets (year-end 1998; $ billion)
Alliance Funds	5.0	2.9
Non-Alliance Funds	16.0	1.6

Solidarity (FTQ) requires investee firms and their employees to buy shares in the fund. This usually takes the form of a savings plan set up by the company for each employee, similar to a 401(k), to which the employer and employee contribute.

This unique distribution system insulated Alliance funds from the drop in sales that occurred in Canada when the tax credit to LSIFs was reduced from 40 to 30 percent in 1996.[5] Workplace sales to unionized and average-income Canadians continued steadily through this period. By comparison, overall sales for the 15 Ontario-based rent-a-union funds fell to $129 million in 1997, compared to sales of $655 million in 1995 before the tax credit change. For funds with a limited social and economic mandate, a reduction in the tax credit caused a dramatic reduction in revenue. By contrast, the Ontario-based Alliance member, First Ontario, had consistent sales each year since its 1995 inception, and Solidarity (FTQ) had its second best sales record in fiscal 1997–1998, raising $361.5 million.

A combination of poor returns and a drop in sales has meant a loss of market for rent-a-union LSIFs since 1997. By December 31, 1998, Alliance funds held the majority of LSIF assets, capturing 64.3 percent of the market in Canada. In other words, Canadians chose to invest $3 billion in financial vehicles controlled by trade union bodies, with the stated purpose of job retention and creation (Table 6.7).

Alliance funds increased their market share during this 2-year period, up from 61.2 percent in March of 1997. This increase represents growth of 13 percent over 2 years. By contrast, the rent-a-union funds lost 3.1-percent market share, declining from total assets of $1.65 billion in March 1997 to $1.63 billion in December 1998.

The social and economic agenda and workplace-based distribution channel put Alliance Funds in the enviable position of gaining market share through their unique characteristics. One of their collateral benefits is to bring new capital investors to the market motivated by progressive values, thus raising savings rates.

CREATING REGIONAL NETWORKS FOR INVESTMENT

Most LSIFs have sectoral expertise and tend to make large investments in firms in the urban clusters of each province. However, only labor-controlled funds deliberately create regional networks for fund investment as part of their mandate (see Table 6.1). Not surprisingly, the largest and most developed of these networks has been established by Solidarity (FTQ) in Quebec.

In the early days of Solidarity's start-up, officials began to realize that many good investments in small firms were overlooked, because these firms were located in regions outside Montreal. Solidarity's fund managers were often unaware of investment opportunities in small communities. At other times, the firms themselves did not approach Solidarity (FTQ), because it was seen as something removed from their community that required travel to Montreal and was focused on opportunities in and around that urban core (Daoust 1998). Solidarity (FTQ), with its commitment to the province as a whole, overcame this barrier by developing a regional network in partnership with the Quebec government. This network now operates seventeen regional funds, each with offices and managers assigned to a local area. Proximity to investment increases the knowledge necessary to select investments and, subsequently, to monitor them effectively. Proximity also builds an atmosphere of trust with local managers and workers. The regional network also aids in the financial education of workers and adds expertise to management.

Each regional Solidarity Fund (FTQ) was initially capitalized at $6 million from Solidarity (FTQ). In 1998, a new partner, the National Bank, joined the network and injected a further $600,000 in capital per selected region. The types of investments undertaken by the regional funds are for projects that require between $50,000 and $500,000 of investment. As of August 31, 1998, the regional funds had directly invested $41.7 million in 155 enterprises across Quebec. Investment in these firms helped maintain and create 3,802 jobs. Despite the small scale of these investments, Solidarity's rate of return at the close of 1998 made it the third best performance in the LSIF class, with an annual return of 8.1 percent.

Commitment to local development does not stop with *les fonds regionaux de solidarité*. Since 1997, the fund has joined in partnership with the Quebec Union of Regional County Municipalities and Local Municipalities to develop a network of local funds geared toward enterprises in the pre-start-up and start-up phases of development. These local funds, or *SOLIDEs*, invest between $5,000 and $50,000 in small enterprises, distributed primarily as loans. There are eighty-six SOLIDEs across Quebec, and to date they have invested in 490 enterprises. Investments of more than $500,000 are handled by Solidarity (FTQ) through its specialty funds, which include sectors such as bioengineering, aerospace, and information technology.

WOF in British Columbia also assists in the development of small, local investment funds (Levi 1998). Working with the Community Futures Development Corporation of Strathcona, a nonprofit corporation, they assist entrepreneurs in rural areas through counseling, training, and small business financing. WOF has been the source of a $1 million line of credit for Community Futures, a regional network that makes small, community-level loans. Between 1995 and 1998, in partnership with WOF, Community Futures made twenty-six loans that totaled $1,125,000. The firms range from forest product manufacturers to water and air transport. Direct employment from these loans has resulted in 150 jobs (sixty-five jobs created; eighty-five jobs maintained) (Perrin, Thorau and Assoc. 1998).

The Crocus Fund invests widely across Manitoba, a province that historically has been far removed from the money centers in Canada (Kreiner 1999). No venture capital investment vehicles existed in Manitoba before the creation of Crocus. In 1997, venture capital investment in this province reached $88 million, growing from $39 million in 1996, a growth rate of 126 percent (see Table 6.4). First Ontario and Workers Investment Fund, the two other Alliance fund members, are also actively developing regional networks. Of the sixteen other Canadian LSIFs, only one fund, Working Ventures, is committed to a broad-base regional strategy for fund development.

SOCIAL AUDITS

Many argue that social audits cloud the judgment of fund managers by introducing irrelevant considerations. This belief is false. The rates of return of the Alliance funds versus non-Alliance LSIFs demonstrate that the use of social screens delivers positive economic benefit. The social audit performed by Alliance funds includes health and safety standards within the firm, as well as environmental and employment practices.

Although Alliance funds are labor-controlled, they do not insist that investee firms be unionized. However, positive labor-management relations mean the firm must be open to unionization if the employees so wish. As Fernand Daoust (1998) of Solidarity (FTQ) commented, "When these firms seek funding from Solidarity they are well aware that we are a fund controlled by the Quebec Federation of Labour. They understand that in accepting investment from us they are opening themselves up for labor's involvement which includes unionization if that is the wish of their employees."

Critics of LSIFs within labor claim that investing workers' savings in nonunion firms is politically unacceptable. Yet, given that many sectors targeted for venture capital investments have very low unionization rates, the greater challenge is, as always, the organizing drives of today's trade unions. Accepting investment from trade union–controlled capital pools often exposes these firms and their workers to the values and benefits of unionization, as well as to the wider social role played by labor and the wealth it generates.

Applying social audit screens helps Alliance LSIFs to avoid investment in firms that are prone to loss of value from future environmental disasters and poor workplace relations. Through the social audit, Alliance LSIF staff members communicate with workers and management about the state of the company and its practices. This communication enables the funds to identify discrepancies between the actual operation of the company and its reported balance sheets before, rather than after, investment has occurred (Daoust 1998).

EDUCATION OF WORKERS

The 1983 act that created Solidarity (FTQ) identifies the education of workers as the second function of the fund, which is "to promote the training of workers in economic matters and enable them to increase their influence on Quebec's economic development."

Solidarity (FTQ) takes seriously its responsibility to train workers. Initially, the fund managers trained workers to build its sales force. Rank-and-file volunteers from unionized workplaces handle sales of the fund across Quebec. By 1989, Solidarity (FTQ) reached the size at which it could begin to offer more formal training to workers in their investee firms, part of the overall philosophy of *transparence* that builds trust between management and labor (Blondin 1998). "Involvement and cooperation presupposes trust, but trust comes with knowledge," said one Solidarity (FTQ) fund officer (Laliberte 1999).

Solidarity (FTQ) also provides workers with financial literacy to enable them to meet increased responsibility for their own retirement savings. Although four other funds within the Alliance have modeled worker education and training aspects on Solidarity (FTQ), they have not yet developed the sophisticated training modules comparable to those in Quebec.

As part of the agreement for investment in a firm, Solidarity (FTQ) requires the company to open its books to its own employees. This *open-book* process becomes part of a 2-day workshop on financial education, which is carried out by the Solidarity (FTQ) staff for the workers in the firm. On the first day, employees are taught how to read a balance sheet and use it to calculate profitability ratios for a firm. The second day is spent examining their company's balance sheet. This process builds an understanding of the macro- and microeconomic environment in which the firm operates. To date, more than sixteen thousand workers in investee firms in Quebec have participated in these 2-day training sessions.

Solidarity's worker training has yielded measurable impacts. In a 1999 study, Pierre Laliberte at the University of Massachusetts found that all the investee companies surveyed reported varying degrees of improvements in communication and trust between labor and management. The survey of management in investee firms found such concrete results as

- A greater flow of cost-saving ideas from workers;
- Easier implementation of quality programs, most notably International Standards Organization (ISO) 9,000 certifications;
- More management attention to health and safety, as well as to worker training;
- The implementation of self-directed work teams.

Surveyed workers who had participated in the training program reported

- Substantial or very substantial impact on their understanding of the company (94 percent);
- Substantial or very substantial impact on their own motivation (73 percent);
- Substantial or very substantial impact on their level of confidence in management (65 percent).

In a 1995 study, Ted Jackson and Francois LaMontagne also found increased labor-management cooperation and increased trust between labor and management as a result of the open-book policy and worker training modules. In the time between the two studies, there has been an increase in positive management responses to the impact of the education component of Solidarity (FTQ). Solidarity (FTQ) also undertakes board-of-director training and education sessions with its regional funds, local SOLIDEs, and investee firms. It continues to train and educate its volunteer sales force on an annual basis.

Although Alliance LSIFs do not intervene directly in collective bargaining or dispute settlement mechanisms in their investee firms, worker-training vehicles and the open-book process established by Solidarity (FTQ) improve labor-management relations. Some firms established or enhanced joint labor-management committees once the fund became involved. In some cases, Solidarity (FTQ) participates in these forums when requested by labor and management.

FACILITATING COOPERATION BETWEEN LABOR AND BUSINESS

Seeking investee firms that have constructive and cooperative labor-management relationships creates rather than erodes shareholder value. This fact also helps Alliance LSIFs to outperform their peers within their asset class; indeed, screened funds are outperforming traditional stock market indices over time. During the 1998 General Motors strike in the United States, market analysts at such Wall Street firms as Solomon Brothers found that, since 1985, General Motors lost share value against Ford and Chrysler due to deteriorating labor relations. The realization that valuing stake-holders increases shareholder return is behind the creation of many new U.S. investment funds that use broader sustainability screens—both labor and environmental—as part of their criteria for investment. Alliance LSIFs under the control of trade unions have always sought investment in firms that value their stake-holders, workers chief among them.

Alliance funds also pursue positive collateral benefits through worker participation within the firm. As discussed, Solidarity (FTQ) promotes a sense of ownership in the firm by requiring the company to establish a savings plan for each employee, who in turn purchases shares in Solidarity (FTQ). This mechanism is designed to create a sense of connection between fund investment in the firm and employee investment in the fund and reflects a larger sense of community in Quebec, a uniquely French-speaking society within North America. However, one study casts doubt on the mechanism's ability to align worker and management interests. In his 1997 survey of workers, Laliberte found that only 57 percent felt strongly that holding Solidarity Fund (FTQ) shares had substantial or very substantial impact on their motivation or commitment, or both.

In contrast, the Crocus Fund in Manitoba actively engages in creating structures within investee firms analogous to ESOPs in the United States. One study performed by the U.S. General Accounting Office found that worker ownership raised productivity by as much as 52 percent within surveyed firms. But Crocus doesn't confine its mandate to ESOP firms only. All of its investments include a component that allows for direct employee ownership in companies, regardless of whether they are ESOPs. Crocus Fund looks for a combination of employee ownership and participative management in investee firms that enhances company productivity. At this writing, the firms in which the Crocus Fund invests have an employee ownership rate of 24 percent. Crocus Fund has been the top-performing Canadian fund in 1997 and the second-best performer in 1998. Its returns can be attributed in part to the productivity gains from these efforts.

WOF takes a slightly different approach to improving labor-management relations. Like more traditional venture capital angel investors, WOF adds value by increasing the management expertise of its firms. Fund officers take positions on the boards of investee companies, normally bringing deep knowledge of particular industrial sectors (Levi 1998). In addition, both WOF and Crocus Fund have established roundtable forums for the senior management of their investee firms to develop their skills further and to share best practice ideas. Solidarity (FTQ) also brings board and management expertise to its investee firms and to its regional and local fund structure. In 1998, it has created a new training program in partnership with a large Quebec philanthropic foundation to assist family-run enterprises in Quebec.

Part of the risk-adjusted returns of Alliance funds results from this virtuous cycle of investing, which encourages cooperation between business and labor to generate productivity gains that in turn increase profits and returns to shareholders.

COST-BENEFIT IMPACT OF LABOUR-SPONSORED INVESTMENT FUNDS

Labor-sponsored funds in Canada use individual investors' contributions to create pools of capital for investment in small- and medium-sized companies. As early as 1983, the federal and provincial governments in Canada recognized the need for more venture capital pools. To encourage individual investment, they offer a tax credit to investors. The tax credit amounts to 30 percent of the investment to a maximum of $1,500 on a $5,000 investment in the funds, with 15 percent coming from each level of government. In addition, the investment can be made within the individual's tax deductible Registered Retirement Savings Plan (RRSP). Governments do not offer the tax credit without the expectation of recouping the cost through the expansion that takes place in the economy. Several detailed studies by independent econometric firms have documented the length of time it takes for both levels of government to recover their costs. Two recent cost-benefit analyses performed on Alliance funds in Canada use conservative modeling to calculate the costs and returns of the LSIF credit. The studies assume that there are direct and indirect benefits from the increase of employment in any single SME. They apportion only the impacts that are equivalent to the level of LSIF investment in the firm.

Although only a corresponding percentage of the investment is attributed to the labor-sponsored fund, LSIF effects are often greater than strict proportionality would suggest. LSIFs often invest first in these projects and then use their position to attract other non-LSIF venture capital investments. A study of WOF estimates that every dollar of WOF investment secures an additional $3.72 from other bodies (Perrin, Thorau and Assoc. 1998).

In a 1996 study of Solidarity (FTQ), the econometric firm SECOR Inc. found that the tax credit was repaid to both levels of government in a period between 1.2 to 2.1 years. Similarly, cost-benefit analysis performed by Regional Data Corporation (RDC) and Perrin, Thorau & Associates of the WOF in British Columbia concluded that total investments from 1992, the year of the fund's inception, by both levels of government were repaid by 1998. From that point, all costs to the British Columbian and federal governments are fully recovered within each year.

Conclusion

An examination of the Canadian experience of LSIFs provides evidence of the positive impact of labor-controlled pools of capital on the economy.

In four of the five provinces that have established funds under provincial legislation, a sole trade union body was named as the sponsor of the fund. In each of these cases, the named body was the provincial federation of labor, the affiliated labor body representing the major part of the trade union movement in that province. In addition to naming the key labor body to act as the fund sponsor, the collateral benefits to be derived from fund investment were incorporated into the legislative framework. These social and economic goals are listed as the primary functions of the fund, with the creation and maintenance of jobs as their primary objective.

In the fifth province, Ontario, the legislation did not name the labor body that was to act as the fund sponsor, nor did it indicate a broad range of social and economic objectives for the funds beyond filling the venture capital gap within the province. As a result, by 1999 fifteen of the twenty-one LSIFs in Canada were incorporated under Ontario legislation. Sponsorship ranges from small professional sports associations to large trade unions. Many of these sponsors are paid a fee by professional money managers who initiate and control the LSIF and its investment decisions. Only the First Ontario Fund in Ontario modeled itself after Solidarity (FTQ), with a corresponding set of broad collateral objectives that include saving, maintaining, and creating jobs in the province. When the objectives were not part of the legislative framework, most other funds did not voluntarily take up this agenda.

The result of the proliferation of funds in Ontario has been the development of two types of funds within this asset class. The five funds that aligned structures with Solidarity (FTQ) are all signatories to a statement of defining principles for labor-sponsored funds. This group has become known as the *LSIF Alliance*. The second group of LSIFs is not signatories to the statement of principles. Only one fund in this group has majority control of the board by labor; the remaining fifteen funds have a mixed board of directors with union or employee associations in the minority and professional money managers in control. Some members of this group receive a fee for their sponsorship, giving rise to their rent-a-union label.

With a 3-year history of these two distinct categories of funds within the LSIF asset class, we can now compare their performance and collateral gains. Critics of ETIs have long maintained that any investing that seeks both risk-adjusted rates of return and a collateral benefit beyond the shareholder does so at the expense of the investors. In 1995, the U.S. Congress Joint Economic Committee presented a report entitled "The Economics of ETIs: Sacrificing Returns for Political Goals." They claimed that, on average, ETIs earn 2 percentage points less than traditional investments. Yet a comparison of Canadian LSIFs points to different conclusions. The performance of Alliance LSIFs demonstrates that funds that deliver collateral benefits often have greater returns, on average, than funds within the same asset class that do not have a corresponding social and community agenda. Furthermore, funds that have labor-controlled boards of directors and labor-directed investment decision making are more likely to generate collateral benefits through their investments.

The social and economic goals of Alliance funds include saving and creating employment, education and training of workers, developing regional investment networks, using a social audit that improves labor relations and encourages environmentally sustainable management practices, inviting the broad participation of working people, and facilitating cooperation between business and labor.

Working with both management and labor within a normative social and economic agenda enables trade union–controlled LSIFs to create additional collateral benefits from their investments. These benefits in turn contribute to increased firm efficiency and productivity. Productivity and efficiency are captured back in profits, which improve the firm's bottom line. That result often gives a greater return to shareholders. This fact is demonstrated when comparing LSIFs in Canada.

Creating collateral benefits generates tangible returns within a virtuous cycle of investment. Defining the goals of the fund and naming a legitimate labor body as its sponsor within the legislative framework has delivered these benefits and generated positive risk-adjusted rates of return.

The significance of Canadian LSIFs, however, extends far beyond their success as worker-friendly venture capital instruments. They offer one more example of the remarkable new creativity emerging from the workers' movement, as labor comes to grip with the rapidly changing forms of contemporary capitalism. We see this creativity surfacing in bold new organizing initiatives across Canada and the United States. We see resurgent political energies in conventional electoral arenas and in coalition-building efforts with new social movements and with young and working people around the globe.

Labor's social impact and transformative potential lies ultimately in its membership and in the militant commitment and intelligence of its activists. But working people have generated, and continue to generate, huge pools of wealth, which casino capitalists use to hold them back. A central part of labor's arsenal must be the willingness to experiment with every good idea that allows workers and their organizations to harness and direct the capital they produce toward useful social purposes.

[VII]

SMALL BENEFITS, BIG PENSION FUNDS, AND HOW GOVERNANCE REFORMS CAN CLOSE THE GAP

Teresa Ghilarducci

Pensions are really about one thing: permitting workers to buy leisure at the end of their working lives. A bad pension system forces older people to keep working when they do not want to. A good pension system secures workers' entitlement to voluntary, comfortable retirements.[1] Although pension funds play vital roles in financial markets and long-term employment contracts, they should ultimately be judged according to whether they deliver secure retirements.

Recent developments of structure, control, and coverage in the U.S. employer-provided pension system are eroding the security that pensions ought to provide. Consider just one aspect of this disturbing trend. Although pension funds have grown by more than 400 percent in 25 years, real benefits have fallen, pension coverage across the population has not budged, and the percentage of middle-class retirement income from pensions has shrunk.

Contrary to popular belief, replacing defined benefit (DB) plans with defined contribution (DC) plans is not the primary threat to workers' retirements. Rather, this chapter shows that changes in the structure of pension governance pose much greater danger. I reach this conclusion by examining several time series composed of data readily available from the Federal Reserve, U.S. Department of Labor (DOL), and the Employee Benefit Research Institute (the latter two draw heavily from the Current Population Reports) and from data on private pension plans compiled at the University of Notre Dame. This time series is drawn from the Internal Revenue Service (IRS) Form 5500 that private sector pension plan sponsors submit annually to the IRS.

These sources of data suggest that there are five major leaks in our current pension fund system: limited pension coverage, losses due to conflicts of interest, administrative costs, inflation, and investment effects. Each has a direct effect on workers' retirement benefits. Based upon a comparison of pension fund governance, I suggest that enhancing worker representation would help stop these leaks.

The following section shows that these leaks threaten the retirement security of those who depend on voluntary employer-based, non–Social Security pensions. I turn next to agency problems. Current pension governance arrangements generate conflicts of interests between pensioners and their representatives and thus threaten pension security. Lastly, I show that, whereas good pension management requires collective worker representation, schemes in which individuals directed their own retirement investments, as in DC plans, erode pension security because they are vulnerable to well-known factors, such as myopia. Mediating organizations, such as labor unions, that stand between workers and final investment choices offer an alternative to improve pension fund governance, as long as they avoid the conflicts of interest that pervade many current arrangements.

Why Are Funds So Large and Benefits So Small?

The ironic and disturbing fact is that, despite vast growth in pension funds and their enormous absolute size, almost equal to U.S. Gross Domestic Product, employer-provided pensions continue to cover only 50 percent of the workforce. Between 1980 and 1998, the value of private pension funds, in real terms, has grown 413 percent, whereas the average real pension benefit has declined by one-third. Coverage has stagnated, and the importance of pension income as a source of retirement income has fallen by 2 percentage points (Table 7.1).

Why has the unprecedented boom in U.S. financial markets in the 1990s done so little for pensioners? Why haven't the gains made by Wall Street flown to Main Street's retiree clubs and pensioners' households? The answer is not that pensions have failed to keep up with financial markets. To the contrary, in absolute terms, pension funds rival gains made by the Standard & Poor's 500 Index. Yet Table 7.1 shows clearly that pension fund generosity has not

TABLE 7.1. Pension Funds Are Large but Benefits Small

Growth in Pension Funds, Coverage, Benefits from Various Years 1979–1998	
Funds	Percentage Growth (%)
Average growth in total U.S. private pension funds (FOF) (adjusted for inflation), 1980–1998[1]	413.0
Cumulative growth in the Standard & Poor's 500, 1980–1999[2] benefits	618.0
Percentage change in average benefit, 1980–1995[3]	−33.0
Change in percent of workforce covered by private pensions, 1979–1993[4]	0.0
Change in percent of income coming from retirement (SSA) (for middle class retirees), 1980–1990[5]	−0.018

FOF, flow of funds; SSA, Social Security Administration.
[1]Federal Reserve, Flow of Funds, various years and tables.
[2]Historical Standard & Poor's 500 record.
[3]Current Population Survey cited in U.S. Department of Labor 1992.24; Employee Benefit Research Institute, 1997:68.
[4]Current Population Survey, various years.
[5]Middle income retirees in 1993 had incomes between $17,208 and $28,714. (U.S. Department of Labor, Pension and Welfare Benefits Administration; Reno, 1993.)

increased. In addition, median pension growth lags behind average growth. Average pension growth is rising, because the pensions of higher-income elderly are growing faster. Yet even that amount is small, particularly after Social Security increases have been indexed to inflation.

The explanation for the disparity between large funds and small benefits lies instead in the way in which pension investment and benefit decisions are made. Corporate pension sponsors who manage 90 percent of DB money are torn between using investment gains to improve pension generosity and financing other vital and pressing corporate needs. These kinds of interest conflicts are often called *agency problems* because there are strong incentives for agents—in this case, those who manage pensions—to act in ways that may harm those whom they represent, the pension beneficiaries

This study shows that the institution of collective bargaining reduces agency problems by allowing worker organizations to monitor these agents and check their conflicts of interest. Two consequences of collective bargaining over pensions are that employers raise their pension contributions and that fund management improves. On the former, worker representation presses employers to allocate more payroll to pensions. Stagnation in pension coverage, the first leak discussed later, partially explains why benefits have not grown as quickly as pension funds. Unionization helps to expand pensions to workers who would otherwise be unlikely to have coverage, such as garment workers, mobile construction and service workers, retail clerks, and others. Worker representatives, namely unions, use their position to ensure that pension fund growth translates into pension improvements and ultimately greater retirement income security. The eye must be on that prize.

Plugging the Leaks—Securing the Pension Promise

Leakage in the pension process reduces pension fund coverage and growth. Five leaks in particular seriously weaken U.S. private pension funds (Figure 7.1). Closing these leaks would expand coverage of pensions among workers even as it increases the value of the benefits paid out. To understand the flow of monies through the pension system, its sources and uses should be considered.

Unlike standard trust arrangements with single incomes, pension funds have two sources: the "real" economy and the "finance" economy. These are depicted at the top and bottom of Figure 7.1. The first major leak is coverage. The proportion of the workforce covered by private pensions has remained between 45 percent and 55 percent since the 1970s. This is an essential drawback to the voluntary, employer-based pension system. As Table 7.2 shows, fewer than half of all workers (47.1 percent) participate in pensions (1993 is the most recent data available from a special survey in the Current Population Reports). Coverage rates are higher than average for middle-aged workers (61.5 percent) and those in large firms (67.3 percent). Unionized and high-income workers have the highest rate of coverage, 78.7 percent and 79.6 percent, respectively. Of the four largest industries in terms of employment, workers in state and local government have the highest coverage rate, 74.4 percent. Black workers, at a 45.3-percent coverage rate, are not far behind white workers, at 47.7 percent.

If employers do not establish institutions that defer current wages for future consumption, voluntary pension contributions will remain small and often inadequate. Workers who lack workplace private pension coverage save at lower rates compared to those who are part of a mandatory contribution scheme. This pervasive absence of coverage reduces income into pension funds and so constitutes a leakage from the first source of income, the real economy.

The second leak occurs when pension fund trustees have multiple and conflicting interests and so fail to represent workers. Such leaks result from agency problems between plan beneficiaries, plan trustees, and money managers. For

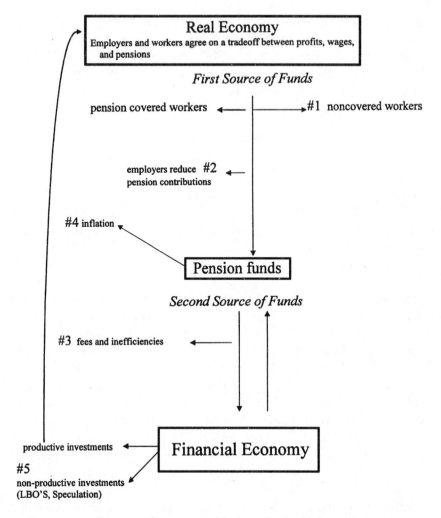

FIGURE 7.1. Sources of income and leakage in the U.S. pension system (leakage denoted by #s 1–5). (LBO, leveraged buyout.)

instance, trustees might use plan surpluses to reduce employer contributions rather than to increase benefits. Another variety of this leak occurs when pension trustees fail to increase pension benefits to offset inflation.

Inefficiencies in money and plan management create the third leak. High annual administrative fees decrease the amount of income flowing to pension funds from investment earnings, the second source of fund income. A further

TABLE 7.2. Who Is Covered by Pensions?
Percent of Workforce Participating in a Pension Plan by Group, 1993

Group of Workers	Percentage of Workers
All	47.1
Full-time	58.5
Middle-aged (41–50)	61.5
Older (51–60)	59.3
Small firms (10–24 employees)	21.1
Large firms (more than 1,000 employees)	67.3
Women	44.0
Men	50.0
Low-income ($5–$10,000)	12.9
High-income (more than $50,000)	79.6
Union workers	78.7
Nonunion	40.5
Largest industries: state and local	74.4
Manufacturing—durable	63.5
Retail trade	24.1
Professional services	42.5
Black	45.3
White	47.7

Source: Employee Benefit Research Institute, Table 10.5:87, 1994.

leak results when professional institutional investors pay too much attention to short-term gains rather than to long-term commitments.

Inflation is the fourth leak. Researchers have found that employers generally will not pay cost-of-living adjustments to retirees when pensions are not well funded (Allen, Clark, and McDermed 1992).

The fifth leak is the *Cheshire cat* problem of pension investments that earn high returns but create no jobs. All that will remain is the "toothy grin" of high rates of return, with no workers left to be covered by pensions. Attention to value-adding investments, rather than speculative and value-extracting investments (Lazonick and O'Sullivan 1996), can increase the employment base and, by extension, expand the base of contributors to the pension system.

Incorporating this principle into the regular operations of investing has been difficult. Employee representation may help money managers to distinguish between comparable investments that create jobs and those that do not. As Jayne Elizabeth Zanglein notes in chap. 8, the 1994 DOL Interpretative Bulletin moves toward a practical way to increase the first source of income into pension plans by arresting this leak.

Agency Problems

Contrary to popular impressions, money managers' selfishness is not the most significant agency problem of pensions.[2] More often, pension sponsors are divided between their roles as agent for firms and agent for workers. The most intense conflicts of interests thus occur when employer sponsors are the sole trustees of their workers' plans.

According to the Employee Retirement Income Security Act's (ERISA's) *duty of loyalty* rule, pension funds are held in trust for the sole benefit of the participants: workers and retirees. Firms qualify for tax exemptions of contributions and earnings by adhering to this fiduciary principle. However, most firms introduce agency problems by integrating their pension decisions with pension funding (Friedman 1983; Francis and Reiter 1987; Mittelstaedt 1989; Ghilarducci 1992; Petersen 1992; Tackett and Drew 1989).

From one view, firms guarantee a certain DB and cannot legally reduce the value of this promised pension. Because such firms assume the full risk of fund loss, integrating pension management with corporate management does not violate the spirit of fiduciary duty. Employers enjoy broad discretion when they act alone; they can either treat the pension trust independently from the corporation (as required strictly by law) or integrate corporate financial goals with pension management.

In other pension funds, however, workers' representatives monitor and help to manage investments and benefits. These watchful eyes can make employers more prone to manage plans in ways aligned with trust law and ERISA's intent that the plan be administered in the sole interest of the participants. Outside the United States, many governments have readily used worker representation to curb these agency problems. In most European nations and Australia, for example, medium- to large-size firms are required to have pension plans for their employees. These plans must have workers represented on the boards.

Who Controls the Pension Fund Universe?— Exposure to Agency Problems

The pension fund universe is divided between funds that have direct, indirect, collective, and individual employee representation. In the United States, more than $6 trillion in pension assets are directly controlled by trustees who must adhere to the 1974 ERISA investment standards of prudence and loyalty to the participants. The bulk of the remaining funds in public sector plans are often managed according to ERISA-type regulations. The dominant policy that guides pension investments under this regime is the *prudent expert rule*, which has been interpreted to require that assets be diversified, experts be carefully chosen and monitored, and investment behavior deviate not too far from the norm.

Only the private, so-called labor-management or jointly trusteed plans established under the Taft-Hartley Act require equal representation of workers and employers on the boards of trustees that invest monies and set benefits. In the United States, these types of structured funds comprise less than 8 percent of assets. They differ from corporate plans in that *excess funds*, which are earnings in excess of expectations, cannot be diverted back to the employers in the form of reduced contributions. However, because there is no safety net from a corporate treasury, boards must freeze benefits when funds perform below expectations.

In the much-larger universe of single-employer, DB plans, which represent more than $1.8 trillion (92 percent) of private DB plans, there is no direct and collective employee representation. The IRS's Form 5500 distinguishes pension funds among single- or multi-employer plans and collectively bargained and noncollectively bargained plans. The most recent Form 5500 data is for 1996, whereas the Federal Reserve flow of funds data reports pension assets in broader categories for 1999. Total pension fund assets, including DC, DB, public, and private, doubled in 5 years to more than $10 trillion at the end of 1999. Private sector assets total $6.5 trillion, the DC plan for Federal workers is valued at $94 billion, and the remaining assets are in state and local pension plans. Surprisingly, DB plan assets grew faster than DC plans, primarily because they typically have higher equity allocations. Employer contributions accounted for only 26 percent of the rise in assets (Anand 2000). In this universe, unions exercise indirect voice in investments and only have a direct say in benefit levels in collectively bargained plans. If funds perform better than expected, unions can evaluate the affordability of better benefits and bargain for them. If a fund performs worse than expected, savvy and well-financed unions can evaluate employers' claims that they cannot afford benefit increases or that workers must forego more wages to bolster contributions.

However, approximately 50 percent of the corporate DB assets—72 percent of the actual plans—is sponsored voluntarily by corporations with no union or employee representatives to monitor investments and benefit distributions. In these cases, the government balances the sometimes competing interests of companies, participants, and the Pension Benefit Guaranty Corporation (*PBGC*), which provides government insurance that guarantees benefits in cases of bankruptcy. All the while, the government must try to encourage corporations to maintain their voluntary plans. To encourage firms

TABLE 7.3. Estimated Distribution of Control

Pension Funds under Direct Influence or Collective Action by Employees ($ billions)

Type of Plan	Direct Collective Employee Representation	Indirect Collective Employee Representation	No Representation or Individual-Directed
Taft-Hartley (labor-management)	247[1]	—	—
Collectively bargained corporate (DB)	—	Est. 1,047[2]	—
Corporate without a union (DB)	—	—	Est. 1,089[2]
Public sector	—	2,094[3]	—
Defined-contribution	—	—	1,792[3]
Total: $6,269	**$247**	**$3,141**	**$2,881**
Share of control	**.04%**	**.50%**	**.46%**

Est., established.

[1]Department of Labor.

[2]The Form 5500 shows that 49 percent of defined-benefit (DB) corporate plan assets are collectively bargained, and that this proportion has been rising. The total in the table is derived from applying 49 percent to the 1997–1996 plan asset figures. The corporate DB assets are estimated by taking the total DB assets in 1997 ($2,136 billion) and netting out the $247 billion of multi-employer assets in 1996.

[3]Quarterly Pension Investment Report, Employee Benefit Research Institute, 1998:1.

to maintain their voluntary pension plans, the legal and regulatory structure imposes a severe tax penalty on firms that divert excess plan assets to corporate treasuries.

In 1995, the $2.1 billion in public-sector DB plans were ERISA exempt, yet many follow ERISA (prudent-expert) rules. Depending on the state, employees and citizens have direct or indirect representation in these pension plans.

Employee representation in DC plans exists through individualizing the investment choices in each employee's retirement plan. Employees make their own portfolio choices and bear the risks of their decisions. Workers select their asset allocation among guaranteed insurance contracts managed by insurance companies and mutual funds. Individuals do not participate in proxy voting or investment management.

Table 7.3 maps the pension universe according to the degree that employees exercise voice.

To summarize, unionized Taft-Hartley plans, which are collectively bargained, jointly managed plans and by far the smallest category of plan assets, are the only category in which owners—that is, workers—have a say in the management of the funds. The others, which contain more than $4 trillion of pension plan assets, although nominally owned by workers and retirees,

Table 7.4. Advantages and Disadvantages of Corporate Plans versus Multi-Employer Plans

Item	Multi-Employer Trusts	Single-Employer Trusts
Importance of a union as coordinator	Vital—unions coordinate the existence of multi-employer trusts.	Not vital.
Agency problems—trustee will not always protect participant	Legal restrictions, transparency, and democratic accountability make the trust serve the participant who votes for the representatives.	Corporations integrate pension finance decisions with corporate decisions, and workers have very little say.

are in fact managed with little employee involvement. Although close to $2 trillion is invested in DC plans in which individuals select broad asset allocations, participants in fact often exercise little real choice, because the range of choices and fund investment decisions are determined without their input. Table 7.4 summarizes agency problems encountered in the administration of pension trusts and the role of unions in jointly controlled trusts and single-employer trusts.

The Taft-Hartley structure is part of a highly evolved set of institutions that solved particular public-good problems in markets in which workers' careers typically involve many short stays with individual employers whose projects and contracts ebb and flow.[3] In these cases, no single employer has the funds or incentives to provide good fringe benefits, yet as a group the employers all benefit when workers are induced by multi-employer health and pension plans to attach themselves to regions and occupations. Collective bargaining provides this public good. Trustees, equally represented from the union and the employers, oversee the trust fund. They operate under clear guidelines, with economic and legal constraints and responsibilities (Gertner 1998).

During the 1950s and 1960s, unions and union plans were under considerable scrutiny, and new legislation imposed requirements that made them more democratic and accountable. These constraints culminated in the 1974 ERISA, which requires all trustees—even single-employer trustees—to manage the nonprofit, tax-favored, pension trust funds explicitly for the interest of the participants (i.e., the workers, their dependents, and retirees) not the employer or the union. The principle, called the *duty of loyalty*, attempts to control agency problems by outlawing them.

Employers' Commitment to Pensions: Coverage
and Cost of Defined-Benefit and Defined-Contribution Plans

Also to be considered is the commonplace belief that corporations are switching from relatively secure DB plans to individualized DC plans. The number of corporate DC sponsors has increased, and relative participation in DC plans has therefore grown. This fact troubles many in the labor movement, policy makers, and others who believe that DC plans are less stable and secure than DB plans. DB plans pay a pension guaranteed for life and can be indexed to inflation. Their benefits are based on years of service and usually reflect an employee's final rate of pay. This formula facilitates long-term labor contracts, because they allow employers to reward employees for their length of career service. By contrast, DC plans are based on separate accounts that are more portable, less cumulative, and afford more options to individual participants. Some argue that the individualized characteristics of DC plans detract from overall retirement security, as these accounts tend to be small, used for other purposes, and expensive to administer.

Many employers, however, have praised the simplicity of DC plans and state their own employees' preferences for them. Employers assert that their workers want DC plans to directly control their investments and ensure portability, because DC plans are more easily understood than DB plans.

However, an annual survey conducted by the employee benefits firm Hay-Huggins, which covered some one thousand medium- to large-size employers (70–80 percent of the same employers are sampled each year), shows DB plans holding their own against the DCs. This survey found that the percentage of corporations sponsoring both DB and DC plans (approximately two-thirds of the respondents) has remained remarkably steady and at a high level since 1985. This survey challenges the assumption that employers are in fact diminishing DB coverage with the increase of DC plans.

Ippolito (1995) draws a similar inference, based on data from the early 1990s. He argues that DC plans are popular supplements to DB plans. He, too, finds that older, larger firms use DCs to complement DB plans, rather than simply substituting them for the more traditional DBs. He finds, however, that both new and small firms are likely to adopt DC plans.

In sharp contrast, data from Form 5500, which tracks 25,000–35,000 firms, shows that, from 1981 to 1996, the Hay-Huggins sample severely underestimates the percentage of firms providing only DC plans and overestimates the percentage of employers offering both DB and DC. Other recent data support the conclusion that DB plans are waning in favor of DC plans. The percentage of employers offering only DC plans is soaring — up from 34 percent in 1981 to

TABLE 7.5. Defined-Contribution Plans Are Gaining Sponsors

Year	Sponsors of Both Defined-Benefit and Defined-Contribution Plans			Sponsors of Defined-Benefit Plans Only		Sponsors of Defined-Contribution Plans Only	
	N = (5500)	Form 5500 (%)	Hay (%)	Form 5500 (%)	Hay (%)	Form 5500 (%)	Hay (%)
1981	26,140	16	—	50	—	34	—
1985	31,488	19	62	38	25	43	10
1988	35,568	19	74	28	10	53	33
1990	37,442	18	—	23	—	60	—
1992	41,103	16	63	19	3	65	14
1995	44,488	15	62	15	2	70	36
1996	33,810	13	—	13	—	75	—

N, sample size approximately one thousand employers for Hay survey.
Sources: Hay-Huggins proprietary data that was presented at the New England Pension Consultants Client Conference by T. Fellows (March 14, 1999, Boston). Form 5500 are calculations from the author.

75 percent in 1996 (Table 7.5). Those offering both plans remained roughly the same, despite a slight decline in the mid-1990s. Papke (1996), using more recent data than Ippolito, supports the substitution hypothesis. He finds that firms offering DC plans were more likely to have terminated a DB plan. This trend represents a definite growth in a flawed retirement system.

Van Derhei and Olson (1997), working under the auspices of the Employee Benefit Research Institute, found two factors for analyzing trends in pensions: changes in the aggregate numbers of plans, and the amount employers contribute to each plan type. Van Derhei and Olson examined the ratio of DC contribution to total contribution when an employer sponsors both types of plans rather than just one. They found that employers contribute more to DC plans compared to DB plans, and they concluded that DC plans are ascendent.

Coverage is not the only indication of employer commitment. What employers actually pay for pensions adds support to the substitution conclusion. On average, and over time, employers who provide only DB plans contribute more per active workers than those who offer both plan types or DC plans alone. The average difference is significant. Firms that only provided DBs paid 50 percent more than DC-only sponsors. Employers could be substituting DC plans for DB plans and adopting DCs to complement DBs, because DC plans establish the environment in which firms can lower their total pension contributions. If more evidence supports this assertion, then adopting

TABLE 7.6. Employer Sponsors with Only Defined-Benefit (DB) Plans
Spend More per Participant, 1985–1996

Year	Employer Sponsors with DB and Defined-Contribution (DC) Plans	Employer Sponsors with Only DB Plans	Employer Sponsors with Only DC Plans	Type of Sponsor That Spends the Most
1985	1,673	931	1,326	Both
1988	1,245	1,786	1,606	DB
1990	1,188	1,423	1,754	DC
1992	1,314	1,648	1,251	DB
1995	1,770	2,126	1,106	DB
1996	1,983	2,204	1,298	DB
Average	$1,529	$1,686	$1,390	DB

DCs is a scheme for reducing employer pension commitment. Table 7.6 shows that employers use DC plans to cut back on total pension spending.

It is reasonable to conclude that employers sponsor DC plans to save pension costs, which means less money is set aside for workers' retirement. On this logic, the shift away from DB plans bodes poorly for the health of the pension system.

In early 1999, for the first time in decades and when most analysts concluded DB plans were dead, DB assets grew faster than DC assets, 20.3 percent compared to 13.8 percent. That trend continued to the end of 1999, when the most recent data were reported. A Federal Reserve official echoed fears that insidious leaks of retirement money out of DC funds, which occur as workers withdraw the funds for nonretirement purposes, caused DC assets to grow more slowly than DB assets (Anand 1999). In contrast, DB monies cannot be spent for any other purpose but retirement.

Indeed, the Federal Reserve official is probably correct. Many studies report that individuals use DC assets for nonretirement purposes. One way to measure this leak is to examine how workers use their DC lump-sum distributions when they change jobs. Forty-one percent of all recipients admit they use the lump-sum DC distribution to buy a home, invest in a business, pay for an education, or simply to buy consumer goods and services. Only 57.9 percent of people with a lump sum equal to $50,000 or more put it in a retirement account (Employee Benefit Research Institute 1997).

Some have contended that the DB plans' superior growth is due to their having more equities and alternative investments in DB portfolios than conservative DC plans. But the actual difference between DC and DB rates of return are quite small, further strengthening the leakage theory. In fact, DCs earned more than DBs in the early 1990s. The 3-year rate of return (1992.3–1995.2) for DC plans averaged 12.2 percent against 11.8 percent for DB plans (Employee Benefit Research Institute 1995).

These leaks from DC plans weaken their capacity to provide retirement security. As shown above, one major flaw is the ability to spend retirement savings before retirement. Another problem is that many workers—approximately half—do not participate in a DC plan, even if their employers offer them. Even when employees participate, contributions to these plans are usually inadequately low. Many studies measure DC adequacy; one rough way to judge is to compare the rule of thumb that workers need to contribute approximately 15–20 percent of their pay to maintain living standards in retirement. The average annual DC contribution is less than $2,000, which is approximately 5 percent of average pay. For these reasons, DC plan growth has not improved pension coverage rates or benefits.

The United States is committed to a well-developed mixture of public and private delivery of the retirement income security system with both voluntary and mandatory components. The pertinent question, then, is how will workers maintain their ability to choose leisure at the end of their working lives?

Control and Workers' Representation Matters

The average contribution that employers make to all pension plans should also be considered. Table 7.7 displays the results from a sample of plans between 1993 and 1996. The sample is unweighted, in contrast to the results in Table 7.6, which are weighted and only capture information on the largest plans. By taking the average this way, we are able to look at the pension world from the point of view of employers rather than workers.

The average employer contribution to DC plans has actually fallen from 1993 to 1996 (the latest data available for individual plans). Yet this average trend hides important facts about management structure. The trend differs considerably, depending on whether the plan is collectively bargained. In 1993, corporate and small-firm sponsors paid more into noncollectively bargained DC plans than into the collectively bargained ones—a whopping $1,469 per head versus just $815. By 1996, per-head contributions to union DC plans had grown significantly, and the contribution differential was less than $200.

DB trends are even more dramatic. Between 1993 and 1996, nonunion employers raised their average per-worker DB pension contribution by just

TABLE 7.7. Employer Contribution per Active Worker in
Defined-Benefit (DB) and Defined-Contribution (DC) Plans
for Union and Nonunion Plans ($ per year—1993 and 1996—
in 1996 constant dollars [unweighted for plan size])

Type of Plan	DB Annual Contributions		DC Annual Contributions	
	1993	1996	1993	1996
Nonunion corporate	1,750 (n = 10,342)	2,062 (n = 6,222)	1,469 (n = 34,738)	1,320 (n = 29,205)
Union corporate	1,874 (n = 4,637)	8,225 (n = 2,943)	815 (n = 2,365)	1,155 (n = 2,216)
Nonunion multi-employer	1,957 (n = 313)	2,137 (n = 181)	1,556 (n = 505)	1,413 (n = 545)
Union multi-employer	2,139 (n = 1,730)	2,420 (n = 943)	1,611 (n = 1,047)	1,657 (n = 709)
Average contributions	**$1,825**	**$3,856**	**$1,434**	**$1,318**

	DB Annual Contributions: Change between 1993 and 1996 (%)	DC Annual Contributions: Change between 1993 and 1996 (%)
Nonunion corporate plan	17.0	−11.0
Union corporate plan	430.0	41.0
Nonunion multi-employer plan	9.0	−10.0
Union multi-employer plans	13.0	2.8

n, sample size.
Source: Calculations based on the Form 5500 universe and research files.

under $300 per head (in real terms, $1,750 in 1993 to $2,062 in 1996), whereas unionized-employer DB plans increased contributions more than fourfold, from $1,874 per head in 1993 to $8,225 in 1996.[4] This is an average of all plans, regardless of size. On the other hand, Table 7.6 samples the largest one thousand corporate plans and shows that the average pension contribution per participant for DB plans is $1,686, well below $8,225.

In the jointly trusteed sector (nonunion multi-employer plans are dominated by not-for-profit agencies), the differences between union and nonunion plans are less stark. However, both union DB and DC plans improved in terms of employer contributions, whereas nonunion pensions did not. Multi-union DC contributions increased by 2.8 percent (adjusted for inflation), whereas the DC plan contributions of nonunion multi-employers fell by a significant 10 percent. Nonunion corporate DC employer contributions also fell by 11 percent, whereas the union corporate DC contribution increased by a huge 41 percent.

Employer contributions are an imperfect measure of employer commitment, however; the pattern shows that, for whatever reason, the presence of a union requires employers to put more priority into employee pensions. Management matters.

Unions also increase pension security by pushing employers to devote larger shares of their payroll to pensions. Researchers commonly use the DOL's Employment Cost Indexes (ECI) to track employer costs. The ECI shows that the percentage of payroll going to pensions has fallen. In 1987, 3.6 percent of total payroll went to retirement and savings plans. By 1996, that share had fallen substantially to 3.1 percent (Employee Benefit Research Institute 1998). The ECI data is one of the few sources that breaks out employer costs by union and nonunion employees, although it does not distinguish between DB and DC plans. According to the DOL's ECI, union employers steadily increased their contributions to retirement plans during the period between 1988 and 1993 by approximately 19 percent (all figures are adjusted for inflation). Although it is not evident from this data source whether the money was going into DB or DC plans, it is known that nonunion employers increased pension contributions by only 5 percent. During that same time period, unionized employers put approximately 15 percent more in wages; nonunion wages went up by approximately 18 percent. Unions raised savings rates, whereas nonunion employers raised wage rates.

The extent of sponsorship and actual dollars spent is not the only gauge of employer commitment to pensions. The growth in DB plan "generosity" is another measure of the employer's commitment to the type of plan that rewards long-tenured workers.

The precise way to evaluate DB pension plan generosity is to examine the plan formula and calculate the amount that workers at various pay levels and years of service would eventually receive. This method is time consuming and restricts the number of plans one can compare. A shorthand way to measure the generosity of a DB formula is to use an actuarial calculation of the extra cost incurred in a plan with the passage of each year. This is called the *normal cost*. The normal cost takes into account the promised benefit and the fact that employees have an additional year of credit, usually at a higher wage.

Fund managers are *fiduciaries*—they manage other people's money—and therefore must adhere to a strict "loyalty standard." A fiduciary would tend to increase generosity when finance markets surge. It is important to note that actuaries determine contributions based on the long term. Therefore, if returns increase over and above the projected return in any given year, the excess could be allocated to a reserve fund or used to increase retiree benefits. Alternatively, managers with divided loyalties might allow employers to reduce contributions or take outright pension holidays in the face of a bull market. This is another version of the agency problem.

The manager is the agent and should act in the sole benefit of the ultimate owner, yet the manager-agent also seeks to satisfy other interests. The management structure of a fund can mitigate or induce agency problems. Table 7.8 illuminates this effect by showing that generosity increased in those funds in which the ultimate owners and recipients were monitoring, influencing, and controlling pension fund managers, or *agents*. Wall Street gains trickled to Main Street in pension funds in which beneficiaries were represented.

MEASURING PENSION SECURITY: MULTI-EMPLOYER VERSUS SINGLE-EMPLOYER PENSION PLANS

Using unpublished data from the Form 5500, I created a sample of the largest pension plans (top one thousand for corporate, largest one hundred for multi-employer plans) in 1984, 1988, 1992, and 1996. I used this data to explore in greater depth the impact of plan type on workers and retirees and to gauge the behavior of the largest firms. These data show three dimensions on which multi-employer pension plans offer greater retirement security compared to single-employer plans.

First, DB union multi-employer plans have increased pension generosity by almost twice as much as corporate plans (Table 7.8). It seems that multi-employer plans structured with a separate trust and workers' representation reduce losses from agency problems. Pension plans with representatives of both union and management are more likely to transmit gains from bull markets to plan beneficiaries than are single-employer plans. Fund managers in single-employer plans often divided their loyalties between the corporation and the trust. The single-employer sponsor can reduce employer contributions; the multi-employer sponsor cannot.

I also determined that only collectively bargained single-employer corporate plans complement DBs with DCs to improve worker pension security. My data shows that these corporations have not been squeezing DB plan generosity as they expand DC plans. In these plans, DB generosity and DC employer contributions have increased 4 percent and 6 percent, respectively (see Table 7.8). In contrast, nonunion employers' DB generosity has fallen by 10 percent, and their contributions to DC plans have also fallen by 6 percent. It is clear that collectively bargained status does matter.

Both pieces of evidence demonstrate that worker representation in pension governance substantially enhances pension security. Union-dominated multi-

TABLE 7.8. Three Ways to Measure Pension Security: Pension Generosity, Employer, and Worker Contributions by Union Status of Corporate Pension Plans (Selected Years) 1984–1986

	Increase (%) between 1988 and 1996	1984	1988	1992	1996
Top 1,000 (by Total Assets) Corporate Plans					
Defined benefit plans					
Total employer contributions per participant	—	2,786.13	1,366.30	1,824.83	1,232.08
Collectively bargained	-33.0	—	2,056.35	2,408.83	1,387.28
Not collectively bargained	9.0	—	1,037.90	1,504.15	1,136.03
Average generosity	—	1,734.41	1,424.23	1,406.16	1,316.35
Collectively bargained	4.0	—	1,150.99	1,195.25	1,200.15
Not collectively bargained	-10.0	—	1,539.19	1,524.02	1,388.41
Defined contribution plans					
Total employer contributions per participant	—	1,309.74	1,369.41	1,259.28	1,313.57
Collectively bargained	6.0	—	1,083.22	974.97	1,153.54
Not collectively bargained	-6.0	—	1,446.14	1,345.83	1,363.71
Worker contributions per participant	—	1,486.78	1,909.56	1,786.38	1,947.52
Collectively bargained	7.0	—	1,813.88	1,679.15	1,932.42
Not collectively bargained	1.0	—	1,935.92	1,817.94	1,953.26
Top 100 (by Assets) Multi-Employer Plans					
Defined benefit plans					
Total employer contributions per participant	-7.0	2,127.98	2,367.21	1,925.26	2,189.99
Average generosity	6.0	658.29	988.89	972.28	1,044.58
Defined contribution plans					
Total employer contributions per participant	-20.0	1,715.10	2,138.20	1,488.09	1,704.62
Worker contributions per participant	-75.0	26.36	549.30	92.04	135.72

All figures weighted by share of active participants in group; dollar figures in 1996 constant dollars.
Source: U.S. Department of Labor, unpublished data (Form 5500 filings).

employer plans have expanded pension generosity, employer contributions, and DC contributions. Moreover, collectively bargained DB and DC plans complement each other with both plan types expanding. Unfortunately, when a union is not present in single-employer plans, DB and DC pension plans contract.

IMPLICATIONS FOR PUBLIC POLICY

Two major public policy problems afflict the U.S. pension system. One is the familiar problem of coverage; as explained later, most workers do not save enough for retirement on their own. The second, less-often-raised problem (but the focus of this chapter), is that the institutional and governance arrangements allow and even encourage some fund managers to act in ways that threaten retirement security.

INDIVIDUAL ACCOUNTS ARE NOT THE ANSWER TO PENSION INSECURITY

The decline in employer-provided pensions would not be important if people were saving in other ways or earning high returns on their assets. Unfortunately, today's savings rates are not enough to secure tomorrow's retirements.

Warshawsky and Amerikas (2000), improving the methodology and data of previous studies, asked the question, "Are Americans financially prepared for retirement?" They estimate that most are not. Even accounting for housing wealth, Social Security and pension benefits, life expectancy, expected college tuition for children, and other factors, they forecast that 52 percent of the individuals in their sample (representing the median household with a full-time working head) would fail to finance their retirement. More than one-third of the households in their sample are predicted to simply run out of assets before they die. Households with greater assets are more likely to fund their retirements successfully, as are those with more education. Low-income households have slightly higher failure rates, as do households with personal loans (not including mortgages). Importantly, households with pensions are more likely to succeed. These results are similar to previous studies, even though they use different methodologies. It is safe to conclude that most U.S. citizens are going to find it difficult to retire.

To be considered are the savings rates needed to achieve 75-percent replacement of current income upon retirement. Forty percent of all households at the bottom end of income distribution would have to save 27 percent of income to retire at age 62, and 13 percent for a retirement at age 65. The median household, in a broad sample of households, has $380,000 worth of wealth. They would still need to save an additional 16 percent of earnings to maintain a stable level of consumption if they were to retire at age 62 (Mitchell, Moore, and Phillips 2000).

Sadly, the national savings rates, approximately 10–15 percent between 1950 and 1970, presently fluctuate between below zero and 3 percent. Although measuring the savings rate may be controversial, its drastic decline is not. Four reasons have been proffered to explain the savings shortfall. First, perhaps high discount rates (people are shortsighted and will borrow for consumer goods at high rates of interest) are the culprit. Second, people underestimate how much they need for retirement. Third, people overestimate how much they will earn on their assets. Fourth, people with lower incomes think they do not have enough income to save.

One study showed, surprisingly, that low income does not cause savings inadequacy. Higher-income individuals want more at retirement, and Social Security has progressive replacement rates. People with high incomes do not have enough wealth to retire in the fashion to which they are accustomed (Mitchell, Moore, and Phillips 2000). Measures of people's value of the future (a low discount rate) are also insignificant factors to explain savings. These factors include whether people report that they plan ahead for long periods of time, request benefit estimates from the Social Security Administration, or have a low preference toward risk. However, divorce causes a savings shortfall for unmarried women. For married couples, being older, having children, and being nonwhite significantly contribute to savings shortfalls.

These examples of conventional savings studies use large national surveys of individuals (the Survey of Consumer Finance and the Health and Retirement Survey), which are designed to measure wealth or health status in detail. None examines the particular institutions that help people to save automatically, to resist consumer temptation, or to develop realistic financial assessments. As noted elsewhere in this chapter, the presence of unions facilitates increased savings rates. Union members are twice as likely to have pensions as nonunion workers, and unionized employers spend more on fringe benefits than nonunion employers, even in the same industry. Also, *antidiscrimination rules*—IRS rules that ensure that tax-favored plans do not skew benefits toward the highest-paid employees—help to spread pensions by forcing large companies that give pensions to management to include lesser-paid workers (Turner and Hinz 1998). Some firms have tried to avoid these rules by leasing employees; Microsoft Corporation offers a prime and well-publicized example. Microsoft is under investigation for defining employees as temporary when they are being used as permanent employees for the purpose of avoiding inclusion in the pension and health plans.

Public policy has many voices. Whether retirement remains a national goal has become controversial in the light of tight labor markets, upward pressure on wages, and the renewed discussion of transforming Social Security into individual accounts. Some taxpayers may care less about whether people can retire and more about the possibility that elders might need government assistance if they run out of assets. Employers faced with tight labor markets may find savings inadequacy to be good news, as older people will want to remain in the workforce longer. Furthermore, vigorous consumer spending and anemic savings cheer those who thrive on economic growth. However, workers hoping for retirement will find the savings shortfall and the shortfall in institutions that promote savings to be bad news.

MANAGEMENT MATTERS

Current public policy solutions for the private pension system include vast, targeted tax breaks to improve coverage but fail to address the agency problems or management structure issues identified previously.

Legislation that required worker representation on all pension boards, not just those of Taft-Hartley plans, would greatly reduce agency problems. Such mandated representation is required by other nations with advanced and funded pension systems (Ghilarducci et al. 1995), and the findings presented previously offer strong empirical reasons for the United States to follow suit. U.S. Representative Peter Visclosky in 1990 and Rep. Marcy Kaptur in the mid-1990s introduced such legislation.

Although agency problems have been outlawed through a variety of legislative acts, these governance changes would mitigate these problems in practice. Some claim that individual-directed accounts are the ultimate solution to agency problems, because they make worker-owners into their own financial agents. Yet individual-directed DC accounts create their own problems. Self-directed DC plans are very seductive for employers and politicians, because they are easily understood and give the illusion of individual control. Yet trust law, also embodied in ERISA, quite wisely specifies the beneficiary as the future pensioner, not the worker of today. Individual workers are notoriously bad at looking after themselves as the ultimate beneficiary, for all the same reasons most people do not save adequately for retirement. These reasons include conflicts with other desires, myopia, and high discount rates.

Individual control is precisely the reason DC plans are poor vehicles for securing retirement. Decades of research on behavioral finance warn against self-directed accounts for the same reasons that physicians cannot operate on close family members. Individuals make bad decisions for themselves, because they cannot possibly meet the prerequisites of a "rational" investor, which are the basis of the efficient market hypothesis.

The reasons for this failure are fascinating and fall into two broad categories. Sometimes, individuals fail to maximize risk-adjusted returns as required of trustees. Beyond this, most people have heuristic and analytic biases that lead to systematic mistakes. In the first category, that of not acting as maximizers, individuals try to avoid regret by holding on to losers too long and selling winners too quickly. People may also feel incompetent and avoid the task, thus maximizing comfort, not wealth.

In the second category, heuristic mistakes made by the plumber in Pittsburgh or the graduate student in Chicago include *representativeness*, which means that people evaluate the probability of a future event based on what happened recently. They overweight new information (Harless and Peterson 1998).

The second heuristic problem is *saliency*, which means that people think infrequent events are more likely to happen if they happened recently. For instance, air travel decreases after a plane crash. Saliency causes overreaction, which is a common observation in finance markets.

The third heuristic mistake is *overconfidence*, known as the *Lake Woebegon effect*—a place where all the children are above average, according to National Public Radio's Garrison Keillor. Psychologists have repeated many experiments that show that 50 percent of a group believes that it is in the nintieth percentile in almost everything, including appearance, ability, athletic skill.

The fourth psychological bias is *anchoring*. People anchor their estimate of value based on previous alleged values of the item. That is why salespersons start negotiations with a high value.

Beyond these systematic cognitive errors, future public-policy debates about individual-directed accounts should consider several additional sorts of risk. *Financial timing risk*, the risk that the market falls when a person turns 65, means that each individual bears more risk than an institution, because the risk is not spread across a group of people with a range of ages. Each individual bears this risk alone.

Individuals also bear *longevity risk*, the risk of outliving one's income. Individuals also suffer the deadweight loss of higher management costs, because they lose economies of scale in financial management. Individuals cannot realistically act as effective responsible owners by participating in proxy voting in any serious and informed way. The flaws associated with individual-directed accounts undermine their future security. Therefore, workers need mediated representation to ensure retirement security.

Conclusion

This chapter attempts to answer the question why are pension funds so large and benefits so small? The answer lies in the problem of agency. Single-employer pensions work against pensions being managed for the sole benefit of the participant—the potential retiree. The current structure of many pension plans produces leaks between the funds and workers. The most critical of these leaks is through "agency" problems. Many employers divert market-based financial gains made by pension funds to their corporate treasuries or deplete them through inefficient and expensive money management.

Although on the surface it may look as if DC plans, especially those that are individual-directed, are the ultimate solution to agency problems, this is not the case. Individual workers poorly represent themselves as future pensioners. Only pension plans that incorporate the effective representation of workers preserve retirement security. Of course, in the face of the fact that the majority of workers do not participate in pensions, the question of how and who manages pension funds may seem less important. Yet worker representation and "accountable" management also ensure expanded coverage. Unionized workers save more in pension plans and have greater representation in their management. As this chapter goes to press, a fight is brewing at General Electric. The fight at General Electric about the company cutting back on contribution has become a contentious issue between labor and management. The union is demanding that General Electric disgorge the excess pension assets and improve benefits. *Business Week* (2000) predicts there will be similar battles in the future as aging workers look longingly at their overfunded pension funds and stagnating pensions. What was not highlighted in the report is that this desire for retirement security will be more easily satisfied when workers are represented in the management of their pension funds.

[VIII]

OVERCOMING INSTITUTIONAL BARRIERS ON THE ECONOMICALLY TARGETED INVESTMENT SUPERHIGHWAY

Jayne Elizabeth Zanglein

The high road economy . . . is built up in layers. At the base are families and workplaces. Strong, union families, and progressive public and private employers provide the foundation for building strong communities. Communities that employ workers in high-wage, high-skill jobs and support families with excellent public services form the next layer of the highway. On these high road communities—or Union Cities—states can build progressive, people-first economies. (AFL-CIO Human Resource Development Institute 1998, 1)

Similarly, the economically targeted investment (ETI) superhighway is built upon three layers. At the base is trustee education. Educated, informed trustees who understand the investment decision-making process, modern portfolio theory, capital markets, and asset allocation will be in a position to demand that fund advisors consider prudent investments that provide collateral benefits to their members. Established ETI programs that allow trustees to easily invest in an ongoing investment program form the next layer of the highway. The third layer is a national center for economically targeted investments that can collect data on established programs and assist regional ETI centers in developing new programs. On these super highways, pension funds can build a secure retirement system within a strong economy.

Beyond providing retirement security for workers after they retire, pension fund assets can also be shifted to help those active in the workforce. Such deliberate shifts are called *economically targeted investments*. Although ETIs are controversial among some investors, others strongly support them, because they can generate important *collateral benefits*—beneficial effects beyond financial returns to investors—such as new or better jobs, housing, infrastructure, and healthy firms. This chapter begins by exploring how the operations of financial markets often leave important "capital gaps" that can be filled by ETIs and then reviews several pervasive misconceptions that prevent pension funds from allocating their assets to ETIs. The third section argues that two measures would greatly reduce the barriers to ETIs and thus open the way to more socially productive investments: better training and education for trustees and their advisors and a national center for collecting and diffusing best ETI practices.

Capital Gaps That Can Be Filled by Prudent Economically Targeted Investments

Although experts claim that financial markets are efficient, "not all investments are discovered by the market, and the markets do not extend their bounty equally to all investment vehicles, given proper returns" (Lurie 1996, 4). Many commentators suggest that an ETI ought to fill needs created by capital gaps. For example, a report issued by the Government Accounting Office states, "An ETI could have little net effect if the company receiving the ETI merely displaced another company that, without the ETI, would have employed the same people, developed the same product, and created the same level of economic activity. Similarly, an ETI could have little net effect if it merely displaced capital that would have been invested anyway by another investor" (U.S. Department of Labor [DOL] 1992, 9). Lawrence Litvak has described this process: "Displacement will occur when a pension fund targets projects so well served by capital markets that the fund only competes with private investors rather than supplying additional capital" (1981, 13). Litvak continues:

> The key to success is concentrating on sectors and enterprises that have been underfinanced due to gaps and inefficiencies in our financial system. . . . Effective yet financially sound development investing first requires identifying situations where the unavailability of capital on competitive terms is impeding development that would otherwise take place. (Litvak 1981, 4)

According to a report issued by the DOL's Advisory Council on Pension Welfare and Benefit Plans, prudent investments exist in an inefficient market and remain unfunded due to information gaps and high administrative costs of consummating and monitoring deals: "To the extent that capital markets are judged to be tradition-bound, rigid or incapable of funding all 'worthy' investments, making funds available from the pension investment pool is seen as addressing capital gaps that would otherwise impede local economic development" (U.S. DOL 1992, 3–4).

The report further states,

> The added costs of acquiring the information needed to make the investment sound must be incorporated in the required rate of return. If the investment can bear these added costs, the ETI strategy may produce additional economic activity in this region. If it isn't able to bear the added costs, the pension fund must: (1) forego the investment, (2) find a third party willing to subsidize some or all of these extra costs, or (3) accept a lower [but still prudent] net return. (U.S. DOL 1992, 9–10)

ETIs have been defined by the DOL as "investments selected for the economic benefits they create apart from their investment return to the employee benefit plan" (U.S. DOL 1994). Collateral benefits obtained through ETIs include "expanded employment opportunities, increased housing availability, improved social service facilities, and strengthened infrastructure" (Berg 1994). ETIs "create new jobs, provide capital to replace loan funds no longer rolling through the bank pipelines, provide startup businesses with access to capital, finance low-cost housing and improve the infrastructures of the nation, all without sacrificing a return on investments or otherwise jeopardizing the pensions of future retirees" (Lurie 1996, 4).

These are true capital gaps: the failure of the market to finance prudent investments. Many investments, such as socially screened stock funds, are touted as ETIs, although they do not truly fill an identifiable gap in the capital markets. An example of a true capital gap is the market's failure to provide venture capital and private placement dollars to established, well-run, medium-sized companies. It is these capital gaps that the DOL encouraged pension funds to fill in its 1994 interpretive bulletin on ETIs. The department's bulletin on ETIs states that a fiduciary may invest plan assets in an ETI "if the ETI has an expected rate of return that is commensurate to rates of return of alternative investments with similar risk characteristics that are available to the plan, and if the ETI is otherwise an appropriate investment for the plan in terms of such factors as diversification and the investment policy of the plan" (U.S. DOL Interpretive Bulletin 94-1, 1994).

Institutional Barriers That Impede Pension Funds from Making Economically Targeted Investments

Despite strong encouragement by the DOL and the American Federation of Labor-Congress of Industrial Organizations (AFL-CIO), pension fund trustees are still reluctant to make ETIs. Seven misconceptions block this high road of investments:

1. ETIs are illegal and concessionary.
2. ETIs are too time-consuming.
3. ETIs are too costly to administer.
4. Competent managers are unavailable.
5. It is impossible to convince trustees and professionals to invest in ETIs.
6. Politics always get in the way.
7. There are no appropriate benchmarks by which to measure the performance of ETIs.

Several studies explore sources of this reluctance. A 1993 study by the Institute for Fiduciary Education concluded that "economically targeted investing is growing only modestly and . . . the subject still elicits strong opinions, both positive and negative, from the pension fund community" (Institute for Fiduciary Education 1993). In the preamble to its interpretive bulletin on ETIs, the DOL recognized that "a perception exists within the investment community that investments in ETIs are incompatible with the Employment Retirement Income Security Act's (ERISA's) fiduciary obligations." The DOL issued the interpretive bulletin to eliminate this misconception and promote ETIs.

In its survey on ETIs, the Institute for Fiduciary Education asked 119 public pension funds to list reasons why they have not made ETIs. Thirty-seven percent of the funds identified conflicts with fiduciary duty as the principal reason for avoiding them. Eleven percent said that ETIs take too much staff time; 11 percent said ETIs are not statutorily authorized; 8 percent said they did not invest in them because "no one asked us to" (Institute for Fiduciary Education 1993, B-2, Table B-8); 4 percent said that their legal counsel had advised against it; and 4 percent said they found no perceived need.

The survey conducted by the Institute for Fiduciary Education listed various aspects of targeted investments and the difficulty involved in the implementation of each aspect (Table 8.1). Liquidity and the procurement of a competent asset manager tied as the most difficult aspect of ETIs. More than 14 percent of plans experienced great difficulty in each of these two areas. Other aspects, such as public opinion and participant opinion, presented no great difficulty.

TABLE 8.1. Perceived Difficulty in Undertaking Economically
Targeted Investments (ETIs)

Aspect	Funds Reporting No Difficulty (%)	Funds Reporting Some Difficulty (%)	Funds Reporting Great Difficulty (%)
Return/risk characteristics	14.3	75.5	10.2
Liquidity level requirements	30.6	55.1	14.3
Board concerns	22.5	70.1	4.0
Internal staff considerations	24.5	69.3	6.1
Political concerns	46.0	48.0	6.0
Public opinion	44.1	55.8	0.0
Participant opinion	38.3	61.7	0.0
Litigation	61.7	36.2	2.0
Procurement of a competent asset manager	14.3	71.4	14.3
Expenses of operation	37.5	60.0	2.5
Development of a performance benchmark	31.7	65.8	2.4
Operating ETI	29.6	68.1	2.3

Source: Institute for Fiduciary Education, Sacramento, California, 1993.

A 1997 survey by Goldman, Sachs & Co. and Frank Russell Capital, Inc., describes the most significant issues for investors. A recent book, *Pension Fund Excellence: Creating Value for Stakeholders* (Ambachtsheer and Ezra 1998) cites ten barriers to excellence (Table 8.2). As stated previously, seven misconceptions seem to block stronger ETIs based upon these investigations. Each misconception is detailed below.

Misconception Number One:
Economically Targeted Investments Are Unlawful

Robert Monks, principal of Lens, Inc. and former pension administrator of the DOL, noted that since ERISA was enacted, trustees and their attorneys "have been driven chiefly by the fear of legal exposure" (Monks 1995). Bill Patterson, director of the AFL-CIO Office of Investments, agrees that trustees have a tendency to make conservative investments. He noted, "There is a premium for not straying from established investment practices. . . . This is worker money and [the trustees] feel obligated to stay with established formulas for creating wealth" (Williams 1998, 20–3). No one has ever been sued by the DOL for making conservative, low-risk, low-return investments. Ambachtsheer and Ezra reached the same conclusion in their survey of fifty senior pension executives. Conservatism was cited by 35 percent of the managers as a barrier to pension fund excellence. Similarly, the Institute of Fiduciary Education Survey showed that 37 percent of funds did not make ETIs, because doing so conflicts with fiduciary duty. This conception is absolutely wrong.

We define ETIs as pension fund investments that earn risk-adjusted market rates of return, provide collateral benefits such as economic development, and provide capital for prudent investments that otherwise might not be financed due to gaps in the capital markets. A pension fund may make an ETI if the investment has a risk-adjusted market rate of return that is commensurate to rates of return on alternate investments with similar risk characteristics that are available to the plan, and the ETI is otherwise an appropriate investment for the plan, taking into account factors such as return, diversification, liquidity, and the investment policy of the plan (Watson and Ferlauto 1995).

ETIs, as defined above, are legal investments under ERISA, and that law's fiduciary duties (given in Section 404[a][1]) determine the propriety of an ETI. ERISA imposes four separate duties on plan fiduciaries: to act solely in the interest of plan participants and beneficiaries (this is the *exclusive benefit rule*), to act prudently, to diversify plan assets, and to act in accordance with plan documents. Misunderstandings of these duties discourage ETI activity.

Table 8.2. Barriers to Excellence

Rank	Barrier	Cited (%)
1	Poor process (including structure, communication, and inertia)	98
2	Inadequate resources	48
3	Lack of focus or clear mission	43
4	Conservatism	35
5	Insufficient skills	35
6	Inadequate technology	13
7	Conflicting beliefs	8
8	Difficult markets	8
9	Lack of innovation	5
10	Suppliers	5

Source: Ambachtsheer, Keith and Dan Ezra. *Pension Fund Excellence: Creating Value for Stakeholders.* New York: John Wiley and Sons, 1998.

EXCLUSIVE BENEFIT RULE

The *exclusive benefit rule*, laid out in ERISA Section 404(a)(1)(A), requires plan fiduciaries to act solely in the interests of plan participants and beneficiaries and for the exclusive purpose of providing plan benefits and defraying reasonable expenses of plan administration. These two requirements, "solely in the interest" and "exclusive purpose," combine to form a statutory duty of loyalty. Under this rule, fiduciaries must act "with an eye single to the interests of participants and beneficiaries" and may not place themselves in a position in which they are required to compromise their duty of undivided loyalty to plan participants (*Donovan v. Bierwirth*, 680 F. 2d 263 [2d Cir. 1982], *cert. denied*, 459 U.S. 1069 1982).

Although the DOL has interpreted Section 404(a)(1)(A) as prohibiting fiduciaries from subordinating retirement assets to "unrelated objectives," (Berg 1994) the DOL has never taken the position that all collateral benefits are prohibited. The DOL has explicitly stated, "There is nothing in ERISA, however, requiring that an investment decision be wholly uninfluenced by the desire to achieve social or incidental objectives if the investment, when judged *solely* on the basis of its economic value to the plan, is equal or superior to alternative investments otherwise available" (Kass 1987, 235–36).

On another occasion, a DOL spokesperson stated that, although the exclusive benefit rule "does not exclude the provision of incidental benefits to others, the protection of retirement income is, and should continue to be, the overriding social objective governing the investment of plan assets" (Lanoff 1980, 387). The DOL has also stated that "under ERISA pension plan investments must be made based upon what is in the economic interest of the plan as a separate and distinct legal entity established for the purpose of providing retirement income, [and] that other considerations can be considered provided that they are incidental and do not compromise the required investment decision" (New York State Pension Investment Task Force 1989, 190–91).

In advisory opinions, the DOL has repeatedly emphasized that plan investments must be made solely in the interest of plan participants and beneficiaries, but that collateral benefits may be considered if the investment is otherwise "equal or superior to alternative investments available to the plan" (Pension and Welfare Benefits Administration [PWBA] Letter 1988). In response to an inquiry made on behalf of the Union Labor Life Insurance Company concerning its *Mortgage Separate Account J*, a mortgage pool for union-built properties, the DOL stated that investment in the J Account would be not prudent if it provided the investor "with less return, in comparison to risk, than comparable investments available to the plan, or if it involved a greater risk to the security of plan assets than other investments offering a similar return"(PWBA Letter 1988). The DOL warned that the interests of participants and beneficiaries cannot be subordinated to unrelated objectives. The DOL stated that the J Account investments would not violate ERISA section 404 if the loans were offered at "rates prevailing in the overall mortgage market" (PWBA Letter 1988). However, the "decision to make an investment may not be influenced by a desire to stimulate the construction industry and generate employment unless the investment, when judged solely on the basis of its economic value to the plan, would be equal or superior to alternative investments available to the plan" (PWBA Letter 1988). Thus, it is not sufficient simply to charge the prevailing rate; the investment must be equal to or better than alternative investments with similar risk and return characteristics.[1]

Courts have agreed with the DOL's interpretation of the exclusive benefit rule. In *Donovan v. Walton* (609 F. Supp. 1221 [S.D. Fla. 1985], *aff'd sub nom.*, *Brock v. Walton*, 794 F.2d 586 [11th Cir. 1986]), the district court for the Southern District of Florida held that "by adopting the 'exclusive purpose' standard, Congress did not intend to make illegal the fact of life that most often a transaction benefits both parties involved."[2] ERISA "does not prohibit a party other than a plan's participants and beneficiaries from benefiting in some measure from a prudent transaction with the plan" (609 F. Supp. 1245).

In *Donovan v. Bierwirth*, (680 F.2d 263 [2d Cir. 1982], *cert. denied*, 459 U.S. 1069 [1982]) the Second Circuit ruled that trustees will not violate their duty of loyalty by "taking action which, after careful and impartial investigation, they reasonably conclude [is] best to promote the interests of participants and beneficiaries simply because it incidentally benefits the corporation, or indeed, themselves . . ." (*Donovan v. Bierwirth* 1982, 271).[3] Similarly, in *Morse v. Stanley*, the Second Circuit held that "it is no violation of a trustee's fiduciary duties to take a course of action which reasonably best promotes the interest of plan participants simply because it incidentally also benefits" another party.[4] Opponents of ETIs, such as Representative Jim Saxton (1995), oppose them "because they violate the law, they lower returns and increase risk for pension beneficiaries." These opponents miss the essential point that ETIs must be prudent and achieve competitive rates of returns. During congressional hearings on ETIs, Saxon asked then Secretary of Labor Robert Reich whether the DOL's interpretation that collateral benefits are permissible contradicts the exclusive benefit rule. Secretary Reich replied:

The statute says exclusive benefit. Does this mean that we cannot consider these other possible advantages of investment, even assuming that we can get the same risk adjusted rate of return? And the DOL, again, in letter after letter, advisory opinion after advisory opinion has said no, that's not what the statute means. Exclusive purpose under the law means that you can't weigh those things against the return, but as long as you perform your obligation as a fiduciary to get that return, it's perfectly appropriate to take into consideration those other things. (U.S. DOL. Hearing on Pension Investments and Economic Growth 1994)

The exclusive benefit rule does not prohibit ETIs, as long as the primary objective is to make a prudent investment with a competitive rate of return for plan participants and beneficiaries.

PRUDENCE RULE

The *prudence rule* is the second fiduciary duty. It requires fiduciaries to act with "the care, skill, prudence, and diligence under the circumstances then prevailing that a prudent man acting in a like capacity and familiar with such matters would use in the conduct of an enterprise of a like character and with like aims" (29 U.S.C. §1104[a][1][B] [1999]). This rule imposes "an extremely high standard of conduct"; this standard is "the highest known to the law" (*Marshall v. Mercer*, 4 Employee Benefits Cas. [BNA] 1523, 1532 [N.D. Tex. 1983]).

The DOL has created a safe harbor for fiduciaries making investment decisions (44 Fed. Reg. 37, 221 [1979]). If a fiduciary complies with the prudence regulation, the investment will be deemed to be prudent. However, if a fiduciary does not comply with the prudence regulation, the investment is not imprudent, per se (44 Fed. Reg. 37, 221 [1979]).

To reach the sanctuary of the safe harbor, the fiduciary must act only after giving appropriate consideration to those

facts and circumstances that, given the scope of such fiduciary's investment duties, the fiduciary knows or should know are relevant to the particular investment or investment course of action involved, including the role the investment or investment course of action plays in that portion of the plan's investment portfolio with respect to which the fiduciary has investment duties. (44 Fed. Reg. 37, 221 [1979])

When considering an investment, the fiduciary must determine whether it reasonably furthers the purposes of the plan, taking into consideration the risk of loss and the opportunity for gain (44 Fed. Reg. 37, 221 [1979]). The regulation states that a fiduciary must consider the following factors in relation to the entire portfolio:

- The composition of the portfolio with regard to diversification;
- The liquidity and current return of the portfolio relative to the anticipated cash flow requirements of the plan;
- The projected return of the portfolio relative to the funding objective of the plan.

The DOL has added a fourth factor: "consideration of the expected return on alternative investments with similar risks available to the plan" (U.S. DOL Interpretive Bulletin 94-1, 1994). The DOL states:

> Because every investment necessarily causes a plan to forego other investment opportunities, an investment will not be prudent if it would be expected to provide a plan with a lower rate of return than available alternative investments with commensurate degrees of risk or is riskier than alternative investments with commensurate rates of return. (U.S. DOL Interpretive Bulletin 94-1 1994)

Thus, a fiduciary may not sacrifice returns to obtain collateral benefits, and proposed investments must be compared with available alternative investments with similar risk and return characteristics.

The prudence rule does not limit fiduciaries to conservative investments. The DOL has stated that the

> relative riskiness of a specific investment . . . does not render such investment either *per se* prudent or *per se* imprudent. . . . Thus, although securities issued by a small or new company may be a riskier investment than securities issued by a "blue chip" company, the investment in the former company may be entirely proper under the Act's "prudence" rule. (44 Fed. Reg. 37, 221 [1976])

The DOL has refused to issue a list of legally permissible investments because "no such list could be complete" (44 Fed. Reg. 37, 221 [1976]). Indeed, the DOL has praised ERISA, because it doesn't specify a legal list of permissible investments: "One of the remarkable things about ERISA as a statute has been its flexibility, because it doesn't prescribe exact investment policies" (U.S. DOL. Hearing on Pension Investments and Economic Growth 1994, 74).

Some opponents of targeted investing have argued that ERISA requires fiduciaries to make investments that will produce the maximum return for the plan with the least amount of risk.[5] Courts have disagreed, however. In *Foltz v. U.S. News & World Report Inc.*, (865 F.2d 364 [D.C. Cir. 1989], *cert. denied*, 490 U.S. 1108 [1989]) a district court ruled that ERISA "section 404 creates no exclusive duty of maximizing pecuniary benefits" (*Foltz v. U.S.*

News & World Report Inc. 1989, 373). In *Anderson v. Mortell,* (722 F. Supp. 462 [N.D. Ill. 1989]) the court observed that a fiduciary has no duty to "achieve the highest possible price" on the sale of securities (*Anderson v. Mortell* 1989, 470). More recently, in *Ershick v. United Missouri Bank,* (12 Employee Benefits Cas. [BNA] 2323 [D. Kan. 1990], *aff'd,* 14 Employee Benefits Cas. [BNA] 1848 [10th Cir. 1991]) the court held that ERISA does not create a duty to maximize pecuniary benefits (12 Employee Benefits Cas. [BNA] 2327). The duty to maximize returns on investment would place an unreasonable and impossible burden on fiduciaries. Return cannot be evaluated in isolation: it depends upon the risks involved. Fiduciaries should optimize returns in comparison to other available investments with similar risk characteristics. They should never sacrifice returns to achieve a collateral objective and the value of the collateral benefit cannot be factored into the rate of return.

Thus, under the prudence rule, it is legally permissible to make ETIs under appropriate circumstances. However, as numerous courts have noted, it is not the success of an investment viewed in hindsight that determines the prudence of the investment.[6] Rather, it is the procedural process by which the investment decision was made that determines its prudence. In *Marshall v. Glass/Metal Association and Glaziers and Glass Workers Pension Plan* (507 F. Supp. 378 [D. Haw. 1980]), the district court for the district of Hawaii held that

> ERISA does not require that a pension plan take no risks with its investments. Virtually every investment entails some degree of risk, and even the most carefully evaluated investments can fail while unpromising investments may succeed. The application of ERISA's prudence standard does not depend upon the ultimate outcome of an investment, but upon the prudence of the fiduciaries under the circumstances prevailing when they make their decision and in light of the alternatives available to them. (*Marshall v. Glass/Metal Association* 1980, 384)

The court held that the fiduciaries failed to satisfy the prudence rule "by committing Plan assets without adequate procedures and evaluation of the risks involved and alternatives available" (*Marshall v. Glass/Metal Association* 1980).[7] Procedural prudence has ten requirements:

1. Refuse to accept below-market rates of returns;
2. Periodically review plan documents to make sure the trustees are acting in accordance with them;
3. Prudently delegate investment duties;

4. Prudently select and monitor experts;
5. Diligently investigate the proposed investment;
6. Diversify investments;
7. Compile a thorough paper trail;
8. Act for the exclusive benefit of plan participants and their beneficiaries;
9. Avoid conflicts of interest; and
10. Avoid transactions with parties in interest.

For a detailed discussion of procedural prudence, see Zanglein, "High-Performance Investing: Harnessing the Power of Pension Funds to Promote Economic Growth and Workplace Integrity" (1995).

DIVERSIFICATION RULE

The third requirement imposed by ERISA Section 404(a)(1) is the duty to diversify plan assets "so as to minimize the risk of large losses, unless under the circumstances it is clearly prudent not to do so."[8] The *diversification rule* requires trustees to reduce exposure to the risk of large losses:

> Diversification of investments is the practice whereby funds are committed to different classes of investments which are characterized by different types of risks. The theory upon which the practice is based is that by allocating funds to different types of investments, the potential losses which might occur in the area due to a particular economic event will be offset by gains in another area. Even if such a loss is not offset, its impact is at least limited to a relatively small portion of the fund.
>
> Conversely, by pursuing a strategy of non-diversification, an investor runs a risk of incurring substantial losses if the particular investment vehicle chosen performs badly, or if one of few large investments chosen performs badly. Under such circumstances a particular negative economic event can devastate the entire plan or a great portion thereof.[9]

ERISA's legislative history provides additional guidance:

> A fiduciary usually should not invest the whole or an unduly large proportion of the trust property in a single security. Ordinarily the fiduciary should not invest the whole or an unduly large proportion of the trust property in one type of security or in various types of securities dependent on the success of one enterprise or upon conditions in one locality, since the effect is to increase the risk of large losses. . . . If he is investing in mortgages on real property he should

not invest a disproportionate amount of the trust in mortgages in a particular district or on a particular class of property so that a decline in property values in that district or of that class might cause a large loss.[10]

Congress "intended that the geographic dispersion be sufficient so that adverse economic conditions peculiar to one area would not significantly affect the economic status of the plan as a whole." Congress indicated that "[b]y spreading asset purchases throughout a number of varying types of securities or investments, a fiduciary may protect to a certain extent against the fortunes of a particular field of business or industry, and thereby minimize the risk of large losses."[11] The Seventh Circuit has adopted modern portfolio theory:

> When investment advisors make decisions they do not view individual investments in isolation. Rather, the goal is to create a diversified portfolio that balances appropriate levels of risk and return for the investor. The risk of a given investment is neutralized somewhat when the investment is combined with others in a diversified portfolio. The risk inherent in the entire portfolio is less than that of certain assets within the portfolio. Ideally, after diversification only market risk remains. Likewise, the return from a portfolio over time should be more stable than that of isolated investments within that portfolio.[12]

The DOL has not established a maximum percentage that can be invested in one geographic area or one type of investment.[13] Diversification depends on the facts and circumstances surrounding each plan and investment.[14] Under certain circumstances, the decision not to diversify might be prudent.[15] In *Donovan v. Mazzola,*[16] the district court for the Northern District of California held that the trustees' general inexperience in real estate loans was not a defense to their imprudent conduct in exposing the pension fund to the large risk of loss resulting from the high concentration of assets in a single type of investment. The loan violated ERISA's diversification rule by subjecting a disproportionate amount (approximately 53 percent) of pension fund assets "in a single investment, subject to a common set of risks associated with a single geographic location, a single product type, and the specific project and property involved."[17]

PLAN DOCUMENT RULE
The final requirement is the *plan document rule*. ERISA Section 404(a)(1)(D) requires fiduciaries to act "in accordance with the documents and instru-

ments governing the plan insofar as such documents and instruments are consistent with the provisions" of ERISA.[18] Plan documents include the plan description, summary plan description, collective bargaining agreement, trust agreement, contract, investment management agreement, investment guidelines, and other instruments under which the plan was established or is operated.

Trustees must frequently review all plan documents to ensure that they do not unintentionally violate any terms. For example, trustees should review their trust agreement, investment management agreement, and investment guidelines before making any investment decisions.[19]

Misconception Number Two:
Economically Targeted Investments Are Too Time Consuming

It is true that direct ETIs are quite time consuming. However, they are often easy to implement. For example, commingled real estate and mortgage accounts are the simplest forms of ETIs for the investor. They provide liquid, diversified investments with certain guaranteed returns (Coyle 1994). Open-end commingled real estate pools are similar to open-end mutual funds. Investors can purchase shares at any time; however, most funds restrict the redemption of shares. Because the capital for redemption is derived from the fund itself, shareholders can redeem their shares if capital is available. If capital is unavailable, the shareholders must wait until enough capital has accumulated (Zanglein 1992b). There are many pooled real estate funds in which a pension fund can invest. Pooled venture capital and private placement accounts are also available to fund investors. These funds provide an easy-to-implement ETI. In contrast, direct real estate investments and private placements are much more time-consuming investments.

Misconception Number Three: Economically Targeted
Investments Are Too Costly

Similarly, direct ETIs suffer from high administrative costs due to their complexity. Some ETIs are based on investments such as mortgages and mortgage-backed securities, which are "standard, insured and salable in the secondary mortgage markets, providing a liquidity not often found in ETIs"

(Zanglein 1992b). These investments entail less administrative expenses and staff time than other types of ETIs (Institute for Fiduciary Education 1993). Additionally, many professionals develop customized mortgage-backed securities programs (Institute for Fiduciary Education 1993).

However, other ETI programs suffer from high administrative costs due to their complexity and the amount of staff time required to develop, implement, and monitor them (Institute for Fiduciary Education 1993). A 1990 report issued by the New York State Industrial Cooperation Council observed that economically targeted investment programs "can be very time consuming and challenging" to establish and administer. Direct investment programs are difficult to manage and consultants often are not easily available. Furthermore, many of these programs are illiquid investments.[20]

Other ETIs, such as pooled funds and linked deposit programs, have very low administrative expenses and are less time consuming. These investments are further explored in chap. 5.

Misconception Number Four: Competent Managers Who Are Willing to Make Economically Targeted Investments Are Not Available

This misconception poses a high hurdle. Certainly, a multitude of expert professionals routinely invest in venture capital and private placements. Their customers, however, are typically sophisticated investors who are not bound by the strict fiduciary requirements of ERISA. A disincentive currently exists for these investment managers to deal with private pension trustees who are unable to make quick investment decisions on complex transactions. Given the choice between a corporate investor and a Taft-Hartley Fund, the investment banker would rather deal with the corporate investor who requires substantially less education and attention, can make rapid decisions, and is subject to less regulation.

I argue later that a national network and database of investment managers can help to address this problem. The AFL-CIO has begun to build just such a network. Richard Trumka, secretary-treasurer of the AFL-CIO, stated, "We want to learn who our trustees are, so we can communicate with them, educate them, and pair them with worker-friendly actuaries, money-managers, lawyers and other professionals" (Industrial Heartland Labor Investment Forum 1996, 10).

Misconception Number Five: It Is Too Difficult to Convince the
Trustees, Their Consultants, and Management Trustees to Make
Economically Targeted Investments

Patrick Cronin, financial manager of the Milwaukee Employee Retirement System, observed that "it would be problematic to find an investment manager who had particular skill investing in ETIs" (P. Levine 1997,
52). This common complaint can only be resolved through education.
Trustees must understand the legal requirements of ERISA and its implications on proposed investment transactions. A solid education allows
trustees to refer uncooperative trustees and advisors to consultants who
are more experienced and knowledgeable with respect to ERISA investment decision making.

Trustees must also be confident enough to demand that an uncooperative trustee or consultant identify the specific obstacle he or she perceives.
The trustee can, in coordination with other knowledgeable consultants,
assist the reluctant trustee in overcoming misplaced fears about ETIs. By
the same token, reluctant trustees should be encouraged to attend educational workshops on the technical aspects of investing in ETIs. More
knowledgeable trustees are better able to fulfill their fiduciary obligations.

Misconception Number Six: Politics Always Gets in the Way

Public pension funds have been criticized for yielding to political pressures to
make unsound investments. A long list of unsuccessful investments made by
public pension funds can easily be chronicled. Although the failure of the
investment is not indicative of the prudence of the investment, losses are routinely publicized by critics.

For example, the Heritage Foundation has compiled a handy list of failed
public fund investments, which it uses as evidence that public funds are susceptible to cronyism and political manipulation (Mitchell 1998). These
high-visibility cases have provided good ammunition to opponents of ETIs.
However, three features distinguish these examples: (a) the investments
were made by public funds whose investments are governed by state law
rather than ERISA's fiduciary duties; (b) the investments are judged solely
by rate of return, a standard rejected by even the DOL—instead, the DOL
measures the prudence of the investment by the thoroughness of the procedural prudence exercised by the trustees at the time the investment decision
was made; and (c) these examples are characteristically risky venture capital

investments, but, when successful, they earn a very high rate of return over a long-term horizon. Such investments are commonly evaluated after 10 years or more.

Misconception Number Seven: There Are No Appropriate Benchmarks by Which to Measure the Performance of Economically Targeted Investments

ETIs are more difficult to evaluate than traditional investments, because there are few established performance benchmarks for these investments. As an example, an equity manager can compare his or her stock returns to the Standard & Poor's (S&P) 500, the Dow Jones Industrial Average, the Wilshire 5000, Russell 2000, and other stock indices. It is more difficult, but not impossible, to develop benchmarks for ETIs.

In its survey of public ETI programs, the Institute for Fiduciary Education compiled a list of benchmarks used by public funds to measure the performance of venture capital funds. Benchmarks used include total return of 20 percent, the S&P 500 Stock Index, a 17-percent annual rate of return on the corporate portfolio, and 5 percent over the S&P Stock Index. Some funds, however, use a benchmark specific to venture capital, such as the rate of return achieved by the fund's external manager for venture capital, venture economics vintage year benchmarks, and venture capital market returns. A 1995 report issued by the General Accounting Office concluded that ETIs maintained by the seven public funds surveyed earned rates of return similar to the selected benchmarks. The General Accounting Office was "cautiously optimistic" about the "ability of public pension plans to earn reasonable financial returns through their ETI programs."

According to a 1998 survey, however, only 2 percent of public funds managers surveyed are concerned about the lack of a suitable benchmark for ETI performance (Reed and Deger), perhaps because the use of benchmarks has become more standardized for ETIs.

Some trustees contend that it is still too difficult to quantify the collateral benefits created by ETIs. This argument is best left unaddressed. Properly designed ETIs are not concessionary. To be prudent, an ETI must be equal or superior to a traditional investment when the risk-adjusted rates of return are compared. Therefore, from a legal perspective, it is unnecessary, and perhaps undesirable, to quantify collateral benefits (U.S. DOL 1992).

Removing Institutional Barriers

Three steps are crucial to the removal of institutional barriers to ETIs. First, trustees and their advisors need to be educated on investment strategies for employee benefit plans. A solid educational program must cover ERISA fundamentals, investment basics, fiduciary duties, and shareholder activism.

Second, trustees must be encouraged to start making ETIs through established pooled programs. These programs offer the advantage of being easily evaluated for prudence and easily administered and monitored. They are also expedient, liquid investments with low transactional costs. These steps counter the ETI misconceptions listed previously.

Third, a national center for ETIs should be developed, staffed, and funded. Regional centers should develop programs and report to the national center, which will maintain a database on ETIs and a network of professionals who are willing to work with trustees on ETIs. The first and third measures are addressed below, whereas the second measure is dealt with more fully in chap. 5.

EDUCATION OF TRUSTEES AND THEIR ADVISORS

Education and control of fund professionals is of paramount importance. According to the conclusions reached by the Industrial Heartland Labor Conference, "Now is the time for workers to stop believing financial professionals who tell them that they face a choice between a job and a pension. Instead, they must identify their own capital resources and demand a voice in how they operate" (Industrial Heartland Labor Investment Forum 1996, 14).

The George Meany Center/National Labor College, in conjunction with the National Coordinating Committee for Multi-Employer Plans and the AFL-CIO's Center for Working Capital, has taken the lead in trustee education. The George Meany Center for Labor Studies offers a four-course certificate program in Investment Strategies and Fiduciary Duties for Employee Benefit Plans.

Robert Georgine, president of the National Coordinating Committee for Multi-Employer Plans and codeveloper of the program, said that the program is designed to "enhance trustees' skills by giving them the background and knowledge necessary to implement an investment program that is in the overall best long-term interest of the participants and beneficiaries they serve. This program can and will flourish into a high-powered educational resource for the stewards of working capital" (Industrial Heartland Labor Investment Forum 1996, 7). Sandra March, a trustee of the New York City Teachers' Retirement System, commented:

Too few funds provide trustees with the education they need to make sure plan assets are managed as well as an owner runs his or her business. Our trustees need to be educated well enough to be able to stand up and pose questions that will knock the socks off any investment manager who is trying to sell a fund some nonsense. The Meany Center program is a step in the right direction. (Industrial Heartland Labor Investment Forum 1996, 14)

The Center for Working Capital has started to serve as a liaison between trustees and consultants. The Center has established four advisory panels: investment consultants, asset managers, legal service providers, and financial advisors (AFL-CIO 1997a). The purpose of the advisory panels is to offer resources for trustee support, create working groups on specific investment issues, participate in annual meetings, and enhance communications between professionals and funds. The panels provide technical assistance on worker-oriented investment approaches. Membership is open to professionals who serve union, Taft-Hartley, and public pension funds that "support the principle that worker savings can and should be invested in ways that promote a sustainable economic future for themselves and their communities" (AFL-CIO 1997a). The panel will "provide a forum for a serious dialogue among [professionals], labor principals, and trustees over the best way of achieving worker investment and economic goals" (AFL-CIO 1997a).

Trustees need more education to (a) gain knowledge and a working vocabulary necessary to communicate with investment managers and other financial advisors and (b) understand capital markets, corporate governance mechanisms, and the prudence required in the investment process, so they can work with professionals to structure solid ETI and shareholder activism programs. Unless trustees can visualize their role in the overall scheme, they will be paving dead-end roads leading off the ETI superhighway.

First, trustees must understand the basic aspects of employee benefit plans, which will affect such investment decisions as the type of plan (e.g., pension or welfare; defined benefit or defined contribution), funding requirements, actuarial factors, the plan's time horizon, hurdle rates, dedicated portfolios, plan objectives, and type of account (i.e., employer directed or participant directed). Each of these aspects influences the investment decision-making process, and trustees must understand these concepts before they can begin to make investment decisions.

Next, trustees must understand the basic financial concepts: type of business entity, equity versus debt financing, capital markets, the effects of inflation, the effect of compounding, types of asset classifications, diversification among and within asset classes, present and historical measures of risk and return, modern portfolio theory, capital asset pricing model (CAPM), and asset allocation. ERISA's prudence regulation adopts a portfolio approach, and trustees must be able to apply such concepts. Trustees must also be able to select performance benchmarks and monitor both investment performance and the performance of their investment professionals. They must possess a basic understanding of different investment styles and be able to evaluate the performance of their investment professionals within those styles. With this knowledge, trustees will have the knowledge and confidence to communicate effectively with investment professionals. They will be able to work competently with these professionals to develop, implement, and enforce an investment policy statement.

Third, trustees must know their fiduciary duties under ERISA so they will not run afoul of these requirements. Trustees must understand the exclusive benefit rule, the prudence rule, diversification, and the plan document rule. Trustees must, in conjunction with their advisors, adopt a policy of procedural prudence. Trustees must learn to recognize parties-in-interest and potential prohibited transactions so they can ensure that plans do not inadvertently enter into prohibited transactions.

Finally, trustees must understand the basics of corporate governance and the fundamental rights of shareholders. They must understand the Security Exchange Commission's shareholder proposal rules so that the fund can successfully launch shareholder proposals. Trustees must also be able to develop proxy voting guidelines. ERISA requires trustees to implement and enforce proxy voting on issues that have an economic impact on plan-held stock. Therefore, before trustees can draft a proxy voting policy, they must be able to identify proxy issues that may have an impact on plan-held stock. They must also be able to monitor corporate performance and coordinate shareholder activism to the extent legally permissible.

Of course, trustees could venture onto the ETI superhighway without the protection of thorough education and training. Because uneducated and misdirected trustees may well venture into imprudent decisions, however, this path may ultimately frustrate the movement for ETIs. If labor is to use its hard-earned capital to influence corporate actions and make job-creating investments, it must be done prudently. Trustee education is one of the only tools that can be used to remove the barriers littered along the high road to investment.

Yet trustee education is only the beginning. The AFL-CIO is working to further investment manager education, another crucial component. Attorneys and consultants also need to be educated. A board of trustees has a much better chance of implementing a high road investment program if labor trustees are educated enough to persuade reluctant management trustees, advisors, consultants, attorneys, and investment managers, that a prudently established, well-monitored ETI program can comply with ERISA's requirements.

NATIONAL CENTER FOR ECONOMICALLY TARGETED INVESTMENTS

The key to establishing and maintaining a comprehensive national ETI program is the creation of a national center for ETIs. The center would provide trustees with a central place from which to find out about existing programs that offer guidance on how to develop similar programs in their region. The center would maintain a database on existing ETIs, solicit investment proposals for national pooled funds, and conduct research on effective ETI programs.

The center must be a place that trustees can call to obtain information on established and new pooled investment programs, examples of prototype plans, and lists of upcoming educational programs on ETIs. The center should act as a liaison between the DOL and funds that plan to establish an ETI program. The center could research proxy issues and assist funds with corporate campaigns. The center might also be a resource for shareholder proposal literature, which would alleviate concerns about the legality and prudence of ETIs and potential prohibited transactions (see Misconception Number One). It should be able to put trustees in contact with other trustees who have developed similar programs. It should maintain a panel of investment managers, financial managers, attorneys, and consultants who are willing to work with funds to develop ETI programs. (This will address Misconception Number Four.)

The center could also play a crucial role in developing new pooled programs, which would allow trustees to diversify their investments in a variety of ETIs. It would be useful for the center to coordinate investments made by regional ETI centers. The national center should negotiate reciprocity agreements between regional centers so that funds can invest in their general geographical region without investing too high a percentage of plan assets in one state or geographic area (see Misconception Number Six).

By coordinating efforts among consultants and funds, the center could alleviate the time constraints involved in many ETIs (see Misconception Number Two) and reduce information costs (see Misconception Number Three). Finally, the center could coordinate educational efforts to educate trustees and their advisors that ETIs can be prudent investments under ERISA (see Misconception Number Five). Educational programs should include the Investment Strategies Program offered through the George Meany Center and capital strategies workshops similar to those currently offered through the Center for Working Capital. These programs allow trustees to meet and work with investment professionals to design new ETI programs and reorient fund professionals to the needs of fund trustees.

Conclusion

Obstacles to ETIs can be overcome by (a) committing resources to trustee/professional education, (b) encouraging trustees to support established ETI programs, and (c) creating a national center for ETIs that would work with regional centers and investment professionals to develop and promote new ETI programs and maintain a database of ETIs.

[IX]

CHALLENGING WALL STREET'S CONVENTIONAL WISDOM: DEFINING A WORKER-OWNER VIEW OF VALUE

Damon Silvers, William Patterson, and J. W. Mason

This final chapter presents the next steps for worker capital by extrapolating from the research presented in the previous chapters. This agenda seeks to organize assets, develop regulatory and legal reforms, and focus the power that flows from those activities to advance a worker-owner view of value in the allocation of capital by firms and markets. We begin by summarizing the perspective on the purposes and governance of the corporation that worker-owners bring to the larger debate on the role of firms and capital markets.

The primary mission of workers' capital is to fund benefits for workers—retirement security, health care, and other vital services (Zanglein 1992b). The fiduciaries of workers' capital have legal duties to manage these funds in the long-term best interest of plan participants. The primary component of that duty is to ensure the best long-term, risk-adjusted rate of return for the plan's assets. The worker-owner view of value articulates this mission by considering the perspective of working families. Such a perspective questions much of the conventional wisdom about both capital markets and the corporation. The preceding chapters have presented a variety of theoretical and empirical work that explains the foundations and implications of the worker-owner view of value.

Worker-owners view the corporation as the cooperation over time of its different constituencies. This cooperation must be based on mutual benefit, respect, and accountability if any of the constituents are to prosper. Worker-owners view capital markets as imperfect. They imperfectly convey information and they imperfectly allocate capital. The worker-owner view stresses that the active involvement of workers and their organizations in the operations of capital markets can reduce the extent of some of these imperfections.

Worker-Owner View of Value

WORKER-OWNER VIEW OF THE CAPITAL MARKETS

The efficient capital markets hypothesis has enjoyed great popularity since it was formulated in the early 1970s (Fama 1970). The hypothesis in its most popular version—the semi-strong form—asserts that the prices of publicly traded securities rationally reflect all publicly available information about the securities (Fama 1970). This hypothesis has a number of quite serious implications, among them (a) that no money manager can legally and systematically outperform the equity markets as a whole, (b) that there is no way to distinguish between short-term and long-term investment strategies, and thus (c) that the immediate market response to an event affecting a company embodies all one can know about the long-term consequences of that event for that company and its investors.

More broadly, efficient market theory predicts that we live in a world of rational investors. Such investors operating in the equity markets should, through the process of maximizing marginal returns, direct capital to its most productive use. Thus, an investment intended to create or retain jobs, for example, is presumed to result only in allocating labor to less-productive uses, lowering returns on the investment, leaving society as a whole worse off, and ultimately, perversely reducing society's overall ability to provide jobs (Zelinsk 1997).

There are good reasons, however, to reject that view of the capital markets. Because information is costly, and because markets are composed of human beings, market operations may systematically "mis-price" certain types of uses. They also may be prey to various irrationalities and thus may fail to direct capital to optimal uses, whether viewed from the perspective of an investor or from that of the society as a whole (Fortune 1991; Grossman and Stiglitz 1980).

To the extent that capital stewardship allows worker representatives to overcome information and agency problems in the capital markets, it may be possible for worker-capital to achieve superior risk-adjusted returns compared with other investments or to produce collateral benefits, such as job creation, without sacrificing returns. In the long run, as the perspective of worker-owners becomes generalized, it may improve the performance of the capital markets as a whole.

In chap. 2, Dean Baker and Archon Fung summarize several critiques of capital market perfection that are central to the worker-owner view of value:

- The relative cheapness and ready availability of information about a firm's short-term profitability and movements of stock price compared to factors affecting a firm's long-term prospects may induce myopia.
- Markets are susceptible to sharp swings from investor sentiment, particularly around issues of risk. Firms, industries, and entire countries can very quickly move in and out of favor.
- Fees, commissions, and other transaction costs may create agency problems for investment managers who may choose to invest in transactions, pursue invest-ment strategies, or focus on entire asset categories that do not enhance returns to the fund but do produce income for the managers.
- The socio-economic circumstances common among investment professionals may leave them subject to biases that make them more attentive to certain sources of value, risks, or costs than to others. For instance, they may overesti-mate the risk of investments in poor or minority communities or unionized companies and underestimate the value of investments in human capital or the opportunities provided by underserved markets.

Each of these critiques applies with additional force to private markets, in which information is much more difficult and costly to obtain and in which there are far greater transaction costs for exit. In private markets, investors must also incur costs of active monitoring to safeguard their investments. These limitations lie at the heart of the problem of capital market gaps. Cap-ital market gaps create significant opportunities for specialized vehicles to overcome the biases and the information, transaction, and monitoring costs that deter other investors.

The preceding studies offer persuasive empirical support for this view. In chap. 8, Jayne Elizabeth Zanglein's review of the institutional obstacles to pension fund investment in economically targeted investments illustrates the actual legal, political, and administrative processes that structure the behavior of important capital market participants. These obstacles have a particularly ironic quality when juxtaposed against the impressive performance of labor-friendly investment vehicles documented by Michael Calabrese in chap. 5.

Calabrese's study accepts the ground rules that return to investors is the proper measure of a project's social utility, as it must be in light of the rules governing the investment decisions of U.S. pension funds. Yet, in a review of Canadian labor-sponsored investment funds in chap. 6, Tessa Hebb and David Mackenzie suggest steps that could be taken by state governments to act on the view that making investment decisions purely a function of return to investors does not always lead to socially optimal results (i.e., socially optimal results can be achieved by providing some firms, industries, and regions subsidized seed capital).

Although the data and experiences recounted in this book by Zanglein, Calabrese, Hebb, and Mackenzie flow largely from the view of capital markets expressed in this chapter, they are incompatible with conventional wisdom that says that capital markets process information with complete efficiency and always yield socially optimal results.

WORKER-OWNER VIEW OF THE FIRM

The worker-owner view of value focuses on firms' long-term capacity to create value and contends that the key to that capacity lies in the relationships between various constituencies—shareholders, lenders, workers, suppliers, customers, government, and the broader community. It sees the firm as a cooperative enterprise, bound together by ties of mutuality that, although shaped in crucial ways by explicit contracts, cannot be entirely captured by their terms (Blair 1995).

Many of the characteristics that create value for a company and its investors are not captured in current accounting and financial reporting standards. Among the most important of these is human capital, which is not counted as an asset at all. Human capital includes not only formal education and training but also more intangible qualities. Much of it is collective and specific to a given firm: workers tend to acquire it only in exchange for a commitment, explicit or more often implicit, that their tenure with the firm will be long enough to make the investment worthwhile (Blair 1995; Shleifer and Summers 1988).

Every successful firm has a core competence that is not captured by the assets on its books, which is why all but the worst performers trade at multiples of their book value. Investors presumably recognize that the investments employees make in individual skills and a collective structure of cooperation increase the value of the firm overall. Much of the talk in corporate America of firm "culture" or "core competence" and the emphasis in business schools on leadership and team building are a way of describing this phenomenon.

Institutions ranging from chartered accounting firms to the Brookings Institution and the Organization for Economic Cooperation and Development are documenting the contribution human capital makes to value creation within the firm and measuring firm investments in its employees. The apparent lack of connection in equity markets between accounting measures of past performance and stock price has fed growing interest in the future-oriented intangibles of firm value (Low 1999).

The strategy of using implicit contracts to encourage a company's workers and other stake-holders to develop firm-specific human capital is sometimes called a *high-road approach*, especially when the strategy hinges, as it usually does, on competition from innovation and quality. However, such firms run a constant risk that one or another of its constituents will see an opportunity to exploit the irreversibility of firm-specific commitments, whether by workers, suppliers, customers, or communities. The shakedown of communities for tax breaks is an important example of this dynamic, as is the tendency of firms of all sizes to cut legal and regulatory corners in pursuit of short-term gains.

To the extent that contracts have legal status, as is the case with collective bargaining agreements or most supplier and customer relationships, their forms incompletely reflect this economic and social content. The corporate constituent pursuing a short-term, exploitative strategy takes advantage of asymmetries of power and information to transfer value to shareholders from other company stake-holders. Such a strategy can, at best, produce brief excess returns for one party at the expense of others.

COMBINING MARKET AND FIRM ANALYSIS

The dangers of exploitative behavior within the firm are exacerbated, as Baker and Fung show, by the nature of the information readily available to shareholders. As the recent history of downsizing shows, capital markets can assimilate some kinds of information more readily than others.[1] It is much easier to calculate the immediate cost savings from a fixed number of layoffs than it is to understand how the functions those employees performed will be carried out, and at what cost. Thus, the short-term signals sent by the capital markets may encourage corporate managers to seek short-term gains for shareholders by exploiting other corporate constituents.

IMPLICATIONS FOR WORKER CAPITAL

If the implications of efficient market theory generally encourage passivity, the worker-owner view of firms and markets is oriented toward action. In light of the tendency of capital markets and firms, combined, to undermine the sources of long-term value, long-term investors can actively shape the governance of the companies in which they invest.[2] Sometimes the challenge is to protect management that, in fact, is committed to sound long-term corporate strategy from the short-term tendencies within the capital markets (Brown 1995). Increasingly, however, worker capital faces the task of holding managers accountable for strategies that encourage value stripping and zero-sum approaches either by investors or, sometimes, by the managers themselves.

Thus, worker-owner activism can appear to have paradoxical qualities. Efforts to ensure managerial accountability to shareholders may appear to favor shareholder dominance but simultaneously aim to challenge management that is pursuing its own narrow self-interest at the expense of the firm's other constituents. On the other hand, efforts to encourage regulatory compliance or collaborative labor relations, which obviously benefit the target firm's employees or the communities in which it is located, typically are motivated by a sense that the firm, and thus its shareholders, would benefit from restored cooperation.

In chap. 4, Marleen O'Connor's survey of labor shareholder activism demonstrates how worker funds have pursued a variety of active ownership agendas in the 1990s. Some of the commentators on that activism whose work she cites, however, look at this activity with an eye toward distinguishing between advocacy on behalf of workers and advocacy on behalf of shareholders. This misses the core of the worker-owner perspective, which views workers and shareholders as sharing a common interest in maintaining a company's focus on long-term value creation through partnerships among corporate constituencies.

For institutional investors with a long-term perspective, *active ownership* necessarily involves tactics other than the "Wall Street Walk" of selling shares. That term embraces the whole continuum of shareholder interventions, ranging from simply selling the stock to acquiring control of a company. Acquiring information about a company's investments, core competencies, and long-run prospects is costly; a shareholder who expects to hold the stock for only a short time has little incentive to acquire such information. Hence, funds with a significant portion of indexed money were among the pioneers of shareholder activism.[3] In addition, the benefits from such interventions are enjoyed by all shareholders, creating a tendency for some to freely ride on the interventions of others. One solution to this collective action problem is leadership from bodies such as national unions, the American Federation of Labor-Congress of Industrial Organizations (AFL-CIO), and the Council of Institutional Investors.

Collateral Benefits, Capital Gaps, and Private Market Investing

The preceding analysis has examined public companies as vehicles for the long-term allocation and management of capital. However, much of this volume has rightly focused on issues in private markets, in which investment decisions have clear and immediate impacts.

Of course, everything in the previous analysis of the imperfections of public capital markets applies in manifold to the private market. These defects suggest that there are opportunities to obtain adequate, if not superior, returns from investing in private companies in capital-starved industry sectors and regions of the country.

Labor-affiliated private capital vehicles may benefit from connection with the labor movement through the recognition of certain kinds of potential value. Many labor-affiliated and labor-oriented real estate funds, for example, invest in projects constructed with 100-percent union labor. Although some institutional investors believe that such a stipulation depresses returns, in chap. 5 Calabrese shows that it may yield long-term cost savings from higher-quality construction and maintenance of the properties.

A second consideration of direct investments is the possibility of collateral benefits. If the collateral benefits sought are socially desirable outcomes that the capital markets do not normally promote, seeking them out may help to identify capital market gaps. To the extent that capital markets show a bias against union employers, for instance, a desire to promote the right of workers to organize as a collateral benefit may help funds identify companies that have been excluded from the capital markets despite their potential to offer good returns. Similarly, a desire to promote investment—affordable housing, for example—in a sector of the economy that has historically been deprived of capital may help to identify undiscovered opportunities for profitable investments in that sector.

In other words, collateral benefits can be more than an afterthought to competitive returns. Although collateral benefits can supercede such returns, seeking them out may lead to higher conventional returns. Viewed from another angle, collateral benefits may not be so collateral: they may be inextricably intertwined with the characteristics of successful private capital investments.

Collateral benefits and capital market gaps reinforce each other in a second way: without the latter, the former are likely to be illusory. Investments in areas already well served by the capital markets are likely to be less effective in job creation and community revitalization. As Zanglein notes, depending on product market conditions, incremental investment in the absence of capital constraints may produce little in the way of additional economic activity.

The view of firms and markets presented in the preceding chapters lies at the heart of the worker-owner view of value as it has been developed within the labor movement since 1980. That view has developed in the context of increasingly powerful and global capital markets matched by growing aggressiveness and sophistication among worker-owners and their funds. Worker capital now is on the verge of asserting power within firms and markets. Whether it achieves that potential depends on worker-owners' ability to meet certain challenges: organizing themselves, improving the regulatory climate, finding their own voice in the world of institutional investors, and, ultimately, taking more control of investment decisions.

Worker–Owner View of Value in Action

DEFINING AN AGENDA FOR WORKER CAPITAL: A HISTORICAL PERSPECTIVE

The labor movement has sought for more than 20 years to organize working families' financial assets. Starting in the 1970s, with *The North Will Rise Again* by Jeremy Rifkin and Randy Barber (1978), labor intellectuals urged workers and their unions to take control of their financial assets. Initially, efforts to put these ideas into practice took widely varied forms. There were efforts to promote union-friendly worker ownership; to obtain union representation on company boards, most significantly at Chrysler; and to reform corporations' business practices through proxy voting, most prominently in relation to investing in South Africa (Blasi 1988; McKersie 1999). This was also the period in which worker-friendly investing developed in earnest in the real estate arena.

In the 1980s, this activity was completely overshadowed by the emergence of extremely dynamic U.S. markets for corporate control, fueled by the boom in junk bond financing and the growth of large institutional investors (Brealey and Myers 1991; Burrough and Helyar 1991; Bruck 1998). In contrast to Germany and Japan, where the presence of a few large institutions as the major shareholders of public companies has helped to constrain the markets for corporate control, the emergence of large pension funds in the United States, and particularly public employee pension funds, seems to have been an important ingredient in the 1980s takeover market (Roe 1994; Roe 1990).

Workers and their unions were generally critical of the role of pension funds in corporate takeovers, particularly in leveraged transactions that led to large job losses and harmed local and regional economies. Many unions supported state antitakeover statutes aimed at giving corporate management wide latitude in opposing takeover attempts (Orts 1992; Anjier 1991). However, two other responses grew in importance as the 1980s drew to a close. First, Taft-Hartley pension fund managers and individual worker-owners began to realize that they shared an agenda with the public pension fund community on issues of corporate governance and managerial accountability.[4] At the same time, several unions began to look at transactions that combined employee ownership with debt financing to rescue troubled employers or remove hostile management. These transactions were particularly important in the steel and airline industries, although they also occurred in apparel and textile manufacturing and the food industry (Blasi and Kruse 1991).

By the early 1990s, the labor movement and its affiliated pension funds played a substantial and growing role in the corporate governance movement, a movement that was being hailed by scholars and corporations as a constructive alternative to the instability of the 1980s.[5] Unions, pension funds, and individual members had become increasingly sophisticated and had developed networks of experts and allies within the capital markets. Large national unions — the United Brotherhood of Carpenters, the United Steelworkers of America, the Union of Needleworkers, Industrial, and Textile Workers (UNITE), the International Brotherhood of Electrical Workers, Plumbers, the International Brotherhood of Teamsters, Hotel Workers, United Food and Commercial Workers, International Association of Machinists and Aerospace Workers, and the Service Employees International Union — had developed sophisticated programs with various degrees of pension fund activism in public companies, worker-ownership initiatives, and investments in worker-friendly economically targeted investments (Georgeson Shareholder Communications 1999).

Labor Shareholder Action Today

In 1997, the AFL-CIO launched its Capital Stewardship Program as an effort to assist and build on the programs at the national union level. Since 1996, the labor movement has sought to organize and activate worker capital in support of the view of value described previously. This activity has taken place in three areas: active ownership; the development of investment products; and interventions in transactional settings such as mergers, acquisitions, and public offerings. This third category of activity has often combined investment activity and active ownership with litigation and legislative, regulatory, and media initiatives.

In the investment area, there has been a dramatic expansion of worker-oriented investment vehicles and investment practices. In 1999 and 2000, the AFL-CIO identified more than fifty of the investment products being marketed to worker pension funds as providing a worker-friendly perspective across asset allocation categories. The list includes such funds as the Multi-Employer Property Trust, the Union Labor Life Insurance Company's J for Jobs real estate fund, and its Separate Account P private capital fund, Heartland funds, and Keilin and Company's KPS Special Situations Fund. On the public equity side are the Amalgamated Bank's LongView Fund and the International Brotherhood of Electrical Worker's National Index Fund, and actively managed equity products include Massachusetts Financial Services' Union Standard Trust. Calabrese reviews many of these vehicles in chap. 5.

In the area of active ownership, union-affiliated funds have become the leading proponents of shareholder proposals in U.S. markets and the leading sponsors of winning proposals (Schwab and Thomas 1998). The late 1990s have seen labor funds, like other institutional investors, turning to more aggressive and innovative strategies for making their voices heard. Such strategies, discussed in the section Next Steps for Worker Capital, include binding by-law proposals, the use of the consent process to present proposals outside of the annual meeting, and the sponsorship of independent-director candidates at companies such as Kmart and Columbia-Health Corporation of America (HCA).

The potential of this activity was demonstrated in 1998 and 1999 by the Hotel Workers and the Teamsters (Rehfeld 1998; Binkley 1998). In the 1998 proxy season, the Hotel Workers led the shareholders of the Marriott Corporation in rejecting a proposed restructuring of the company that would have left the Marriott family in control in perpetuity through a dual-class voting structure. Despite holding a token thirty-five shares themselves, the Hotel Workers gained the support of key proxy advisory services and large institutional shareholders. Initially, Marriott had tied the dual-class voting structure to a broader restructuring proposal that was clearly advantageous to shareholders. Under pressure from institutions, analysts, and the financial press, Marriott separated the two proposals. In the ensuing proxy fight, the Hotel Workers obtained the support of the vast majority of institutional investors and a significant portion of individual shareholders, many of whom had long-standing ties to the Marriott Corporation and the Marriott family. The proposal was defeated by a 53-percent vote (Rehfeld 1998).

This campaign was followed by a campaign at Santa Fe Gaming in the spring of 1999. A coalition of Hotel Workers with preferred shareholders launched a successful effort to elect dissident directors jointly by the Hotel Workers and the largest holder of preferred shares in Santa Fe Gaming. It was the first successful effort by a union to elect directors over the opposition of management at a public company (*Las Vegas Sun* 1999).

In the summer of 1998, the International Brotherhood of Teamsters waged a very different campaign that targeted the initial public offering of Overnite Freight. Union Pacific, Overnite's parent, needed cash to fund the escalating costs of integrating its railroad acquisitions and sought to sell Overnite to the public (Rockel 1998). Meanwhile, the Teamsters had organized many of Overnite's largest and most strategic facilities and were without contracts at all of them (Securities and Exchange Commission [SEC] 1998a). The Teamsters organized a counter–road show, visiting the same initial public offering market participants as the company, to inform them about labor relations at Overnite and the wave of unfair labor practice strikes (*Business Week* 1998b). In the face of this activity and the worsening conditions in the initial public offering market, Union Pacific withdrew the offering in August 1998 (Watson 1998).

On a different front, the Carpenters union has led an effort by several Ohio building trades pension funds to develop relationships with the Ohio companies in which they invest (Monk 1999). This program seeks to combine worker-owners' commitment to managerial accountability with the funds' commitment to the Ohio economy. The trades' funds are seeking to open a dialogue with the interlocking boards of leading Ohio companies. They seek terms on which their funds can support Ohio companies' efforts to build regional prosperity. In essence, they challenge the business leaders of their communities to make a long-term commitment to their communities in exchange for patient capital (Durkin 1999).

During the fall of 1999, the Carpenters and several other building trade unions and their affiliated pension funds broadened this effort to include a number of industrial, retail, and financial services companies. Their agenda combined proposals that challenged executive pay and sought greater access to the proxy for institutional investors with proposals that sought to insulate management from short-term capital market pressures.

Worker capital has shown that it can operate with sophistication and success in the capital markets, particularly through corporate governance initiatives and efforts to set the agenda for public debate, such as the AFL-CIO's Executive Paywatch Web site (*Wall Street Journal Reports* 1999). Labor has also shown that it can defend worker-owners' rights against managerial counterattacks. The most important such recent counterattack was the failed effort by the business community to change the SEC's rules governing shareholder proposals to exclude proposals sponsored by workers and their benefit funds.

Yet, as significant as these accomplishments are, labor's capital has not yet approached its potential power as an advocate for the worker-owner's view of value. Several reasons explain this limited success.

First, worker assets remain underorganized. Despite the efforts of national unions, the AFL-CIO, and other groups, labor pension fund trustees do not have sufficient and timely access to information. They lack information about either time-sensitive issues in the companies in which they invest or the broader debate on the sources of long-term value creation for beneficiaries.

Second, the larger disclosure and financial accounting system, which in many ways has been one of the great regulatory successes of modern U.S. history, nonetheless fails to provide the kinds of information worker-owners and their representatives need to assess the business strategies of corporations. An interesting example of this problem is the accounting treatment of investments in employee training and development. Currently, these expenditures are booked as expenses under the Financial Accounting Standards Board rules. This stands in contrast to investments in fixed assets or software, which in many circumstances are capitalized and depreciated over time. It is especially ironic that goodwill generated by acquisitions is capitalized, whereas the actual investments in human capital are treated as an expense.

Third, labor funds have yet to speak with a distinct voice in the corporate governance arena. Worker-owners have built up influence in corporate boardrooms and annual meetings by collaborating with other investors on basic issues of investor rights—questions such as confidential voting at annual meetings or the annual election of all directors. Although these issues are important, they merely create mechanisms of managerial accountability. They do not infuse those mechanisms with content. Worker-owners need to develop content-driven initiatives while retaining the support of other large shareholders and resisting the temptation to micromanage companies.

Next Steps for Worker Capital

TRUSTEE AND BENEFICIARY EDUCATION

Worker-owners and their representatives cannot be effective advocates for their own views unless the labor movement as a whole elaborates a version of the worker-owner perspective that engages debates around business-oriented corporate governance and corporate finance and challenges its underlying assumptions. The chapters in this book contribute to that project, but they are necessarily only a beginning. Worker-owners need empirical data, critical analysis, and accessible curriculum materials that communicate the important work of scholars in economics, finance, and law to trustees and beneficiaries.

The worker trustee who understands how executive stock option grants dilute his or her pension funds' investment in a given company, and who can put a price tag on that dilution using Black-Scholes, is in a far better position to argue that his or her fund should sponsor a shareholder proposal or act as lead plaintiff in litigation seeking to rein in excessive pay. Similarly, the trustee who understands both the uses and the limits of efficient market theory will be far better able to argue for active ownership against active money managers who suggest that large pension funds should express their displeasure by selling stock.

At the most basic level, there are still serious misconceptions about the implications of the Employment Retirement Income Security Act's implications for proxy voting and other forms of active ownership, economically targeted investments, and the pursuit of collateral benefits for beneficiaries as a secondary objective.

All of the institutions involved in trustee training are working together to address these concerns. These include both institutions committed to the worker-owner perspective and more broadly focused groups, such as the International Foundation of Employee Benefit Plans and the Council of Institutional Investors.

The Center for Working Capital, a nonprofit organization sponsored by the AFL-CIO, seeks to make its mark in the area of the worker-owner perspective. The center sponsors research projects that investigate and measure the long-term outcomes associated with varying corporate strategies and approaches to corporate governance. The center also holds conferences and forums that bring together fund trustees, managers, consultants, and lawyers in discussions about broader theoretical issues as well as topical initiatives in both active ownership and investment management. At the close of 1999, the center received a grant from the Ford Foundation to pursue this agenda globally. This commitment is reflected by the presence on the center's board of Ebrahim Patel of the Congress of South African Trade Unions; Mavis Robertson, the executive chair of the Conference on Major Superannuation Funds; and Anne Simpson, a founder of the London-based pension advisory firm Pension Investment Research Consultants (PIRC) and now senior private sector development specialist with the World Bank Group.

FUND GOVERNANCE

As Teresa Ghilarducci points out in chap. 7, the scope of workers' assets is by no means matched by the scope of workers' voice in managing those assets. The vast majority of private pension plan assets are in either single-employer defined-benefit plans, in which control rests in trustees appointed by the employer, or in defined-contribution plans, in which control of the assets rests in the hands of mutual fund managers, despite the rhetoric of choice.

The governance of single-employer funds has its roots in philosophical approaches toward benefit provisions that differ between the industrial and the craft unions, in part because employment patterns differ between service and construction sector jobs and industrial jobs (Rifkin and Barber 1978). Increasingly, however, unions that have negotiated single-employer pension plans are trying to increase worker voice in their management through collective bargaining. The AFL-CIO has established an interunion working group on collective bargaining initiatives for pension plans to assist these efforts (AFL–CIO 1999a).

However, these efforts do not address pension governance for the nonunion workforce or 401(k) participants. In contrast to funded pension systems in other industrialized countries, the U.S. legal system is noteworthy in that it requires no participant involvement in plan governance (U.S. Department of Social Security 1999). This problem requires a uniform legislative solution. In the interim, there are incremental steps that can be taken by the regulatory authorities. The Department of Labor should consider ways of encouraging plan sponsors to provide mechanisms for participant involvement in governance. The 1999 effort by the SEC to make mutual fund governance more transparent illustrates the potential for regulatory initiatives to enhance the quality of fund governance (SEC 1999).

INVESTMENT PROFESSIONAL RELATIONS

The experts—fund attorneys, fund consultants, or the actual investment managers—who advise benefit funds on investment matters exercise great power. This power is enhanced by the prudent expert rule in Employment Retirement Income Security Act jurisprudence (*Donovan v. Bierwirth,* 680 F.2d 263 [2d Cir. 1982], *cert. denied,* 459 U.S. 1069 [1982]). That rule places the burden on a plan's fiduciaries of exercising the care and judgment not of a prudent person of affairs (as in the rule governing the obligations of a corporate director), but the judgment of an expert.[6]

Pension fund money managers have a variety of reasons for being reluctant to support active ownership initiatives by pension fund clients. In comparison with being an arbitrageur or a trial lawyer, investment management is not a conflict-driven profession. Investment managers may manage large sums for corporate pension funds that are under the control of corporate managers who do not want to encourage shareholder activism.[7] The individuals who control the particular money management firm may not support a worker-owner perspective. Finally, investment managers may believe that such activity lies beyond their expertise.

The AFL–CIO has been attempting to align fund professionals more closely with beneficiary interests. Two examples of this effort have included the AFL–CIO's Key Votes Survey of 1998–2000 and the AFL–CIO's Investment Product Review. The Key Votes Initiative surveys investment managers, tracking how they vote plan proxies on a variety of proposals that represent a worker-owner view of value. The survey is intended to help trustees fulfill their fiduciary duty to monitor how managers vote their proxies.

The Investment Product Review brought together pension trustees, union leaders, and staff from nineteen unions in an unprecedented project to review the reality of the promises of collateral benefits made by investment products that were being marketed as worker friendly. The review committee drafted criteria for evaluating products in four categories—public equity, private capital, real estate, and international investments—and graded the products with a narrative evaluation and a rank of *excellent, good, satisfactory,* or *poor.*

These efforts have revealed how far we have to go. For example, the 1998 Key Votes Survey revealed that major managers of union fund assets had voted against proposals supporting the worker-owner view of value more often than they had voted for such proposals; these managers included significant Taft-Hartley managers, such as JP Morgan. These initiatives aim not merely to prevent managers from voting against their clients but to encourage them to develop investment products that meet worker-owners' needs, whether for appropriate asset class diversification, active ownership, or collateral benefits such as job creation.

GOING GLOBAL: ORGANIZING WORKER CAPITAL

Capital markets draw on savings and invest them in companies and projects without regard for borders. On the other hand, companies that appear to be domestic, such as General Electric or Citigroup, are in fact global institutions in their operations and their investor base (Reich 1991).

At the same time, worker assets globally are growing. Although the United States continues to dominate the list overall, the top three hundred pension funds globally are based in eighteen countries, and the largest is in the Netherlands (Kelly 1999). There is a need for a global dialogue among workers, unions, and funds about the role of worker capital in global markets. The role that the Heartland Forum has played in educating U.S. unions about Canadian private capital initiatives is a noteworthy example of the potential of this dialogue.

This dialogue is particularly urgent as a defense against attacks on worker retirement security and workers' role in corporate governance globally. Just as Social Security has been under attack in the United States, similar systems of social retirement provision are besieged in other countries. At the same time, some U.S. institutional investors and financial institutions seek to impose the U.S. model of corporate governance on countries around the world whose systems differ (Tagliabue 2000). Some efforts appear to be aimed specifically against systems of worker involvement in corporate governance, such as the German codetermination system.[8]

The challenge for worker capital is to construct a global dialogue that promotes workers' view of value and worker interests without inadvertently contributing to either attacks on social retirement provision or on partnership-based corporate governance systems. As a first step in that direction, a meeting of labor movement leaders from nineteen countries with existing privately funded pension systems was held in November 1999 in Stockholm. The result was agreement on an action agenda focused on a continuing effort to map worker assets, improve worker trustee education, and conduct cross-border shareholder initiatives. After that meeting, the International Confederation of Free Trade Unions established a permanent committee on pension investment issues.

Even as the Stockholm meeting adjourned, worker capital became involved in the largest hostile takeover ever attempted, the hostile bid by Britain's Vodafone PLC for the German conglomerate Mannessmann AG. The bid, opposed by Mannessmann's employees; their Works Council; their representatives on Mannessmann's supervisory board; and their union, IG Metall, also met with skepticism from worker capital in the United States (Atkins and Simonian 1999). AFL–CIO President John Sweeney issued a statement opposing the bid, and the AFL–CIO's Office of Investment issued a lengthy critique of the proposed deal and met with a number of large U.S. institutional holders to discuss the issues presented by Vodafone's bid. At the time of this writing, the situation remains unresolved, but press reports indicate that a number of large U.S. shareholders remain skeptical of Vodafone's bid.

IMPROVING THE LARGER WORLD: ACCOUNTING, DISCLOSURE, AND SECURITIES REGULATION

Much of the challenge of organizing worker assets behind a worker view of value stems from deficiencies in information available to worker-owners. For worker-owners to understand and evaluate the strategies pursued by the companies in which they invest, they need better information in accounting statements and in the broader disclosure required of public companies under the Securities Exchange Act.

The Organization for Economic Cooperation and Development has sponsored an initiative on the accounting and disclosure treatment of investments in intangible assets, foremost among which is human capital (Organization for Economic Cooperation and Development 1999). Although still in its initial stages, this measure has already met resistance from the corporate community and the accounting profession. Nevertheless, it constitutes an important first step toward correcting the biases of our accounting and disclosure system against investments in workers and communities.

The recent fights over accounting and disclosure of executive compensation show the extent of this problem. Despite an overwhelming consensus among corporate finance scholars that stock options granted to executives are a corporate expense whose value can be reasonably approximated using the

Black-Scholes option-pricing method, there continues to be neither mandatory disclosure of the Black-Scholes values of options nor any recognition of these awards as expenses in company financial statements. Compounding the problem, the New York Stock Exchange has sought to weaken its prohibition on the adoption of executive stock option plans without a shareholder vote.

More ambitiously, a 1999 article in the Harvard Law Review (Williams 1999) suggests major revisions that the SEC could make in its disclosure system. These changes would facilitate a more complete understanding by investors and the general public of companies' business practices and their effect on the partnerships that make up the corporation and on the corporation's prospects for long-term success.

Yet the need for regulatory reform does not stop with disclosure. Worker-owners' ability to change company behavior depends greatly on what legal and regulatory limits are placed on managerial power. As just noted, the business community is seeking to remove such limits on boards' power to award stock options to management. In other arenas, however, unions are moving to challenge management's dominance of corporate governance. One such effort, discussed by O'Connor in chap. 4, has been to establish shareholders' right to propose binding bylaw amendments affecting company antitakeover devices.

A regulatory initiative with broader implications arose in the context of the changes made to Rule 14a-8 by the SEC in 1998. In the draft regulation, the SEC proposed that the prohibition on shareholder proposals addressing ordinary business issues, which has historically been interpreted to exclude most employment-related proposals, could be overridden if 3 percent of a company's shareholders supported the proposal's inclusion in the meeting agenda (SEC 1997). This provision was dropped from the final rule in the face of strong opposition from some elements of the business community. However, the AFL-CIO has continued to raise it as an important initiative to which the SEC should return.

GETTING THE CONTENT RIGHT: MOVING WORKER CAPITAL'S SUBSTANTIVE AGENDA

Organizing worker capital and reforming the regulatory climate create an environment in which worker-owners can make changes in the way their money is invested and in the way the companies in which they invest behave. Yet that does not resolve what the content of those changes should be.

Workers as owners see businesses as long-term partnerships, and are skeptical of the capital markets' short-term ability to assess corporate strategies. Worker funds, however, are also skeptical of managers and want them held accountable to investors and to other corporate constituencies. This aspect of the worker-owner agenda has been highly successful, because it has been shared increasingly with a wide variety of other investors, and, to a limited extent, it has been embraced by the business press and corporate finance academics. Yet the fundamental worker view of the corporation and the market is by no means a consensus held among U.S. investors, although it enjoys considerable appeal in Europe.[9]

Thus, the great programmatic challenge is to develop initiatives that forward the worker-owner view of value and to organize support for them beyond the Taft-Hartley community. Several recent initiatives indicate promising directions.

In 1997, the California Public Employees' Retirement System (CalPERS) adopted a responsible contractor policy for its real estate investment portfolio. This policy required that contractors providing construction and maintenance services to properties in which CalPERS invests respect labor rights and provide reasonable wages and benefits to their employees. The adoption of this policy followed a study conducted in the Miami area that suggested that the value of commercial property was negatively affected by the use of maintenance contractors who paid substandard wages and provided no benefits. Since then, a number of other public pension funds and real estate investment managers have adopted similar policies.[10]

On the shareholder initiative side, the General Electric (GE) Coordinated Bargaining Committee (1999) submitted a shareholder proposal to GE that asked the company to adopt the International Labor Organization's (1998) core standards as corporate policy globally. These standards bar child and forced labor and protect workers' right to organize. At the annual shareholders' meeting of GE, the proposal was moved by a Malaysian trade unionist, who spoke of the repression of GE workers in Malaysia and who received a standing ovation (Bohner 1999). Although the proposal received only 7 percent of the vote, that percentage represented more than $20 billion in GE stock and included the votes of leading institutional investors, such as CalPERS and the New York State Common Fund, investors more commonly associated with procedural initiatives. GE worker-owners are resubmitting the proposal to the 2000 annual meeting.

Also during 1999, the Steelworkers worked in coalition with public pension funds and foundation endowments to nominate former Senator Howard Metzenbaum and former White House Counsel and D.C. Circuit Court Judge Abner Mikva as independent directors for the board of Maxxam. Maxxam is an energy company with serious problems in corporate governance, labor rights, environmental issues, and indigenous peoples' rights, both in the United States and in South America. The two candidates received 24 percent of the vote. This is an impressive figure, given that Maxxam Chief Executive Officer Charles Hurwitz controlled the majority of the company's stock. This initiative shows that coalitions can campaign with both procedural and substantive platforms.

These initiatives suggest that there is space to build alliances between Taft-Hartley, public pension funds, worker funds globally, foundation and religious investors, and the socially responsible investment community, with the goal of reforming companies that pursue dangerously shortsighted business strategies. These coalitions can then attract broader support from money managers, if they choose their issues carefully and aggressively seek the support of such companies' entire shareholder bases. As of this writing, efforts are under way at several global corporations to bring together worker-owners, their unions, and pension funds with other shareholders and advocacy groups in corporate governance campaigns.

BRINGING IT ALL TOGETHER:
THE TRANSACTIONAL CHALLENGE

At the end of the day, worker capital can organize itself, the regulatory environment can improve, and our efforts can become more focused on forwarding our view of value. Yet worker-owners will not be effective agents of change, until the worker-owner view of value drives the allocation of capital through markets or firm decisions. That is the final and most difficult challenge facing worker capital today. One of the distinctive characteristics of worker capital's agenda is the wide range of responses to managerial and market behavior, including investment screening, informal dialogue, shareholder proposals, and independent-director candidacies. Yet worker capital will be a consequential market force only to the extent that it can decisively influence both large and small transactions.

Investment decisions are not necessarily multibillion-dollar deals and do not necessarily involve public companies. One of the most important ways worker capital can affect the shape of the corporate economy is by investing in smaller companies, companies with potential for growth and companies with records of long-term stable profitability.

Many of the most interesting initiatives now being undertaken by worker capital can be seen as responses to this challenge. We have already discussed the Marriott and Overnite initiatives. Worker-oriented screened funds offer a different approach to the same issue; among their objectives is to affect capital allocation decisions and corporate strategies through the mechanism of secondary market prices. These funds offer an interesting laboratory for determining the impact of stake-holder relations on stock price performance.

The growing interest among both Taft–Hartley and public funds in private market investing vehicles is yet another response to this challenge.

Conclusion

Union members and their representatives generally agree about the defects in capital market and corporate management interactions. They also share criticisms of the resulting decisions about the allocation of workers' savings and strategic directions of the firms in which they invest and work. This viewpoint stands in marked contrast to the views of U.S. capital market professionals, corporate finance academics, and the business press. Among these groups, confidence in the beneficent power of the capital markets has reached levels not seen since before the First World War.

This book presents arguments and strategies for aligning workers' values with the management of workers' money. These arguments are constructed with the concepts and methods of markets themselves. There are a number of initiatives that worker capital is pursuing—initiatives whose intellectual roots lie in the critique of the efficient market hypothesis, the analysis of capital gaps, and studies of the importance of pension funds and corporate governance.

Although we have focused on the activities of the larger funds, national unions, and the AFL–CIO, an effective capital stewardship program depends on the cooperative action of many decentralized funds, investors, and, ultimately, workers. These initiatives rest on thousands of separate funds voting their proxies, holding their managers accountable, rethinking asset allocations, considering worker-friendly investment products, and choosing to be advocates for their beneficiaries. Although this effort to use labor's capital is well under way, it is far from complete. Extending it requires intensifying education, innovation, action, and organizing in the spirit of the programs and strategies described above.

Acknowledgment

The authors of this chapter thank Toby Sheppard Bloch for his invaluable research assistance.

NOTES

[11]

Collateral Damage: Do Pension Fund Investments Hurt Workers?

1. Robert Shiller (1992) surveyed approximately 400 investment managers in 1990 on the time horizons of expectations placed on them. Fifty percent believed that their own short-term performance received too much attention, 4 percent believed that short-term performance received too little attention, and the remainder had no opinion.

2. According to *Pensions & Investments* magazine, the pension funds that experienced the most explosive asset growth in the 1990s had high commitments to domestic equities (Barr and Williams 1997).

3. The $8.00 cost per trade is the commission charged by the brokerage house. In addition to this commission, there typically is a margin between the "asking price" paid by the buyer and the "bid price" paid by the seller. This fee is collected by the specialty traders who actually run the market in specific stocks.

4. A *derivative* is a financial asset that gets its value based on another asset. For example, an option is a commonly used derivative. An option allows its holder to purchase (or sell) another asset at a particular price at some date in the future. The value of an option to buy shares of stock in General Motors at $50 each in thirty days will depend on what people expect the price of General Motors stock to be in thirty days.

5. Karpoff (1987) presented a survey of the state of the literature on the relationship between trading volume and volatility. Of the twenty studies he examined, nineteen found a positive relationship between volatility and trading volume, strongly suggesting that more trading increases volatility.

6. As a compromise, corporations must include a footnote that indicates the number of new shares that can be issued as a result of the options given to its executives.

[223]

[III]

Social Funds in the United States:
Their History, Financial Performance, and Social Impacts

1. See the Social Investment Web site at www.socialinvest.org for the full report.
2. According to the *Pensions & Investments* annual directory of investment advisors, total internal U.S. institutional tax-exempt assets grew from $3.149 trillion to $5.811 trillion between 1995 and 1997, a growth rate of 84 percent for pension/retirement assets, based on a survey of 791 firms. This growth figure includes both market appreciation and new cash inflows into all investment asset classes managed within retirement plans in the United States.
3. All Lipper mutual fund average data from *Wall Street Journal*, January 7, 1999, R3.
4. The Parnassus Equity Income Fund was known as the Parnassus Income Fund Balanced Portfolio before April 1, 1998.

[IV]

Labor's Role in the Shareholder Revolution

1. Throughout this article, I use the phrase *union pension fund* to refer to multi-employer plans covered under the Taft-Hartley Act. Under these plans, unions have a strong voice in strategic decision making. Although unions have some voice with respect to public pension funds, these funds are not included in the term *union pension fund* because they cannot effectively control decision making. An exception, however, is the New York City Employees Retirement System (NYCERS), in which three out of seven union representatives can effectively veto decisions. I include NYCERS as a union pension fund. In this article, I concentrate on using the disclosure power of the securities laws to further workers' interests. Another option for promoting change through workers' pension power is to invest in economically targeted investments (ETIs). For a discussion of ETIs, see Calabrese (chap. 5) and Patterson (1994).
2. Damon Silvers, of the American Federation of Labor-Congress of Industrial Organizations (AFL-CIO) Department of Corporate Affairs, asserted (Institutional Investors and Compensation 1999) the following:

    I think that from the perspective of worker-owners that we have an additional point of view, which is that excessive executive compensation is a sign that management may be running the company in a way that is likely to be divisive. Our members and their counterparts, America's working families who are participating in creating value in this company, may look at the company and say, "This is not really a team. This is really something that's being run by a couple of disconnected big shots." And that's not, in our view from a shareholder perspective, the kind of culture in an organization that's going to be producing value in the long run.

3. Richard Ferlauto explained, "On the shop floor, they lose out on pay increases and investments in training and capital equipment—which boosts their productivity and incomes—while the value of their pension trust assets are diluted by misguided option grants to CEOs."

4. It is hard to tell the effect of the results, because some money managers segregate their votes—that is, they vote proxies differently for different clients. The 1998 Key Votes Survey, "The AFL-CIO Proxy Voting Guidelines discourage this practice, since it results in votes effectively canceling each other out, dissipating this plan's assets." The 1998 Key Votes Survey designates that five of 106 funds segregated their votes. Leo Gerard refers to this practice as *double breasting*. He stated, "[A] fund manager may use investment guidelines; yet follow investment practices in another situation of a kind positively short-term and highly destructive to workers" (Gerard 1997).

5. Employee Ownership Letter from William Patterson and Bartlett Naylor to SEC, November 16, 1995.

6. Historians have long debated the issue of why socialism did not develop in the United States. I highlight two of the most prominent factors. First, unlike the movements in Europe, the AFL did not set as its prime goal the improvement of the working class as a whole. Labor historians emphasize that the U.S. labor movement did not develop a strong working class consciousness, because the United States has a heterogenous population and a greater possibility of upward class mobility. Second, during the decades around the turn of the nineteenth century, the U.S. courts narrowly interpreted many labor statutes, dimming the trade unionists' views of what was possible through political action. These narrow judicial interpretations were not just the result of hostility to labor but stemmed from the courts' perspective of its role in relationship to the legislature and an unwillingness to serve as arbiter of labor disputes (Forbath 1991; Brody 1993).

7. In 1997, the Teamsters submitted a resolution to DuPont that asked managers to appoint a labor representative to the board of directors. The resolution received a 3.5-percent vote, compared to 4.9 percent support in 1996 (Investor Responsibility Research Center 1997).

8. Schwab and Thomas (1998, 1089): "Our analysis suggests that if unions are successful in mobilizing shareholder support for their voting initiatives, they may be able to get boards to consider labor's interests as part of their pro-

cesses of considering shareholder interests without any dramatic changes in legal rules."

9. For excellent articles on the notion of global corporate governance, see Coffee (1999) and Cunningham (1999). ("The law in U.S. and Germany contemplate that directors act in the best interests of the 'shareholders and the corporation as a whole.' In short, U.S. practice more nearly resembles German practices than it resembles U.S. rhetoric and German practices more nearly resembles U.S. practice than it does German rhetoric. . .") (Cunningham 1999, 58).

10. In Germany, German-style codetermination has roughly the opposite characteristics of workers-ownership. Codetermination provides for substantial worker participation in corporate governance but requires no equity investments; the rights are rewarded in recognition of human capital investments. Although workers do not have the power to block any decisions, managers respect the workers' opinions, because they appreciate the value of labor peace.

11. For recent publications discussing intellectual capital, see Edvinsson and Malone (1997), Stewart (1997), Kaplan and Norton (1996), Brooking (1996).

12. The proponent of the proposal challenged the U.S. Securities and Exchange Commission (SEC) decision in *Cracker Barrel* in federal court. The district court issued an injunction against the SEC, which prohibited the issuance of any ruling at variance with the court's construction of the 1976 Interpretive Release unless and until the SEC amended Rule 14a-8(c)(7) in a rule-making proceeding in accordance with the requirements of the Administrative Procedures Act. *NYCERS v. SEC,* 843 F. Supp. 858 (S.D. N.Y. 1994). On appeal, the Second Circuit reversed the district court, holding inapplicable the notice and comment requirements of the Administrative Procedures Act and determining that the plaintiffs had an effective alternative to suing the SEC—they could sue to enjoin the company to include their proposal in its proxy materials. *NYCERS v. SEC,* 45 F.3d 7 (Ad. Cir. 1995).

13. In the National Securities Markets Improvement Act of 1996, Congress included a requirement to study the proxy rules and expressed concern about "the ability of shareholders to have proposals related to corporate practices and social issues included as part of proxy statements." Former Commissioner Steven Wallman, an outspoken critic of the *Cracker Barrel* policy, proposes that the securities law provide a cap on the number of shareholder resolutions a company would have to accept based on its shareholder base (Wallman 1996; *Securities Law Daily* 1996). In addition, Wallman suggests that the SEC automatically allow *core*, or traditional, corporate governance proposals on the proxy statement. Shareholders could submit *other*, or social policy, concerns on a lottery basis, but managers could not

submit a proposal if at least 3 percent of the shareholders supported it. The only subjective decision left for SEC staff would be to decide whether a proposal is frivolous.

14. *SEC Survey Shows Cracker Barrel Still Controversial; Some Responding Issuers Seek Tougher Access Threshold*, BNA Corp. Coun. Wkly., Apr. 30, 1997, p. 10 (10 corporations advocated maintaining the *Cracker Barrel* position). One draft of the new rules would have eliminated the ordinary business exceptions of the proxy rules and limited the number of proposals to three. The draft would have allowed an override of the cap in cases in which "serious" proposal by "significant" shareholders were presented. In the discussion process, then–SEC Commissioner Stephen Wallman stated: "Expanding their shareholder rights to engage in a wide-ranging and important dialogue of matter of importance to their company's business (by rescinding the (c)(5) and (c)(7) exclusion) will outweigh the perceived advantage of having the right to make an unlimited number of proposals on relatively narrow issues."

15. Ken Bertsch, *SEC Release on Shareholder Proposal Rule Reform Sparks Much Controversy*, XIV Corp. Gov. Bull. Oct.–Dec. 1997, p. 7. One of the main areas of controversy concerned raising the resubmission rules. The proposal would raise the minimum voting support requirement for resubmission to 5, 20, and 35 percent; the current thresholds are 3, 6, and 10. The goal was to eliminate repeat submissions of "frivolous" proposals, but it would have eliminated the great majority of social issues resolutions, which often get less than 10 percent support.

16. The most persuasive argument against *Cracker Barrel* is that it runs counter to Brandeis' (1914) maxim: "Sunlight is said to be the best disinfectant; electric light the most efficient policeman."

[V]

Building on Success: Labor-Friendly Investment Vehicles and the Power of Private Equity

1. Half of this total ($9 billion) is in a number of stock index funds enhanced by active management of proxy voting rights; most of the other $9 billion is spread among a wide variety of investments in private equity, mortgage-backed securities, real estate equity, project finance, and other direct lending to companies and real estate projects.

2. An exception is Poland Partners Fund LP, which began operating in 1993. That fund, organized by Landon Butler & Company, provides start-up and

expansion capital to companies in Poland, particularly firms projected to expand export markets for unionized U.S. companies. Although this chapter does not profile any international fund, the AFL-CIO Corporate Affairs Department recently identified ten international funds that describe themselves as union friendly.

3. See "Public Funds Earmark $9.3 Billion for Investment in Private Equity," *The Private Equity Analyst*, February 1992. A survey by *The Private Equity Analyst*, the leading periodical that tracks private equity, showed that by year-end 1991, the 56 largest public pension funds already had allocated an average 4.3 percent of total assets to private equity. The nine largest public plans each had between $800 million and $2 billion in private equity in 1998.

4. Partnerships are the dominant format for private equity investing because of their ability to accommodate both pension and nonpension investors, favorable tax treatment, limited liability, and well-established legal precedent and familiarity. In LPs, the general partner is almost always itself organized as a partnership or corporation. Two alternative vehicles are the commingled trust (Union Labor Life Insurance Company's [ULLICO's] model) and the limited liability company, which is a new but increasingly common structure described as a hybrid between a corporation and a partnership. References to LPs in this chapter include limited liability companies, because they are similar from a fiduciary perspective.

5. Although the investment vehicles profiled here include the largest funds investing domestically, this list is by no means exclusive. In October 1999, the AFL-CIO published an *Investment Product Review* that describes and grades forty investment products "that market themselves as providing collateral benefits to workers," including ten international funds (p. 1). The *Review* applies a uniform system of criteria and rankings "that can be used by trustees and other fiduciaries to judge the claims of 'worker-friendly' products" (p. 1). Among the forty products reviewed, fifteen invest in real estate debt and equity, seven in public equities, eight in private debt or equity (five of which are just starting up), and ten overseas ventures.

6. Prohibited Transaction Class Exemption 90-1 (insurance company–pooled separate accounts), 55 Fed. Reg. 2891 (Jan. 29, 1990). When pension trustees delegate investment authority to a qualified private asset manager, as defined by the Employment Retirement Income Security Act (ERISA), the underlying investments within a commingled fund are exempt from many rules prohibiting transactions with potential conflicts of interest, such as transactions that benefit "parties in interest," including participating employers, service providers, and fiduciaries.

7. The advantages are similar to those described in the note above, with respect to ULLICO's commingled account. From a trustee's perspective, investing

through a qualified asset manager is a protected delegation under ERISA, because the commingled fund's underlying assets are not considered to be plan assets. This allows the partnerships to invest without regard to most ERISA restrictions. A Taft-Hartley plan investing directly in LPs can achieve this result—without the extra layer of management involved in a fund of funds—but only if each individual partnership qualifies as a venture capital operating company, or if employee benefit plans represent less than 25 percent of the equity in the partnership. (See 29 C.F.R. section 2510.3-101[a][2][ii].) In 1980, the U.S. Department of Labor (DOL) granted private equity partnerships a "safe harbor" exemption from plan asset restrictions if they qualify as *venture capital operating companies*. To qualify, partnerships must not have more than 100 investors and must actually exercise contractual management rights over one or more of the operating companies or LPs in which it invests. (See, e.g., William M. Mercer, Inc., "Key Terms and Conditions for Private Equity Investing," a study commissioned by eight large public pension funds [1996].)

8. The U.S. Department of Housing and Urban Development's Federal Housing Administration guarantees mortgages on qualified low-income housing. The Government National Mortgage Association packages these mortgages into securities (bonds) with a guaranteed fixed-income stream and sells them to investors. The Federal National Mortgage Association and the Federal Home Loan Mortgage Corporation are federally created entities, now privately operated, that likewise purchase, securitize, and insure repayment on pools of qualifying mortgages purchased from private lenders nationwide. By pooling the mortgages and arranging to repurchase them as securities issued by these agencies—rather than holding individual mortgages—ProLoan (like the AFL-CIO Housing Investment Trust [HIT]) virtually eliminates the risk of default.

9. FHA loans account for nearly half of the HIT's portfolio, with Fannie Mae, Ginnie Mae, and Freddie Mac securities accounting for the rest. See Gregory Sandler, "HIT Puts the Union Label on America's Housing," *Multifamily Executive*, May 1997, p. 56.

10. According to HIT financial statements, the trust has outperformed both the Salomon Mortgage Index and the Lehman Aggregate Bond Index over the past 1-, 3-, 5-, and 10-year periods by a significant margin. HIT's total gross rate of return for the year ending December 31, 1998, was 8.71 percent, exceeding the Salomon Mortgage Index (6.99 percent) by nearly 2 percent. Over the trailing 5-year and 10-year periods, the trust eclipsed both industry indices by more than one percent annually on average (AFL-CIO HIT, *1998 Annual Report*). HIT's total expenses have fallen to 39 basis points (0.39 percent) due to economies of scale, its nonprofit character, and the fact that its professional staff members are compensated at rates generally below market

because of their commitment to the trust's goals, according to HIT Executive Vice President Mike Arnold (1999).

11. Interview with Kennedy (1999). Commercial mortgage loans typically provide higher yields than publicly traded bonds. In 1997, prime commercial mortgages yielded an average 160–basis point spread (1.6 percent) over 10-year U.S. Treasury bonds and a 55-point spread over AAA-rated corporate bonds. Commercial mortgage loans also tend to be less sensitive to interest rate fluctuations, because they frequently call for adjustable rates and reduce prepayment risk by imposing penalties. See General American, Commercial Mortgage/Plus Fund, *Prospectus.*

12. ULLICO, *J for Jobs Quarterly Report,* Third Quarter 1999, page 2. Over the most recent 5-year period, the J Account returned an annualized 8.4 percent compared to 7.8 percent for the Lehman Brothers Aggregate Bond Index.

13. Although one or two companies may be added to or deleted from the Standard & Poor's 500 Index in a particular year, the composition is generally stable. Indeed, the widely accepted efficient market theory maintains that passive indexing should yield higher returns than the average actively managed portfolio over long periods, net of expenses. Other benefits associated with indexing include broad diversification, lower transaction costs, and investment fees.

14. See the "Avon letter," DOL Opinion Letter (Feb. 23, 1988), *reprinted in* 15 Pens. Rep. (BNA), 391; and the "Monks letter," DOL Opinion Letter (Jan. 23, 1990), *reprinted in* 17 Pens. Rep. (BNA), 244. ERISA requires trustees to monitor investment managers to ensure that proxies are voted on a timely basis in the best interest of plan participants.

15. Wilshire Associates, Inc., *Long-Term Rewards from Corporate Governance,* a report commissioned by the California Public Employees Pension Fund (CalPERS) Board of Trustees (1994). The CalPERS Corporate Governance Program, which continues to target relatively poorly performing large companies for shareholder activism, is described at www.calpers.ca.gov/invest/corpgov/corpgov.htm.

16. The AFL–CIO's *Model Guidelines for Delegated Proxy Voting Responsibility* were adopted by the AFL–CIO Executive Council in February 1991. They are designed specifically for the occasion when proxy voting authority is delegated by plan trustees to an investment manager or other fiduciary, to ensure that shareholder rights are exercised on behalf of plan participants and not neglected or voted in unthinking deference to corporate managements.

17. One of many such proposals during the early 1990s was presented by the National Infrastructure Investment Commission, created under the Intermodal Surface Transportation Efficiency Act of 1991. In January 1993, the commission called for a $30 billion investment in sewage plants and fiber optic infor-

mation highways funded by federal guarantees for bonds acquired voluntarily by pension funds. The AFL–CIO supported this approach, provided that "guarantees and other credit enhancements" ensured that pension funds received a market rate of return. See testimony of Thomas R. Donahue, secretary-treasurer, AFL–CIO, before the Commission on Infrastructure Investment (November 19, 1992).

[VI]

Canadian Labour-Sponsored Investment Funds: A Model for U.S. Economically Targeted Investments

1. Recent legislation in Manitoba created a new fund in 1998. This single fund, Ennis, was named in the new Act of the Manitoba Legislature rather than opening the floodgates to any sponsorship arrangement as part of the labour-sponsored investment fund (LSIF) program.
2. Eighty-five percent of all venture capital investing in Canada was in privately held companies in 1996. Economic Impact of Venture Capital, Business Development Bank of Canada, 1997, p. 11.
3. Working Ventures at the time of the survey had majority control by a trade union body. Since then, the Canadian Federation of Labour has disbanded, leaving the fund with a mixed board of elected representatives, fund officials, and money managers.
4. It should be noted that this fund returned −29.5 percent in 1998.
5. In 1996, the maximum annual tax credited LSIF contribution was reduced to $3,500 from $5,000. The substantial drop in LSIF investment over the next 2 years meant that in 1998, the contribution was returned to its $5,000 limit.

[VII]

Small Benefits, Big Pension Funds, and How Governance Reforms Can Close the Gap

1. By this measure, the U.S. pension system is a success. The labor force participation rate of men older than age 55 has fallen dramatically, from 68.9 percent in 1950 to 37.6 percent by 1995. Scholars attribute the fall to voluntary retirement made affordable by increased pension coverage and, most important, Social Security benefits (Hobbs and Damon 1996).

2. In the real world, money managers must compete against other managers to obtain clients' business. Money managers do not want to be caught with performance much below the average; if so, there may be a new manager in the following year. The authors find that money managers as a group fail to obtain the highest risk-adjusted return because of these concerns. They *herd*, or tend not to hold extreme positions so that they do not increase their chance of falling too far below a benchmark. Money managers' "clinging to the benchmark" is potentially a cost to the sponsors (Lakonishok, Shleifer, and Vishney 1992).

3. In the 1940s, more unions and employers entered into collective bargaining agreements to contribute to these fringe benefit plans. The 1947 Taft-Hartley Act required that they be controlled by equal numbers of representatives from labor and management (Ghilarducci et al. 1995). The plans flourished under legalized collective bargaining and became highly regulated under the Employment Retirement Income Security Act of 1974.

4. The unusually high number of $8,225 is due in part to major auto companies', which are unionized, catching up on funding in the early 1990s by contributing their own stock to their pension plans. The high union figure is also due to unions' persistently driving up the cost of pensions by negotiating better benefits, as evinced by the generosity increases as seen in Table 7.7.

[VIII]

Overcoming Institutional Barriers on the Economically Targeted Investment Superhighway

1. See also Pension and Welfare Benefits Administration (PWBA) Letter to Gregory Ridella, Chrysler Corporation (A.O. 88-16A) (Dec. 19, 1988), in which the U.S. DOL stated, "A decision to make an investment may not be influenced by non-economic factors unless the investment, when judged solely on the basis of its economic value to the plan, would be equal or superior to alternative investments available to the plan."

2. F. Supp. at 1245. See also *Martin v. Feilen*, 15 Employee Benefits Cas. (BNA) 1545, 1556 (8th Cir. 1992) (holding that an "ESOP [employee stock ownership plan] fiduciary is not prohibited from being on both sides of a transaction involving the ESOP's assets, but he must serve both masters [or at least the ESOP] with the utmost care and fairness" and "[w]hen a fiduciary has dual loyalties, the prudent person standard requires that he make a careful and impartial investigation of all investment decisions").

3. In *Trenton v. Scott Paper Co.*, the Third Circuit held that "the fact that a fiduciary's actions incidentally benefit an employer does not necessarily mean that the fiduciary has breached his duty." 832 F.2d 806, 809 (3d Cir. 1987), *cert. denied*, 485 U.S. 1022 (1988).

4. *Morse v. Stanley*, 732 F.2d 1139, 1146 (2d Cir. 1984). Most violations of the exclusive benefit are blatant. Examples of breach of the duty of loyalty include the following: *Marshall v. Kelly*, 465 F. Supp. 341 (W.D. Okla. 1978) (in which plan made a loan to a fiduciary); *Donovan v. Daugherty*, 550 F. Supp. 390 (S.D. Ala. 1982) (concerning when trustees unlawfully extend benefits to themselves); *Wright v. Nimmons*, 641 F. Supp. 1391, 1402 (S.D. Tex. 1986) (concerning when a fiduciary treats plan assets as if they were his own property); *Marshall v. Mercer*, 4 Employee Benefits Cas. (BNA) 1523 (N.D. Tex. 1983), *rev'd on other grounds*, 747 F.2d 304 (5th Cir. 1984) (concerning when a trustee fails to take action to collect loans made by the plan to himself and his corporation); *Dasler v. E.F. Hutton & Co.*, 694 F. Supp. 624, 632 (D. Minn. 1988) (concerning when a fiduciary broker churns a plan account to receive greater commissions). See also *Investment of Pension Plan Assets: Hearings Before the Subcomm. on Oversight of the House Comm. on Ways and Means*, 100th Cong., 2d Sess. 181 (1988) (testimony of William Posner, Assistant Director; Employee Plans Technical and Actuarial Division. Internal Revenue Service, U.S. Department of the Treasury).

5. Interpretive Bulletin 94-1 makes clear that investments are to be compared to comparable investments: a plan cannot make an investment if the return would be less than other investments of similar risk, and the plan cannot make an investment if the risk would be greater than investments of similar return. The bulletin does not require the investment to have the best of both worlds: the highest return and the lowest risk. Instead, the comparison is the highest return of investments with similar risk characteristics.

6. *Debruyne v. Equitable Life Assur. Society*, 720 F. Supp. 1342, 1349 (N.D. Ill. 1989), *aff'd*, 920 F.2d 457 (7th Cir. 1990) (stating that "[t]he fiduciary duty . . . requires prudence not prescience."); *GIW Industries, Inc. v. Trevor, Stewart, Burton & Jacobsen, Inc.*, 10 Employee Benefits Cas. (BNA) 2290, 2300 (S.D. Ga. 1989), *aff'd*, 895 F.2d 729 (11th Cir. 1990) (holding that a "court must consider the conduct of the fiduciary not the success of the investment, . . . and the court must evaluate the fiduciary's conduct, from the perspective of the time of the investment decision 'rather than from the vantage point of hindsight.'" [citations omitted]); *Donovan v. Walton*, 609 F. Supp. 1221, 1238 (S.D. Fla. 1985), *aff'd sub nom.*, *Brock v. Walton*, 794 F.2d 586 (11th Cir. 1986) (stating that "[o]ne must resist the knee-jerk reflex to pronounce an investment prudent or imprudent based on the success of the venture, for ERISA is concerned with the soundness of the decision to invest" (quoting

Leigh v. Engle, 727 F.2d 113, 124 [7th Cir. 1984]). See also *New York Hearings*, at 198 (testimony of David Walker, assistant secretary of labor for Pension and Welfare Benefits Administration, U.S. DOL, stating "What we don't do in ERISA is we don't second-guess people. We don't employ hindsight.").

7. See also *Donovan v. Mazzola*, 2 Employee Benefits Cas. (BNA) 2115 (N.D. Cal. 1981), *aff'd*, 716 F.2d 1226 (9th Cir. 1983), *cert. denied*, 464 U.S. 1040 (1984), in which the court held that plan trustees acted imprudently when they made a loan without obtaining or reviewing basic documentation, including financial statements, project plans, and an accurate market study. The court also found that the trustees failed to monitor the use of the loan proceeds after the loan was made.

8. U.S.C. §1104(a)(1)(C) (1999).

9. *Donovan v. Guar. Nat'l Bank*, 4 Employee Benefits Cas. (BNA) 1686, 1688 (S.D. W.Va. 1983).

10. H.R. Report Number 1280, 93rd Cong., 2d Sess. 304 (1974), *reprinted in* 1974 U.S.C.C.A.N. 5038, 5085.

11. *GIW Industries, Inc. v. Trevor, Stewart, Burton & Jacobsen, Inc.*, 10 Employee Benefits Cas. (BNA) 2290, 2303 (S.D. Ga. 1989), *aff'd*, 895 F.2d 729 (11th Cir. 1990).

12. *Leigh v. Engle*, 858 F.2d 361, 368 (7th Cir. 1988), *cert. denied sub nom.*, *Estate of Johnson v. Engle*, 489 U.S. 1078 (1989).

13. *Lanka v. O'Higgins*, 810 F. Supp. 379 (N.D. N.Y. 1992). The Conference Report states that "[t]he degree of investment concentration that would violate this requirement to diversify cannot be stated as a fixed percentage, because a prudent fiduciary must consider the facts and circumstances of each case." H.R. Report Number 1280, 93d Cong., 2d Sess. 304, *reprinted in* 1974 U.S.C.C.A.N. 5038, 5084.

14. See *Marshall v. Glass/Metal Ass'n*, 507 F. Supp. 378, 383 (D.Haw. 1980).

15. ERISA §404(A)(1)(C) imposes an obligation to diversify "unless under the circumstances it is clearly prudent not to do so." 29 U.S.C. § 1104(a)(1)(C) (1994). See *Reich v. King*, 18 Employee Benefits Cas. (BNA) 1801, 1804 (D. Md. 1994) (trustees have the burden of proving that their decision not to diversify is "clearly prudent"; prudence under the diversification rule is the same as the prudent person rule of ERISA § 404[A][1][B]). In *Reich v. King*, the district court denied the Secretary of Labor's motion for summary judgment, which claimed that the trustees' failure to diversify is a *per se* violation of the diversification rule. The trustees had invested 75 percent of plan assets in mortgages and notes, 72 percent of which was secured by residential real property in one county. *Id.* at 1802. The remaining mortgages were secured by real estate in three neighboring counties. *Id.* The court refused to grant summary judgment, holding that nondiversification is not a per se violation of the diversification rule

and that a material fact existed as to the prudence of the trustees' decision not to diversify. *Id.* at 1805-06. Later, the court granted the trustees' motion to dismiss, holding that the trustees had met the burden of showing that the decision not to diversify was clearly prudent. *Labor Department Loses Lawsuit Over Trustees' Failure to Diversify*, 21 Pens. & Benefits Rep. (BNA) 2281-2 (Dec. 5, 1994).

16. Employee Benefits Cas. (BNA) 2115 (N.D. Cal. 1981), *aff'd*, 716 F.2d 1226 (9th Cir. 1983), *cert. denied*, 464 U.S. 1040 (1984).

17. Several cases have involved such high percentages of plan assets in one type of investment it is not surprising that the Department of Labor challenged the investment. In *Freund v. Marshall & Illsley Bank*, 485 F. Supp. 629, 636 (W.D. Wis. 1979), the court noted, "it can hardly be disputed that the investment of virtually all of the Plan's assets in loans to affiliated companies, on its face, represents a complete failure to diversify the investments of the Plan." In *Marshall v. Mercer*, 4 Employee Cas. (BNA) 1523, 1535 (N.D. Tex 1983), *rev'd on other grounds*, 747 F.2d 304 (5th Cir. 1984), the court observed, "it should be obvious that a concentration of 85% to 90% of the Plan's assets in a single class of investments is little or no diversification at all." In *Marshall v. O'Donnell*, Civ. Action No. R-81-28 (D. Md. Jan. 28, 1981), the court held that loans of 99 percent of plan assets to parties in interest violated the diversification rule.

18. See, e.g., ERISA §104(b)(2), 29 U.S.C. §1104(b)(2) (1999). Courts have ruled that plan documents also include a deadlock arbitration award, *Ironworkers Local 272 v. Bowen*, 695 F.2d 531 (11th Cir. 1983); and a memorandum in which the trustees' instructions are described, *Clark v. Bank of New York*, 687 F. Supp. 863 (S.D. N.Y. 1988). See also *Schoenholtz v. Doniger*, 628 F. Supp. 1420 (S.D. N.Y. 1986); *Delgrosso v. Spang & Co.*, 769 F.2d 928 (3d Cir. 1985), *cert. denied*, U.S. 1140 (1986); *Donovan v. Daugherty*, 550 F. Supp. 390 (S.D. Ala. 1982); *Winpisinger v. Aurora Corp. of Ill.*, 456 F. Supp. 559 (N.D. Ohio 1978).

19. This basic ERISA principle was overlooked by Grace Capital, an investment manager for the Fur Manufacturing Industry Retirement Fund. *Dardaganis v. Grace Capital, Inc.*, 664 F. Supp. 105, 107 (S.D. N.Y 1987), *aff'd in pertinent part*, 889 F.2d 1237 (2d Cir. 1989), *on remand*, 755 F. Supp. 85 (S.D. N.Y. 1991). In its investment management agreement with the Fund, Grace Capital agreed to "manage the Account in strict conformity with the investment guidelines promulgated by the Trustees . . . and with all applicable Federal and State laws and regulations." The investment guidelines limited investment in common stocks to "25% of the cost of the securities in the Account." Later, the limitation was increased to 50 percent.

Although Grace Capital recommended an additional increase to invest more than 50 percent in equities, the trustees refused to increase the limit. Over a 15-month period, equity investments steadily increased from 54 percent to 81 percent.

The trustees sued Grace Capital. The court held that by agreeing to act as the Fund's investment manager, Grace Capital had assumed the statutory obligation to act in accordance with plan documents, including the investment management agreement. The court further held that Grace Capital had breached its fiduciary duty to the Fund by exceeding the 50-percent limitation established in the investment management agreement. The court rejected the defense raised by Grace Capital that in the investment business, "percentage guidelines merely establish a rough demarcation zone to assist the manager in portfolio allocation."

20. Institute for Fiduciary Education, p. 15. Most funds expect to hold an ETI investment (other than mortgage-backed securities) until maturity. *Id.* Some funds avoid the problem of illiquidity by making short-term ETIs: 3-year or 3-month certificates of deposit, or 2- to 5-year mortgages. *Id.* Approximately 7.5 percent of the ETI surveyed were investments that matured in 1 year or less.

[IX]

Challenging Wall Street's Conventional Wisdom:
Defining a Worker-Owner View of Value

1. Event studies suggest a short-term positive correlation between downsizing announcements and stock prices. Yet longer-term studies that focus on downsizing's effect on productivity call into question whether mass layoffs generate value. David Levine, *Reinventing the Workplace: How Business and Employees can Both Win.* Brookings Institution, 1995; Martin Baily, John Haltiwanger, and Eric Bartelsman, "Downsizing and Productivity Growth: Myth or Reality?" National Bureau of Economic Research Working Paper: 4741, May 1994; Terry Wagar, *Exploring the Consequences of Workforce Reduction*, Canadian Journal of Administrative Sciences, 15(4), December 1998, pp. 300–309.

2. Although the traits common to worker-owners as a group, such as a high tolerance for constructive conflict borne of collective bargaining or an appreciation for the synthetic nature of value creation, may predispose them toward effective active ownership, worker-owners—with the exception of employee stock ownership plan participants—should not have systematic firm-specific information advantages over other owners, given the diversification of fund portfolios. See chap. 4 by Marleen O'Connor for more information.

3. For example, the California Public Employees' Retirement System's equity portfolio is approximately 80-percent indexed. Nelson's Institutional Market-

place CD-ROM, Nelson Information, 1998. See also the Amalgamated Bank's LongView Fund, marketing materials prepared for the AFL-CIO Investment Product Review Public Equity Working Group, July 23, 1999.

4. AFL-CIO, *Investing in Our Future: An AFL-CIO Guide to Pension Investment and Proxy Voting,* 1992. Compare with Council of Institutional Investors, *Core Policies, General Principals, Positions, and Explanatory Notes,* March 29, 1999.

5. Martin Lipton and Jay Lorsch, "A Modest Proposal to Improve Corporate Governance," Business Lawyer (Nov. 1992, vol. 48, no. 1) 55-77; Ronald Gilson and Reiner Kraakman, "Reinventing the Outside Director," Stanford Law Review, April 1991, pp. 863–906; William T. Allen, "The Evolving Role of Corporate Boards 10," Address at the Harvard University Graduate School of Business Administration, Leadership Workshop: Making Corporate Boards More Effective 10 (June 24, 1994) (on file with The Delaware Journal of Corporate Law).

6. It is noteworthy that although the duties of pension plan trustees and the duties of corporate directors share an origin in the common law of trusts, they have evolved very differently in the area of the duty of care. Under Delaware law, a corporate director may be indemnified by the corporation for breaches even of the "prudent man standard." There appears to be a clear basis for this development in the different postures toward risk of the corporation and the Employment Retirement Income Security Act fund, but it still has the effect of creating quite different power relationships between decision makers and experts. 8 Del. Code Annotated 102(b)(7).

7. Conflicts of interest between the interests of corporate pension plan participants and corporate managers were the occasion for the DOL's Advice Letter to Robert Monks, which first defined the fiduciary duty to vote proxies. Letter from DOL to Robert A. G. Monks of Institutional Shareholders Services, Inc. (January 23, 1990), *reprinted in* 17 Pens. Rep. (BNA) 244, 245 (January 29, 1990).

8. The most noteworthy example of this activity has been the Organization for Economic Cooperation and Development's (OECD's) efforts to develop corporate governance guidelines in the aftermath of the crisis in emerging markets. An initial draft of that document clearly advocated the Anglo-American model of shareholder-driven corporate governance at the expense of both European and Japanese approaches that focus on building structures of collaboration between different corporate constituencies. However, in the January meeting, the draft was extensively revised to be neutral between these systems and to acknowledge explicitly the importance of stake-holders. Compare Draft OECD *Principles of Corporate Governance* (October 1988) with Draft OECD *Principles of Corporate Governance* (February 1999).

9. The Local Authority Pension Fund Forum, *The Role of the Forum*, London, 1998; Hermes Investment Management Limited, *Statement on Corporate Governance and Voting Policy*, July 1998; ABP Corporate Governance Guidelines, Amsterdam, 1999.

10. *AFL-CIO Investment Product Review*, AFL-CIO, Washington, D.C., October 1999; California Public Employees' Retirement System, Responsible Contractor Policy, 1996; New York Common Retirement Fund, Contractor Selection Policy, 1997; Service Employees International Union National Pension Fund, Responsible Contractor Policy, 1998.

BIBLIOGRAPHY

Act to Establish the Fonds De Solidarité des Travailleurs du Quebec. 1983. Quebec General Assembly.

Activist Shareholders. 1999. 15 (January): 23 Inst. Inv. and Compensation.

American Federation of Labor-Congress of Industrial Organizations (AFL-CIO). 1999a. *Executive Council Resolution.*

AFL-CIO. 1999b. *Investment Product Review: Report of the Investment Product Review Working Group.*

AFL-CIO. 1998. *1998 Key Votes Survey.*

AFL-CIO. 1997a. *Investment Managers Leadership Panel.*

AFL-CIO. 1997b. *10 Key Votes Survey.*

AFL-CIO. 1997c. *Proxy Voting Guidelines.*

AFL-CIO. 1993. *Pensions in Changing Capital Markets, A Report and Guidelines for Domestic and International Issues.* Washington, D.C.

AFL-CIO Building Investment Trusts. 1999. *Semi-Annual Report.*

AFL-CIO Human Resource Development Institute. 1998. Economic Development: A Union Guide to the High Road.

Allen, Steve G., Robert L. Clark, and Ann A. McDermed. "Post-Retirement Benefit Increases in the 1980s." *Trends in Pensions* (1992): 319–42, ed. John A. Turner and Daniel J. Beller. Washington, D.C.: U.S. Government Printing Office.

Ambachtsheer, Kenneth P.D., and Don Ezra. *Pension Fund Excellence: Creating Value for Stakeholders.* New York: John Wiley and Sons, 1998.

Anand, Vineeta. "Labor Learns Lesson Well: Unions Use Activism As Tool Against Target Companies." *Pensions & Investments* (April 3, 1995): 8.

Anand, Vineeta. "Market Contributions Boost Pension Assets." *Pensions & Investments* (October 19, 1998): 97.

Anand, Vineeta. "Defined Benefit Assets surge by 20.3%." *Pensions and Investment Age* (March 22, 1999): 1.

Anand, Vineeta. "U.S. Pension Assets Cross $10 Trillion." *Pensions & Investments* (March 20, 2000): 46.

Anjier, John C. "Anti-Takeover Statutes, Shareholders, Stakeholders and Risk." *Louisiana Law Review* 51 (1991): 561–622.

Arnold, Corinna. "Recent Scandals Place German Boards Under Attack." *Corp. Gov. Bul.* 13, no. 16 (July–September 1996).

Arnold, Mike. 1999. Interview by author. Washington, D.C., 11 February.

Atkins, Ralph, and Haig Simonian. "Germany Calls for New Rules to Govern European Takeovers." *Financial Times* (November 23, 1999).

Atlanta Journal. "Overperked, Overpaid." Editorial. (April 13, 1998): A10.

Baker, Stephen. "The Yelping Over Labor's New Tactics." *Business Week* (October 23, 1995): 75.

Baldwin, Bob. "Unions and Pension Fund Investments." *Jobs Now!* (February 1998).

Baldwin, Bob, David Levi, Ted Jackson, and Michael Decter. March 1991. Worker Investment Funds Issues and Prospects. Paper presented at Canadian Labour Congress.

Barkema, Harry, and Luis Gomez-Mejia. "Managerial Compensation and Firm Performance: A General Research Framework." *Academy of Management Journal* 41 (April 1998): 135–45.

Barnes, John A. "Should Government Be Directing Pension Funds?" *Investor's Bus. Daily* (August 21, 1995): B1.

Barr, Paul G., and Fred Williams. "Equity-Rich Pension Funds Win Big with Long Bull Run." *Pensions & Investments* 25, no. 5 (March 3, 1997): 1.

Barry, Dave. 1999. Chairman, Retail Food Industry Joint Labor-Management Committee, United Food and Commercial Workers. Interview by author. Washington, D.C., 9 March.

Becker, Brian E. "Union Rents as a Source of Takeover Gains Among Target Shareholders." *Industrial & Labor Relations Review* 49, no. 1 (October 1995): 3–19.

Berlau, John. "The Risks of Political Investing." *Investor's Bus. Daily* (February 2, 1999): A1.

Berg, Olena. Assistant Secretary of Labor in testimony *Hearing on Pension Investments and Economic Growth Before the Joint Economic Committee,* 103 Cong., 2d Sess., 1994, *reprinted in Federal Document Clearing House Congressional Testimony* (22 June).

Bernstein, Aaron. "Sweeney's Blitz: He Wants to Turn Labor into a Lean, Mean Recruiting Machine." *Business Week* 56 (February 17, 1997a).

Bernstein, Aaron. "Working Capital: Labor's New Weapon?" *Business Week* (September 29, 1997b): 110.

Bhagat, Sanjai, Andrei Shleifer, and Robert Vishny. "Hostile Takeovers in the 1980s: The Return to Corporate Specialization." In Brookings Papers on Economic Activity (1990).

Binkley, Christina. "Marriott Plan for New Stock Is Voted Down." *Wall Street Journal* (May 21, 1998).

Black, Bernard. "Shareholder Activism and Corporate Governance in the United States." *Corp. Gov. Advisor* 14 (January–February 1999).

Black, Bernard. "Agents Watching Agents: The Promise of Institutional Investor Voice." *UCLA L. Rev.* 39 (1992): 911.

Blackburn, Robin. "The New Collectivism: Pension Reform, Grey Capitalism and Complex Socialism." *New Left Review* 233 (January–February 1999).

Blair, Margaret. 1995. Ownership and Control: Rethinking Corporate Governance for the Twenty-First Century. Washington, D.C.: Brookings Institute.

Blair, Margaret. 1996. Wealth Creation and Wealth Sharing: A Colloquium on Corporate Governance and Investments in Human Capital.

Blair, Margaret. Firm-Specific Human Capital and the Theory of the Firm. Working Paper (February 1997).

Blair, Margaret, and Lynn Stout. "A Team Production Theory of Corporate Law." *Va. L. Rev.* 85 (1999): 247–328.

Blasi, Joseph. *Employee Ownership: Revolution or Ripoff?* Cambridge, Mass.: Ballinger Pub. Co., 1988.

Blasi, Joseph, and Douglas Kruse. 1991. *The New Owners: The Mass Emergence of Employee Ownership in Public Companies and What It Means to American Business.* New York: Harper-Business, 1991.

Blondin, Michel. 1998. Information Director, Solidarity (Federation de Travailleurs du Quebec). Interview by author. Montreal, Quebec, Canada, 9 November.

Bohner, Chris. 1999. Interview by author. Washington, D.C.

Brancato, Carolyn Kay. *Institutional Investors and Corporate Governance*, vol. 87 (1997).

Brandeis, Louis Dembitz. *Other Peoples Money, And How The Bankers Use It.* New York: Stokes, 1914.

Braverman, Harry. *Labor and Monopoly Capital: The Degradation of Work in the Twentieth Century.* New York: Monthly Review Press, 1974.

Brealey, Richard A., and Stewart C. Myers. *Principles of Corporate Finance.* New York: McGraw-Hill, 1991: 846–47.

Breen, Kerry. "Board Focus Charts Varied Terrain of Corporate Governance Abroad." *Corp. Gov. Bul.* 13, no. 15 (July–September 1996).

Brody, David. *In Labor's Cause: Main Themes on the History of the American Worker.* New York: Oxford University Press, 1993.

Brooking, Annie. *Intellectual Capital.* New York: International Thomson Business Press, 1996.

Brown, Warren. "Chrysler's Profits Fell 37% in First Quarter; Analysts See Implications for Kerkorian Bid." *Washington Post* (April 14, 1995).

Bruck, C. *The Predator's Ball: The Junk Bond Raiders and the Man Who Stalked Them.* New York: Simon and Schuster, 1998.

Builders Fixed Income Fund. 1998. *ProLoan Program*, marketing presentation.

Builders Fixed Income Fund. 1999. *Prospectus* (29 January).

Burrough, Brian, and John Helyar. *Barbarians at the Gate: The Fall of RJR Nabisco.* New York: Harper-Collins, 1991.

Burton, Edward. 1996. *Derivatives: Is There Any Future for Them in Pension Funds?* Presented at the Pensions and Investments' Investment Management Conference (Washington, D.C., June 19, 1996).

Bushee, Brian J. "The Influence of Institutional Investors on Myopic R&D Investment Behavior." *Accounting Review* 73, no. 3 (July 1998): 305–33.

Business Development Bank of Canada. 1997. *Economic Impact of Venture Capital, 5th Annual Survey.*

Business Week. "Working Capital: Labor's New Weapon?" (September 29, 1997).

Business Week. "Special Report: Executive Pay." (April 20, 1998a): 84–5.

Business Week. "Road Hazard for an IPO." (July 20, 1998b).

Business Week. "Who Needs a Money Manager?" (February 22, 1999): 27–132.

Business Week. "GE's Pension Fund Runneth Over, So Do Tempers." (June 5, 2000): 68.

Bute, Joe. *Industrial Heartland Labor Investment Forum: Our Money, Our Jobs* (June 14, 1996). (www.heartlandnetwork.org.)

Butler, Landon. 1999. Policy Board member and marketing director, Multi-Employer Property Trust (MEPT). Interview by author. Washington, D.C., 21 February.

Calabrese, Michael. "Q: Would Economically Targeted Investments Trigger a Pension Crisis?" *Insight* (September 16, 1996): 25.

Calvert Social Investment Fund. 1998. *Prospectus*: 28.

Calvert Social Investment Fund. 1999. *Calvert Policy: Labor and Human Rights Standards.* (www.calvertgroup.com).

Carey, Mark et al., 1993. *The Economics of the Private Placement Market,* Staff Studies 166, Board of Governors of the Federal Reserve System (Washington, D.C.).

Carleton, Willard et al. "The Influence of Institutions on Corporate Governance Through Private Negotiations: Evidence from TIAA-CREF" *J. of Fin.* 30 (1998): 1335.

Chubb Corporation. 1999. *Definitive Proxy Statement* (DEF 14A) (March 24).

CIGNA America Fund. 1999. *Review* (January).

CIGNA America Fund. 1999. Marketing brochure with performance data for the periods ending July 31, 1999.

Clark, Gordon. 1997. *Pension Fund Capitalism: A Casual Analysis.* Oxford University, England: School of Geography.

Clark, Gordon. 1998. *Contested Terrain: Republican Rhetoric, Pension Funds and Community.* Oxford University, England: School of Geography.

Coffee, John. 1991. "Liquidity Versus Control: The Institutional Investor as Corporate Monitor," *Colum. L. Rev.* 91: 1277.

Coffee, John. 1997. "The Folklore of Investor Capitalism," *Michigan Law Review* 95: 1970.

Coffee, John. 1999. The Future as History: The Prospects of Global Convergence in Corporate Governance and Its Implications. Columbia University Working Paper.

Cossette, Jeff. "A Consolidated Effort," *Inv. Rel.* (June 1, 1995): 10.

Coyle, Stephen. Chief executive officer of AFL-CIO Housing Investment Trust. 1994. Testimony before the Joint Committee. 103 Cong. 2nd Session. Washington, D.C.

Cunningham, Lawrence A. "Commonalities and Prescriptions in the Vertical Dimension of Global Corporate Governance." *Cornell Law Review* 84 (July 1999): 1133–94.

Daly, Brian. 1999. Fund Manager Trust Company of the West. Interview by author. New York City, 10 February.

Daoust, Fernand. 1998. Vice president, Solidarity (FTQ). Interview by author. Montreal, Quebec, Canada, 9 November.

DeCarlo, John. 1999. General counsel, United Brotherhood of Carpenters. Interview by author. Washington, D.C., 25 February.

Delaney, Ken. 1998. Chief executive officer, First Ontario Fund. Interview by author. Toronto, Ontario, Canada, 4 December.

Denkenberger, Amy. "Shareholders Speculate on Implementation of Dutch Governance Reforms." *Corp. Gov. Bul.* 15, no. 21 (January–March 1998).

Depenbrock, John M. 1999. Senior vice-president, Multi-Employer Market, CIGNA Retirement & Investment Services. Interview by author. Silverspring, Md., 23 February, 9 November.

De Villiers, Les. *In Sight of Surrender: The U.S. Sanctions Campaign Against South Africa, 1946–93.* Westport, Conn.: Praeger, 1995.

"New Proposal Impinges on Board Power." *Director's Alert* 1 (March 1999): 3.

"AFL-CIO Fights Boards on Exec Comp and Independence." *Director's Alert* 3 (January 1999).

"Study Proves Board Independence Irrelevant." *Director's Alert* 4 (March 1999): 3.

Director's Monthly. 1999. *Corp. Gov. Rev.* 23, no. 1 (January). (Statement by Charles Elson, a prominent shareholder activist, *citing* Ken West, TIAA-CREF.)

Domini, Amy, and Peter Kinder. *Ethical Investing.* Reading, Mass.: Addison-Wesley Publishing, 1986.

Domini Social Equity Fund Web site. 2000. (www.domini.com/DSEF.html).

Donovan v. Bierwirth, 680 F.2d 263, 271 (2d Cir. 1982), *cert. denied,* 459 U.S. 1069 (1982).

Dreyfus Third Century Fund. 1998. *Prospectus*: 4.

Drucker, Peter. *The Unseen Revolution: How Pension Fund Socialism Came to America.* New York: Harper and Row, 1976.

Drucker, Peter. *The Pension Fund Revolution.* New Brunswick, New Jersey: Transaction Publishers, 1996.

Durkin, Ed. 1999. United Brotherhood of Carpenters. Interview by author. Washington, D.C.

Duskas, Andrea. 1997. "Gearing Up for the EMU, Germany Contemplates Governance Changes," *Corp. Gov. Bul.* 14 (October–December 1997): 19.

Dymski, Gary, and John Veitch. 1996. "Credit Flows to Cities." In *Reclaiming Prosperity: A Blueprint for Progressive Economic Reform.* Washington, D.C.: Economic Policy Institute.

Edelstein, Ryan. "Groups Are Poised For Next Step After Final Hampel Report," *Corp. Gov. Bul.* (October–December 1997): 25.

Edvinsson, Leif, and Michael S. Malone. *Intellectual Capital: Realizing Your Company's True Value By Finding Its Hidden Roots.* New York: Harper Business, 1997.

Employee Benefit Research Institute. 1995. *Quarterly Pension Investment Report* (June).

Employee Benefit Research Institute. 1998. *Quarterly Pension Investment Report* (September).

Employee Benefit Research Institute Databook on Employee Pensions. 1997. 4th ed., chap. 17. Washington, D.C.: Employee Retirement Research Institute.

Employee Investment Act. 1989. Legislative Assembly of the Province of British Columbia, Canada.

Employment Cost Index. Various years. U.S. Department of Commerce. (http://stats.bls.gov/search/search.asp).

Falconer, Kirk. 1995. *The Role and Performance of Labour-sponsored Investment Funds in the Canadian Economy: An Institutional Profile.* Ottawa, Canada: Canadian Labour Market Productivity Centre, 1995.

Falconer, Kirk. 1997. Survey of LSIFs, Background documentation, meeting hosted by Solidarity and the FTQ. Paper presented at Labour-Sponsored Investment Fund (LSIF) Alliance meeting. Montreal, Quebec, Canada, 5 June.

Fallick, Bruce, and Kevin Hassett. "Unionization and Assets." *Journal of Business* 69, no. 1 (1996): 51–73.

Fama, Eugene. "Efficient Capital Markets: A Review of Theory and Empirical Work." *J. of Fin.* 25 (1970): 383.

Fenn, George W., Nellie Liang, and Stephen Prowse. 1995. *The Economics of the Private Equity Market,* Staff Studies 168, Board of Governors of the Federal Reserve System. (Washington, D.C.).

Ferlauto, Richard. "Confronting the Impact of Exorbitant Executive Pay." *Labor & Corp. Gov.* (December 1998a): 1, 3.

Ferlauto, Richard. "Labor Campaigns Target Executive Compensation." *Issue Alert* (December 1998b): 5, 15.

Fisch, Jill E. "Relationship Investing: Will It Happen? Will It Work?" *Ohio St. L.J.* 55, no. 1009 (1994):1029–34.

Forbath, William E. *Law and the Shaping of the American Labor Movement.* Cambridge, Mass.: Harvard University Press, 1991.

Fortune, Peter. "Stock Market Efficiency: An Autopsy?" *New England Economic Review* (March–April 1991): 17.

Francis, J., and S. Reiter. "Determinants of Corporate Pension Funding Policy." *Journal of Accounting and Economics* 9 (April 1987): 35–60.

Freeman, Allan. "Tax credit boosts labour fund's allure," *Globe and Mail* (January 23, 1995): B1.

Friedman, Benjamin. "Pension Funding, Pension Asset Allocation and Corporate Finance." In *Financial Aspects of the United States Pension System,* ed. Zvi Bodie and John B. Shoven. Chicago: University of Chicago Press, 1983.

"Ethical Investing, on the Side of the Angels." *The Futurist* (March 1999).

General Electric. 1999. *Definitive Proxy Statement (DEF 14A)* (March 12).

Georgeson Shareholder Communications, Inc. 1998. *Georgeson Report, Annual Meeting Wrap-up.*

Georgeson Shareholder Communications, Inc. 1999. *Corporate Governance: Annual Meeting Season Wrap-up.*

Gerard, Leo. 1997. *Worker Funds: Possibilities and Initiatives,* LCC Conference (June 11–12).

Gertner, Mark. *Trustees Handbook: A Basic Text on Labor–Management Employee Benefit Plans, Fifth Edition.* Milwaukee: International Foundation for Employee Benefit Plans, 1998.

Ghilarducci, Teresa. *Labor's Capital: The Politics and Economics of Private Pensions.* Cambridge, Mass.: MIT Press, 1992.

Ghilarducci, Teresa. "U.S. Pension Investment Policy and Perfect Capital Market Theory." *Challenge* (July–August 1994).

Ghilarducci, Teresa, Peter Phillips, Garth Magnum, and Jeff Petersen. *Portable Pension Plans for Casual Labor Markets.* Westwood, Conn.: Quorum Books, Greenwood Publishing Group, Inc., 1995.

Ghilarducci, Teresa. "Labor's Paradoxical Interests and the Evolution of Corporate Governance." *J. L. & Soc.* 24 (1997).

Ghilarducci, Teresa. "*Who Controls Labor's Capital and Why It Matters.*" Heartland Labor Capital Project Conference Proceedings (April 1999).

Gilpin, Kenneth. "A Labor-Friendly Fund Helps to Channel the Power of Unions." *New York Times* (September 6, 1998).

Gilson, Ronald J. "Corporate Governance and Economic Efficiency: When Do Institutions Matter?" *Wash. U. L.Q.* 74 (1996): 327–41.

Gilson, Ronald J. Globalizing Corporate Governance: Convergence of Form or Function. Working Paper. (December 5, 1997).

Goldman Sachs and Frank Russell Company. *1999 Report on Alternative Investing By Tax Exempt Organizations.* New York, 1999.

Gordon, Jeff. "Duetsche Telekom, German Corporate Governance, and the Transition Costs of Capitalism." *Colum. Bus. L. Rev.* 185 (1998).

Gordon, Lilli et al. 1994. *Report to the California Public Employees' Retirement System: High-Performance Workplace: Implication for Investment Research and Active Investing Strategies,* May 30. The Gordon Group, Inc.

Government Accounting Office. 1995. *Public Pension Plans: Evaluation of Economically Targeted Investment Programs.* Reprinted at www.access.gpo.gov/su_docs/aces/aces.160.shtml.

Graebner, Lynn. "Social Investing Grows in Strength." *Bus. J.* (January 6, 1997): 12.

Greenwich Associates. *What Now? U.S. Investment Management.* Greenwich, Conn., 1998.

Grossman, Sanford, and Joseph E. Stiglitz. "On the Impossibility of Informationally Efficient Markets." *Amer. Econ. Rev.* 70: 393 (June 1980).

Guerard, John B. Jr. *Is There a Cost to Being Socially Responsible in Investing?* Muslowitz Prize Winning Paper. Social Investment Forum, 1996. Reprinted at www.socialinvest.org/areas/research.

Hall, Bronwyn. 1988. Effect of Takeover Activity on Corporate Research and Development. In *Corporate Takeovers: Causes and Consequences.* Chicago: University of Chicago Press, 1988.

Hamilton Lane Advisors. 1999. *Presentation Book*: 8. Hamilton Lane-Carpenters' Partnership Fund, LP.

Hansmann, Henry. *The Ownership of Enterprise.* Cambridge: Harvard University Press, Belknap Press, 1996.

Hansmann, Henry, and Reinier Kraakman. 2000. *The End of History for Corporate Law?* Working Paper.

Hanson, Dave. 1999. Chief Investment Officer, Boilermakers & Blacksmiths National Pension Trust. Interview by author. Washington, D.C., 26 February.

Harless, David W., and Steven P. Peterson. "Investor Behavior and the Persistence of Poorly Performing Mutual Funds." *Journal of Economic Behavior and Organization* 37 (November 1998): 3.

Harrison, Joan. "M&A is a key source of corporate layoffs." *Mergers and Acquisitions* 33, No. 4 (January–February 1999): 7–8.

Hartzell, Scott. 1999. Managing Director, ProLoan Builders Fixed Income Fund. Interview by author. Washington, D.C., 19 February.

Heard, James. "Global Governance Reform Is Key to Global Finance." *Director's Monthly* 22, no. 18 (October 1998).

Heinzl, John. Globe and mail. Toronto, Ontario, Canada. (April 3,1998). Editorial.

Hitt, Michael A., Robert E. Hoskisson, Richard A. Johnson, and Douglas D. Moesel. "Market for Corporate Control and Firm Innovation." *Academy of Management Journal* 39, no. 5 (1996): 1084–119.

Hirschman, Albert O. *Exit, Voice and Loyalty: Response to Decline in Firms, Organization and States.* Cambridge, Mass.: Harvard University Press, 1970.

Hobbs, Frank B., and Bonnie L. Damon. 1996. Chapter 4: Economic Characteristics. In *65+ in the United States: Current Population Reports Special Studies.* U.S. Department of

Commerce and U.S. Department of Health and Human Services. Washington, D.C.: U.S. Government Printing Office, April. 4-1: 23–190.

IBEW–NECA Equity Index Fund. 1999. *Update* (through January 31, 1999).

ILO. 1998. *ILO Standards*. Geneva. (www.ilo.org/public/english/about/mandate.htm).

Industrial Heartland Labor Investment Forum. 1996. *Our Money, Our Jobs* (June 14). (www.heartlandnetwork.org.).

Institute for Fiduciary Education. 1993. *Economically Targeted Investments: A Reference for Public Pension Funds*. Sacramento, CA.

International Brotherhood of Teamsters v. Fleming Cos., Okla., no. 90,185, January 26, 1999.

"Government Investment Is Fraught with Peril." *Investor's Bus. Daily.* (January 11, 1999): A26.

Investor Responsibility Research Center. 1996. *The High-Performance Workplace.* (March): 24.

Investor Responsibility Research Center. 1997. *Corporate Governance Highlights* 8, no. 21 (May 23).

Investor Responsibility Research Center. 1999. *Social Policy Shareholder Resolutions in 1998: Issues, Votes and Views of Institutional Investors* (January): 8.

Ippolito, Richard A. "Toward Explaining the Growth of Defined Contribution Plans." *Industrial Relations* 34, no. 1 (January 1995).

Jackson, Ted, and Francois Lamontagne. *Adding Value: The Economic and Social Impacts of Labour-sponsored Venture Capital Corporations on their Investee Firms.* Ottawa, Canada: Canadian Labour Market Productivity Centre, 1995.

Jacobs, Michael. "A Cure for America's Corporate Short-Termism." *Planning Review* 20, no. 1 (January–February 1992): 4.

Jeffers, Michelle. "Here Come the Consultants." *Forbes ASAP* (April 1998).

Jareski, Laura. "Report on Wisconsin investment board recommends tighter internal controls." *Wall Street Journal* (June 1, 1995): C20.

Jensen, Michael. "Takeovers: Their Causes and Consequences." *Journal of Economic Perspectives* 2, no. 1 (Winter 1988): 21–48.

Jensen, Michael. 1989. Corporate Time Horizons. In *U.S. Congress. Joint Economic Committee Hearings on Corporate Time Horizons.*

Jones, Luther. 1999. Managing Director, Hamilton Lane Advisors. Interview by author. Washington, D.C., 10 February.

Kamiat, Walter. 1999. AFL-CIO Housing and Building Investment Trusts special counsel. Interview by author. Washington, D.C., 26 January.

Kaplan, Robert S., and David P. Norton. *The Balanced Scorecard: Translating Strategy Into Action.* Boston: Harvard Business School Press, 1996.

Karpoff, Jonathan M. "The Relation Between Price Changes and Trading Volume: A Survey." *Journal of Financial and Quantitative Analysis* 22 no. 1 (March 1987): 109–37.

Kass, Dennis. 1987. Assistant Secretary of Labor, Pension and Welfare Benefits Administration. Current Developments at the Department of Labor. Address at the Annual Conference in Las Vegas sponsored by the International Foundation of Employee Benefits Plans (November 1986). *Reprinted in* International Foundation of Employee Benefits Plans, Employee Benefits Annual (1987): 235, 236.

Kelly, Bruce. "The Particulars: Growth of Largest Pension Funds Slowed in 1998; World's Biggest 300 Funds Had More Than $5.2 Trillion in Assets." *Pensions & Investments* (September 20, 1999).

Kennedy, Jim. 1999. Vice president, Union Labor Life Insurance Company. Interview by author. Washington, D.C., 25 January.

Kinder, Lydenberg, Domini & Co. 1998. *Domini 400 Social Index Statistical Review* (December).

Kinder, Lydenberg, Domini & Co. Nov. 1999. *The Corporate Social Ratings Monitor, Dayton Hudson profile.*

Koppes, Richard. Editorial. *New York Times* (May 19, 1996): 36.

Kraakman, Reinier. The Mystery of Unions Shareholder Activism: Commentary on Schwab and Thomas. In *Employee Representation in the Emerging Workplace. Proceedings of New York University 50th Annual Conference on Labor,* ed. Sam Estreicher, 1997. New York City.

Kreiner, Sherman. 1999. Chief executive officer, Crocus Fund. Interview by author. Ottawa, Ontario, Canada, 5 February.

Kristof, Nicholas D., and Edward Wyatt. "Who Sank, or Swam, in Choppy Currents of a World Cash Ocean." *New York Times* (February 15, 1999): A1.

Kristof, Nicholas D., and David E. Sanger. "How U.S. Wooed Asia to Let Cash Flow In." *New York Times* (February 16, 1999): A1.

Kuttner, Robert. "Soaring Stocks: Are Only the Rich Getting Richer?" *Business Week* (April 22, 1996).

Labor & Corp. Gov. 1998. "How the AFL-CIO Key Vote Survey Creates Shareholder Value." Vol. 1.

Labor & Corp. Gov. 1998 (December*).* "Labor Flexes Newly Found Muscle."

Labor & Corp. Gov. 1999a. (February). "Poison Pills.": 11.

Labor & Corp. Gov. 1999b. (March*).* "Labor Pushes An International Corporate Governance Program": 1.

Labor & Investments. 1987. "Pension-Backed Housing Expands." 7, no. 8 (October).

Labour Sponsored Venture Capital Corporations Act. 1992. Legislative Assembly of the Province of Ontario, Canada.

Lakonishok, Josef, Andrei Shleifer, and Robert W. Vishny. *"The Structure and Performance of the Money Management Industry."* Brookings Papers on Economic Activity; Microeconomics (1992): 339–79.

Laliberte, Pierre. 1999. Agency Problems in the Capital Markets and in the Employment Relationship. Ph.D. diss., University of Massachusetts, Amherst.

Lally, Rosemary. 1997. "CalPERS Breaks New Ground with Global Governance Principles," *Corp. Gov. Bull.* 13, no. 17 (October 1996–January 1997).

Langbein, John. 1985. Social Investing of Pension Funds and University Endowments: Unprincipled, Futile, and Illegal. In *Divestment: Is It Legal, Is It Moral, Is It Productive?* Washington, D.C.

Langevoort, Donald. 1998. "Commentary: Stakeholder Values, Disclosure and Materiality," *Cath. L. Rev.* 43, no. 93 (1998): 93–94.

Lanoff, Ian. *"The Social Investment of Private Pension Plan Assets: May It Be Done Lawfully under ERISA?"* Lab. L. J. 31 (1980): 387–389.

Las Vegas Sun. 1999. "Culinary, Lesser Claim Win at Santa Fe Gaming." (May 4).

Lazonick, William, and Mary O'Sullivan. 1996. Big Business and Corporate Control. In *The International Encyclopedia of Business and Management,* ed. Malcolm Warner. New York: Routledge Press.

Levi, David. 1998. CEO, Working Opportunity Fund. Interview by author. Vancouver, B.C., 18 September.

Levine, Marc. 1997. *The Feasibility of Economically Targeted Investing*. Madison: University of Wisconsin, for the International Foundation of Employee Benefits.

Levine, Phil. 1997. "Where There's a Will, There's an ETI." *Pensions & Investments* (November 10): 52.

Lewis, Daniel. 1996. "Unions Seeking Leverage as Shareholders." *Boston Globe* (April 7).

Lichtenberg, Frank, and Siegel, Donald. 1989. Effect of Takeovers on the Employment and Wages of Central-Office and Other Personnel. National Bureau of Economic Research. Working Paper no. 2895, Cambridge, Mass.

Lichtenberg, Frank R. *Corporate Takeovers and Productivity*. Cambridge, Mass.: MIT Press, 1992.

Lipin, Steven. "Investors Find Gold Mine in Global Crossing Stock." *Wall Street Journal* (March 19, 1999): C1.

Litvak, Lawrence. *Pension Fund and Economic Renewal*. The Council of State Planning Agencies (1981): 13.

Low, Jon. 1999. "*Valuing Intangibles: Results and Implications*." Heartland Labor Capital Project Conference Proceedings (April). (www.heartlandnetwork.org.).

Lowenstein, Louis. "Financial Transparency and Corporate Governance: You Manage What You Measure." *Colum. L. Rev.* (1996).

Lubin, Joann, and Sara Calian. "Activist Pension Funds Create Alliance Across Atlantic to Press Lackluster Firms." *Wall Street Journal* (November 23, 1998): A4.

Lublin, Joann. "Labor Unions Brandish Stock to Force Change." *Wall Street Journal* (May 17, 1996).

Lublin, Joann. "Poison Pills Are Giving Shareholder A Big Headache, Union Proposals Assert." *Wall Street Journal* (May 23, 1997).

Lublin, Joann. "Oklahoma Court Affirms Holders' Right to Pursue a Binding Bylaw Proposal." *Wall Street Journal* (January 28, 1999): B2.

Luraschi, Ron. 1999. Senior vice president, Pension Trust Department, Amalgamated Bank of New York. Interview by author. New York, 18 February.

Lurie, Alvin. "ETIs: A Scheme for the Rescue of City and County with Pension Funds." *J. Pens. Planning & Compliance* 1 (1996): 4.

Macdonald and Assoc. 1998. *Venture Capital in Canada: Annual Statistical Review* (June).

The Manitoba Employee Ownership Fund Corporation Act. 1991. Legislative Assembly of the Province of Manitoba, Canada.

McGuire, Jean. "Legitimacy through Obfuscation: The Presentation of Executive Compensation." *International Journal of Organizational Analysis* 3 (1997): 115–33.

McGurn, Patrick. "Controversy Swirls around Labor Unions' Shareholder Activism." *Corp. Gov. Bull.* (January–February 1994): 3.

McGurn, Patrick. "1999 Proxy Season Preview: Governance in a Changing Market." *Issue Alert* 14, no.1 (January 1999).

McKersie, Robert B. 1999. Union-Nominated Directors: A New Voice in Corporate Governance. Task Force Working Paper no. WP08 (April 1). Cambridge, Mass.: MIT Sloan School of Management.

McNichols, Maureen, and Mark Lang. 1997. Institutional Trading and Corporate Performance. Stanford Graduate School of Business Research Paper no. 1460. (October).

Medina, Eliseo. 1998. Executive vice president, Service Employees International Union, International Corporate Governance Network. 9 July.

Mercer Management Consulting Inc. 1998. *U.S. Study of 800 Firms 1991–1996.*

Meredith, Robyn. "Executive Defends Downsizing." *New York Times* (March 13, 1996): D4.

Mergerstat. 1997 (October). (www.mergerstat.com).

MFS Union Standard Equity Fund. 1999a. *Investing in Labor-Sensitive Companies* (January 1999a).

MFS Union Standard Equity Fund. 1999b. *Prospectus* (February 1, 1999b).

Mills, Mike. "Two Telecom Powers to Merge: Global Crossing Buys Frontier Corp." *Washington Post* (March 18, 1999): E1.

Minnesota IMPLAN Group. 1998. *The Impact of Multi-Employer Property Trust Investments Across the United States.* Prepared for MEPT (July 8, 1998).

Mishel, Lawrence, Jared Bernstein, and John Schmitt. *The State of Working America 1996–7.* Armonk, NY: M.E. Sharp Press, 1996.

Mishel, Lawrence, Jared Bernstein, and John Schmitt. *The State Of Working America, 1998–99.* Ithaca, NY: ILR Press, 1999.

Mitchell, Daniel J. "Why The Government Should Not Invest Americans' Social Security Money." *The Heritage Foundation Backgrounder* (December 23, 1998).

Mitchell, Olivia S., James F. Moore, and John W. Phillips. 1999. Projected Wealth and Savings Adequacy. In *Forecasting Retirement Needs and Retirement Wealth,* ed. Olivia S. Mitchell, P. Brett Hammond, and Anna M. Rappaport. The Pension Research Council: 68–94, 139–66. Philadelphia: University of Pennsylvania Press. 2000.

Mittelstaedt, H. Fred. "An Empirical Analysis of the Factors Underlying the Decision to Remove Excess Assets from Overfunded Pension Plans." *Journal of Accounting and Economics* 11 (November 1989): 399–418.

Moberg, David. "Union Pension Power: Labor Is Mobilizing Its Investment Power to Pressure Corporate America." *The Nation* (June 1, 1998): 16.

Monk, Dan. "Labor Groups Push Change at Local Firms." *Cincinnati Business Courier* (March 29, 1999).

Monks, R., and N. Minnow. *Corporate Governance.* Cambridge, Mass.: Basil Blackwell, 1995.

Monks, R. 1995. House Economic Subcommittee on Employer-Employee Relations, *Economically Targeted Investments,* (Testimony) June 15, 1995, *reprinted in* Federal Document Clearing House Congressional Testimony, June 15, 1995.

Morgenson, Gretchen. "Seeing a Fund as Too Big to Fail, New York Fed Assists Its Bailout." *New York Times* (September 24, 1998): A1.

Multi-Employer Property Trust. 1998. *1998 Year-End Report* (December 31): 10, 14–15.

Multi-Employer Property Trust. 1999. *Trust Report* (January).

Nelson's Directory of Investment Managers. 1997.

Neumark, David. "Rents and Quasi Rents in the Wage Structure: Evidence from Hostile Takeovers." *Industrial Relations* 35, no. 2 (April 1996): 145–179.

New York State Pension Investment Task Force. 1989. Pension Investments: Public Hearing. Testimony of David Walker, Assistant Secretary for Pension and Welfare Benefits, U.S. Department of Labor. (March 3): 190–91.

Nomani, Asra. "CalPERS Says Its Investment Decisions Will Reflect How Firms Treat Workers." *Wall Street Journal* (June 16, 1994): 8.

O'Barr, William M., John M. Conley, with Carolyn Kay Brancato. *Fortune or Folly: The Wealth and Power of Institutional Investing.* Homewood, Ill.: Richard D. Irwin, 1992.

O'Connor, Marleen. "Restructuring the Corporation's Nexus of Contracts: Recognizing a Fiduciary Duty to Protect Displaced Workers." *N.C. L. Rev.* 69 (1991): 1196, 1201.

O'Connor, Marleen. "Organized Labor as Shareholder Activist: Building Coalitions to Promote Worker Capitalism." *Univ. Rich. L. Rev.* 31 (1997): 1345.

O'Connor, Marleen. "Symposium: Corporate Malaise: Stakeholders Statutes Cause or Cure?" 2 (1992): 21.

Organization for Economic Cooperation and Development. 1999. Intellectual Capital Reporting by Enterprises: Prospects for Advancing the State of the Art. In Draft Program, Organization for Economic Cooperation and Development, *Measuring and Reporting Intellectual Capital: Experience, Issues, and Prospects.* Draft Annotated Agenda, (March 19).

Oregon Steel Mills Investor Relations. Press Release—Oregon Steel Mills Shareholders Defeat Union-Sponsored Proposals. (www.oregonsteel.com/consent.htm).

O'Reilly, Charles et al. 1996. Overpaid CEO's and Underpaid Managers: Equity and Executive Compensation. Research paper 1410 (October).

Orts, Eric W. "Beyond Shareholders: Interpreting Corporate Constituency Statutes." *George Washington Law Review* 61, no. 1. (November 1992): 14–135.

O'Sullivan, Mary. 1999. "*Shareholder Value, Financial Theory and Economic Performance,*" Heartland Labor Capital Project Conference Proceedings, April 1999. (www.heartlandnetwork.org).

Papke, Leslie. 1996. Are 401(k) plans replacing other employer provided Pensions? Evidence for Panel Data. National Bureau of Economic Research Working Paper, no. 5736.

Patterson, Jeanne. "Public Pension Funds and Economically Targeted Investments." *Pub. Bud. & Fin. Mgmt.* 6 (1994): 566.

Pax World Fund. 1998. *Prospectus.*: 7. Portsmouth, New Hampshire.

Pension and Welfare Benefits Administration Letter to James S. Ray. 1988 (July 8).

"Unions and Proxies." *Pensions & Investments* (May 4, 1998). Editorial, p. 12.

Perrin, Thorau & Assoc. 1998. *Analysis of Fiscal Costs and Fiscal and Economic Benefits of the British Columbia Working Opportunity Fund 1992 to 1998.* (November).

Perrone, Ronald. 1999. Managing Director, Allied Investment Advisors. Interview by author. 19 February

Petersen, Mitchell. "Pension Reversions and Worker-Shareholder Wealth Transfers." *Quarterly Journal of Economics* 107 (August 1992): 1033–56.

Phan, Phillip H., and Charles W.L. Hill. "Organization Restructuring and Economic Performance in Leveraged Buyouts: An Ex Post Study." *Academy of Management Journal* 38, no. 3 (1995): 704–39.

Pistor, Katharina. Co-Determination in Germany: A Socio-Political Model with Governance Externalities. In *Corporate Governance Today,* ed. Mark Roe, 1998.

Plan Sponsor. *1997 (July–August).* "Editorial Comment: Social Investing—It's Everywhere.": 2.

Pollin, Bob, Dean Baker, and Marc Schauberg. 1999. "The Case for a Securities Transactions Tax: Taxing the Big Casino." Draft manuscript, University of Massachusetts, Amherst. (April 1999).

Pontiff, Jeffrey, Andrei Shleifer, and Michael Welsbach. "Reversions of Excess Pension Assets After Takeovers." *Rand Journal of Economics* 21, no. 4 (Winter 1990): 600–613.

Porter, Michael E. *Capital Choices: Changing the Way America Invests.* Cambridge: Harvard Business School, 1992.

PR Newswire. 1998. "Institutional Investors—Especially the Top 25—Are Gaining More Power and Control Over the Largest U.S. Companies" (August 20).

"Funding Sets Fifth Annual Record, Surging 53% to Exceed $85 Billion." *The Private Equity Analyst.* 1 (January, 1999): 46.

Quarter, Jack. *Crossing the Line.* Toronto, Canada: James Lorimer and Co., 1995.

Ravenscraft, David, and William Long. "LBOs, Debt and R&D Intensity." *Strategic Management Journal* 14 (1993): 119–35.

Reed, Jennifer Lea, and Renee Deger. "Public Plans Lead Private Equity Frenzy." *Venture Cap. J.* (January 1, 1998).

Rehfeld, Barry. "A Suite Victory for Shareholders." *Pensions & Investments* (July, 1998).

Reich, Robert. *The Work of Nations: Preparing Ourselves for 21st Century Capitalism.* New York: Alfred A. Knopf, 1991.

Reich, Robert. "The New Power." *American Prospect* 11, no. 1 (November 23, 1999).

Reno, Virginia. The Role of Pensions in Retirement Income. In *Pensions in a Changing Economy.* Washington, D.C.: Employee Benefits and Research Institute, 1993.

Rifkin, Jeremy, and Randy Barber. *The North Will Rise Again: Pensions, Politics and Power in the 1980s.* Beacon Press, 1978.

Rock, Edward. "America's Shifting Fascination with Comparative Corporate Governance." *Wash. U. L.Q.* 74 (1996): 367.

Rockel, Douglas. 1998. "Union Pacific Corporation," ING, Barinf, Furman, Selz, LLC, (August 11, 1998).

Roe, Mark. "Political and Legal Restraints on Ownership and Control of Public Companies." *Journal of Financial Economics* 27, no. 1 (September 1990).

Roe, Mark. "The Modern Corporation and Private Pensions." *UCLA L. Rev.* 41 (1993): 75, 93.

Roe, Mark. *Strong Managers, Weak Owners: The Political Roots of American Corporate Finance.* Princeton University Press, 1994.

Roe, Mark. "German Codetermination." *Colum. Bus. L. Rev.* 170 (1998).

Rogers, Joel. 1996. Labor and Economic Development. Prepared for pre-HRDI Conference, Labor Strategies in Economic Development, Training, and Modernization. San Francisco, December 7, 1996.

Romano, Roberta. "Public Pension Fund Activism in Corporate Governance Reconsidered." *Colum. L. Rev.* (1993): 795.

Rose, Robert. "Labor Has Discovered the Perfect Issue for Galvanizing Workers: CEO Pay." *Wall Street Journal* (April 9, 1998).

Rosett, Joshua G. "Do Union Wealth Concessions Explain Takeover Premiums?" *Journal of Financial Economics* 27 (1990): 263–82.

Russell Reynolds Associates. *Corporate Governance a Growing Investor Concern on a Global Scale, New Study Shows.* News Release (April 6, 1998).

Rutledge, John. "You're A Fool if You Buy into This." *Forbes ASAP* (April, 1998).

Sabel, Charles. 1996. *Ungoverned Production: An American View of the Novel Universalism of Japanese Production Methods and Their Awkward Fit with Current Forms of Corporate Governance.* Columbia Law School Working Paper (Feb. 1996).

St. Louis Post-Dispatch. 1995 "Orange County Treasurer Says Broker Did It." (January 19): 8C.

Salter, Malcolm S., and Wolf A. Weinhold. "Corporate Takeovers: Financial Boom or Organizational Bust?" In *Knights, Raiders and Targets: The Impact of the Hostile Takeover,* ed. John C. Coffee et al. New York: Oxford University Press, 1988.

Sandler, Gregory. "HIT Puts the Union Label on America's Housing." *Multifamily Executive* (May 1997).

Saxton, Rep. Jim. 1995. "*Economically Targeted Investments.*" Testimony before the Joint Economic Committee, House Economic Employer-Employee Relations, June 15, 1995, *reprinted in* Fed. Doc. Clearing House Congressional Testimony.

Scherer, F.M. 1988. "Corporate Takeovers: The Efficiency Arguments." *Journal of Economic Perspectives* 2, no. 1 (Winter, 1988): 69–82.

Schwab, Stewart J., and Randall Thomas. 1998. "Realigning Corporate Governance: Shareholder Activism by Labor Unions." *Mich. L. Rev.* 96 (1998): 1018.

Schwartz, Donald. "The Public-Interest Proxy Contest: Reflection on Campaign GM." *Mich. L. Rev.* 69 (1971): 419.

Schwartz, Donald. "Toward New Corporate Goals: Co-Existence with Society." *Geo. L.J.* 60 (1971): 57.

Securities and Exchange Commission (SEC). 1983. Capital Cities Communications, SEC No-Action Letter, March 16, 1983, reconsidered March 24, 1983.

SEC. 1984. Louisiana-Pacific, SEC No-Action Letter, March 6, 1984.

SEC. 1985. Gannett Company, SEC No-Action Letter, March 11, 1985.

SEC. 1997 (September 19). *Amendments to Rules on Shareholder Proposals.* Release no. 34-39093.

SEC. 1998a (May 20). Overnite S-1 Registration Statement.

SEC. 1998b. Shiva Corporation, LEXIS 1005, SEC No-Action Letter. (May 1).

SEC. 1999 (October 15). Proposed Rule S7-23-99. Release No. 34-42007.

"Wallman Proposes Broad Changes to SEC's Shareholder Proposal Rule." *Securities Law Daily* (October 9, 1996).

SECOR. 1996. "*Retombees Economiques et Fiscales Des Investissements Du Fonds de Solidarité des Travailleurs du Quebec (FTQ), 1984–1995.*"

Shiller, Robert. "Do Stock Prices Move Too Much to Be Justified by Subsequent Changes in Dividends?" *American Economic Review* (1981) 71: 421–36.

Shiller, Robert. *The Report of the Twentieth Century Fund Task Force on Market Speculation and Corporate Governance.* New York: Twentieth Century Fund Press, 1992.

Shleifer, Andrei, and Lawrence Summers. Breach of Trust in Hostile Takeovers. In *Corporate Takeovers: Causes and Consequences.* Chicago: University of Chicago Press, 1988.

Sirower, Mark. *The Synergy Trap: How Companies Lose the Acquisition Game.* New York: Free Press, 1997.

Sirower, Mark. "Manager's Journal: What Acquiring Minds Need to Know." *Wall Street Journal* (February 22, 1999): A18.

Snow Spalding, Kirsten, and Matthew Kramer. 1997. What Trustees Can Do under ERISA. Paper presented at conference. University of California, Berkeley.

Snow Spalding, Kirsten, and Elizabeth C. Rudd. 1998. *"Culture Clash: Labor's Economic Agenda and Taft-Hartley Trustees' Interpretation of ERISA."* Berkeley Center for Labor Research and Education, Institute of Industrial Relations. (October): 45.

Social Investment Forum. 1998. *1997 Report on Responsible Investing Trends in the United States* (January).

Social Investment Forum. 1995. *After South Africa: The State of Socially Responsible Investing in the United States.*

Social Investment Forum. 1999. *1999 Report on Responsible Investing Trends in the United States* (November).

Solidarity Fund, 1998. Growing Opportunities Annual Report, Montreal, Quebec, Canada.

Stanford, Jim. *"Labour-Sponsored Funds: Examining the Evidence."* Toronto, Canada: Canadian Auto Workers, 1999.

Steed, Michael. 1999. Senior vice president, Union Labor Life Insurance Company. Interview by author. Washington, D.C., 5 March.

Stewart, Thomas A. *Intellectual Capital: The New Wealth of Organizations.* New York: Doubleday, 1997.

Stone, Katherine. "Labor and the Corporate Structure: Changing Conceptions and Emerging Possibilities." *U. Chi. L. Rev.* 55 (1988): 73.

Super 2000 and International Labour Forum on Superannuation and Pension Funds' Investment Strategies. 1994. *Conference Proceedings.* Evatt Foundation for Australian Council of Trade Unions. Sydney, Australia.

Suret, Jean Marc. *The Fonds de Solidarite des Travailleurs du Quebec: A Cost-Benefit Analysis.* Vancouver, B.C.: Fraser Institute, 1994.

Survey of Current Business. August 1988. Tables 6.4 and 6.7. New York, N.Y., The Conference Board.

Sweeney, John. Address, *Working Capital* 1 (1998): 1.

Sweeney, Paul. 1996. *Clash By Proxy.* Conf. Board (May 1).

Tackett, Michael, and Christopher Drew. "Pension Funds Become a Bonanza for Companies." *Chicago Tribune* (December 4, 1989).

Tagliabue, John. "Resisting Those Ugly Americans; Contempt in France for U.S. Funds and Investors." *New York Times* (January 9, 2000).

Taylor, Frederic. *The Principles of Scientific Management.* New York: Harper & Brothers, 1911.

Thomas, Randall, and Catherine Dixon. 1998. *Aranow and Einhorn's Proxy Contests for Corporate Control. Sec. 16.*

Thomas, Randall, and Kenneth Martin. 1999. Should Labor Be Allowed to Make Shareholder Proposals? In *The Effect of Shareholder Proposals in Executive Compensation* (Working Paper).

Tocco, Frank. 1999. Senior regional vice president, General American. Interview by the author. 19 February.

Trumka, Richard. 1996. Forum Keynote Speaker: Summary of Industrial Heartland Labor Investment Forum: *Our Money, Our Jobs* (June 14): 10.

Trumka, Richard. 1996. *Capital Strategies, Leveraging Financial Resources to Strengthen Our Workplaces and Communities.* AFL-CIO Washington 1 (October).

Turner, John A., and Richard Hinz. "Why Don't Workers Participate?" In *Living With Defined Contribution Plans*, ed. Olivia S. Mitchell and Sylvester J. Schieber. Philadelphia: The Pension Research Council, University of Pennsylvania Press, 1998: 15–37.

Union Labor Life Insurance Company (ULLICO). *Separate Account J: Report on Audits of Financial Statements*, two years ended December 31, 1997a.

Union Labor Life Insurance Company (ULLICO). "Separate Account P: The Union Labor Life Insurance Company Private Capital Fund," *Confidential Update* (June 30, 1997b).

Union Labor Life Insurance Company (ULLICO). "*Overview: Mortgage Separate Account 'J for Jobs'*" (January 1999).

U.S. Department of Commerce, Bureau of the Census. 1998. *Statistical Abstract of the United States 1998*. Table 794: 512. Washington, D.C.

U.S. Dept. of Commerce, Economics and Statistics Administration, Bureau of Economic Analysis. 1998. *Survey of Current Business*. Washington, D.C.

U.S. Department of Labor (DOL). 1992. *Economically Targeted Investments: An ERISA Policy Review*. Washington, D.C.: Advisory Council on Pension Welfare and Benefit Plans.

U.S. DOL. 1994. Hearing on Pension Investments and Economic Growth Before the Joint Committee. 103 Cong. 2nd Session. Washington, D.C.

U.S. DOL. 1994. *Interpretive Bulletin 94-1 on Economically Targeted Investments*. 59 Fed. Reg. 32,606 (June 23, 1994), *codified in* 29 C.F.R. '2509.94-1 (1994). Washington, D.C.

U.S. DOL. *Interpretive Bulletin 94-2 on Proxy Voting*.

U.S. DOL. *Trends in Pensions*, ed. John A. Turner and Daniel J. Beller. Washington, D.C.: U.S. Government Printing Office. 1989.

U.S. Department of Social Security. 1999. "*Occupational Pensions Strengthened By New Bill.*" Press Release (December 1). Washington, D.C.

Useem, Michael. *Investor Capitalism: How Money Managers Are Changing the Face of Corporate America*. New York: Basic Books, 1996: 277.

Van Derhei, Jack, and Kelly Olson. 1997. "Defined Contribution Dominance Grows across Sectors and Employer Sizes, while Mega-Defined Benefit Plans Remain Strong: Where We Are and Where We Are Going." Washington, D.C.: Employment Benefit Research Institute (October). EBRI Special Report SR-33.

Vogel, Thomas T. Jr. "Connecticut's Pension Fund May Incur Loss of Up to $25 Million on Derivatives." *Wall Street Journal*. (March 28, 1995): B4.

Wall Street Journal Reports. 1999. "Executive Pay." (April 9).

Wallman, Steven M.H. 1996. *Reflections on Shareholder Proposal: Correcting the Past: Thinking of the Future, The Council of Institutional Investors*. Speech. (October 8).

Warshawsky, Mark J. Financial Accounting and the Funding Status of Plans. In *Trends in Pension, 1992*, ed. John A. Turner and Daniel J. Beller. Washington, D.C,; U.S. Government Printing Office, 1992: 497–508.

Warshawsky, Mark, and John Amerikas. 2000. How Prepared Are Americans For Retirement? In *Forcasting Retirement Needs and Retirement Wealth*, ed. Olivia S. Mitchell, P. Brett Hammond, and Anna M. Rappaport. Philadelphia: The Pension Research Council, University of Pennsylvania Press, 2000: 33–67.

Watson, Isamu, and Rich Ferlauto. *Investment Intermediaries: Model State Programs*. Washington, D.C.: Center for Policy Alternatives, 1995.

Watson, Rip. "Overnite Spinoff Postponed; Owner Cites Falling Stock Prices." *Journal of Commerce* (August 3, 1998).

Williams, Cynthia A. "The Securities and Exchange Commission and Corporate Social Transparency." *Harv. Law Rev.* 112 (April 1999): 1199.

Williams, Terry. "Big Union Funds Still Avoiding Private Equity." *Pension & Investments* (May 4, 1998): 20.

Working Capital 10. 1998. "Worker Capital Finds Its Ownership Voice in 1998.": 1.

Working Capital 5. 1999. "Which Worker-Friendly Funds Live Up to Their Name?": 2.

Working Opportunity Fund Newsletter. 1998. no. 6, 7, and 8.

Zahra, Shaker A. "Corporate Entrepreneurship and Financial Performance—The Case of Management Leveraged Buyouts." *Journal of Business Venturing* 10, no. 3 (May 1995): 225–47.

Zanglein, Jayne. 1992a. "Who's Minding Your Business." *Hofstra Labor Law Journal* 10, no. 1 (Fall 1992).

Zanglein, Jayne. 1992b. "Solely in Our Interest: Creating Maximum Benefits for Workers Through Prudent Pension Investments." 102–104 AFL-CIO Lawyers Coordinating Committee 1992. *Reprinted in Labor Law Exchange,* no. 11, 1992.

Zanglein, Jayne. "High-Performance Investing: Harnessing the Power of Pension Funds to Promote Economic Growth and Workplace Integrity." *Labor Lawyer* 11 59 (1995): 101–27.

Zanglein, Jayne. "Protecting Retirees While Encouraging Economically Targeted Investments." *Kansas Journal of Law & Public Policy* 5, no. 2 (Winter 1996).

Zanglein, Jayne. 1998. "From the Wall Street Walk to the Wall Street Talk: The Changing Face of Corporate Governance." *DePaul Bus. L.J.* 11 (1998): 43.

Zelinsk, Edward A. "Economically Targeted Investments: A Critical Analysis." *Kansas Journal of Law & Public Policy* (Winter 1997).

CONTRIBUTING AUTHORS

Dean Baker is currently a Senior Research Fellow at the Premble Center and a Research Associate at the Economic Policy Institute, both in Washington, D.C. Previously, he was a Senior Economist at the Economic Policy Institute. He does work in macroeconomics, financial markets, and Social Security. He is the author of the *Economic Reporting Review* (ERR), a weekly on-line commentary on media coverage of economic issues (http://www.fair.org/).

Eric Becker, C.F.A., is an equity analyst and Assistant Portfolio Manager and Editor of *Investing for a Better World*. Before joining Trillium Asset Management (formerly known as *Franklin Research & Development Corporation*) in Boston, Massachusetts, in 1993, he worked for Cultural Survival in Cambridge, Massachusetts, a human rights organization. Eric serves on the board of Interlock Media, a non-profit human rights and environmental media organization also based in Cambridge. He earned his B.A. from Haverford College in Haverford, Pennsylvania. He is a chartered financial analyst, and is a member of the Association for Investment Management and Research and the Boston Security Analysts Society.

Michael Calabrese is Director of the Public Assets Program at the New America Foundation, a non-partisan public policy institute in Washington, D.C. He has served previously as General Counsel of the Congressional Joint Economic Committee and as a Pension and Employee Benefits Counsel at the national American Federation of Labor-Congress of Industrial Organizations (AFL-CIO) in Washington, D.C. He has an M.B.A. and law degree from Stanford University in California and received a B.A. in Economics and Government from Harvard College in Cambridge, Massachusetts, in 1979.

Archon Fung is an Assistant Professor of Public Policy at Harvard University's John F. Kennedy School of Government in Cambridge, Massachusetts. Before this appointment, he was a Senior Associate at the Center on Wisconsin Strategy (COWS) in Madison. He writes on the deliberative-democratic reorganization of large public institutions, such as urban school and police systems and environmental agencies. He co-edited *Institutions of Justice: Constitutionalism, Democracy, and State Power* (Edward Elgar, 1996) with Joshua Cohen. At COWS, he worked on the Milwaukee Jobs Initiative, a project that moves vulnerable workers into family supporting careers, and the Labor-Capital Initiative, a project that explores the responsible investment of worker pension funds. He recently earned his Ph.D. in Political Science from the Massachusetts Institute of Technology in Cambridge, Massachusetts, and received an S.B.s in Physics and Philosophy from the Massachusetts Institute of Technology in 1990.

Teresa Ghilarducci is an Associate Professor of Economics at the University of Notre Dame in Indiana. She is a presidential appointee on the Pension Benefit Guaranty Corporation's Advisory Board and was appointed by Indiana Governor Frank O'Bannon to serve on the Board of Trustees of the State of Indiana Public Employees Pension Fund. Professor Ghilarducci directs the Higgins Labor Research Center, a multidisciplinary center at the University of Notre Dame that focuses on scholarship and teaching about the living standards of workers. Her book, *Labor's Capital: The Economics and Politics of Employer Pensions* (MIT Press, 1992), won an American Publisher Association's award for business books of 1992. In 1995, she co-authored a study of multi-employer pension plans, *Portable Pension Plans for Casual Labor Markets* (Greenwood Press), with an introduction by former Labor Secretary Ray Marshall.

Tessa Hebb was Co-Chair of the Research Task Force for the Heartland Labor Capital Project. She is an independent consultant and President of Hebb, Knight and Associates in Ottawa, Canada. Ms. Hebb is a Visiting Scholar at Carleton University, Ottawa, Canada, where she is developing a national Pension Fund Trustee Education Program. She has an extensive background in public policy research. As an independent economic consultant, Ms. Hebb works with trade unions in Canada and the United States with a particular focus on investment and pension funds. Ms. Hebb is President of the Douglas-Coldwell Foundation, a foundation for research and education in support of the social democratic movement in Canada. She is also the President of the Virtual Institute, an Internet-based think tank that explores current policy issues and the values that drive policy choices. She obtained her M.A. in Public Administration, specializing in International Finance, from Harvard University in Cambridge, Massachusetts. Recent publications include *Just Making Change,* a collection of essays on Canada's financial sector (The Golden Dog Press, 1999).

David Mackenzie works for the Canadian section of the United Steelworkers of America as Executive Director of the Steelworkers Humanity Fund. He has previously served the union as an organizer, a political and legislative representative, and as an executive assistant to two of the union's national directors. He has been a member of the board of directors of Ontario's Workers Compensation Board (1989–1990), and has served as a special advisor to the Premier of Ontario (1994–1995). He was a member of the national executive of the New Democratic Party from 1985 to 1995.

J. W. Mason is completing his doctoral studies at the University of Massachusetts at Amherst. He was Editor of *Working Capital*, the newsletter of the Center for Working Capital in Washington, D.C. Prior to this position, he edited *Rebuilding Chicago*, a newsletter monitoring the city budget and public services. His articles have appeared in publications including *The American Prospect*, *The Nation*, and the *Chicago Reader*. He has a B.A. in History from the University of Chicago.

Patrick McVeigh is the Executive Vice President and Senior Portfolio Manager for Trillium Asset Management (formerly known as *Franklin Research & Development Corporation*) in Boston, Massachusetts. In addition, he serves as Managing Editor of Trillium's *Investing for a Better World* investment newsletter. He has been employed at Trillium since its founding in 1982. He also serves on the Board of Directors of SEED, a community development loan fund that supports new business development among the peasant community in Haiti. He has written and spoken extensively in the field of socially responsible investing.

Marleen O'Connor is a Professor of Law at Stetson University College of Law in St. Petersburg, Florida. She has also practiced securities law as an Associate at the law firm of King and Spalding in Atlanta, Georgia. She joined the Stetson faculty in August 1988. Her fields of interest include real property, business associations, securities regulation, and law and economics. She has published several articles concerning the role of employees in the corporate structure. Professor O'Connor graduated first in a class of 999 at DePaul University in Chicago, Illinois.

William Patterson is the Director of the American Federation of Labor-Congress of Industrial Organizations (AFL-CIO) Office of Investment in Washington, D.C. He was hired in 1996 by the new leadership of the AFL-CIO to create a new office to provide investment management and corporate governance services to collectively bargained pension and benefit plans. The Office of Investment provides assistance in proxy voting and shareholder advocacy and works with investment professionals and fund service providers. It evaluates investment performance and investment vehicles to meet fund objectives, provides asset allocation strategies, and offers legal, regulatory, and legislative advice and membership financial services. Mr. Patterson served as Co-Chair of the Council of Institutional Investors from 1994 to 1996 and has been a member of its Executive Committee since 1988.

Joel Rogers is the John D. MacArthur Professor of Law, Political Science, and Sociology at the University of Wisconsin-Madison, where he also directs the Center on Wisconsin Strategy (COWS), a policy research institute and project incubator dedicated to promoting sustainable development. Rogers has written widely on American politics and public policy, political theory, and U.S. and comparative industrial relations. His most recent books are *What Workers Want* (Cornell University Press, 1999) and *Metro Futures* (Beacon Press, 1999). A long-time social and political activist, Rogers was the founder and First Chair of Sustainable America in New York, New York; the Center for a New Democracy; and the New Party in Brooklyn, New York. A recipient of one of the MacArthur Foundation's "genius" grants, he was recently identified by *Newsweek* as one of the one-hundred Americans most likely to affect U.S. politics and culture in the twenty-first century.

Damon Silvers is an Associate General Counsel for the American Federation of Labor-Congress of Industrial Organizations (AFL-CIO) in Washington, D.C. Mr. Silvers works closely with the AFL-CIO's Office of Investment and the Center for Working Capital and has represented the AFL-CIO and the Trade Union Advisory Committee to the Organization for Economic Cooperation and Development. Before working for the AFL-CIO, Mr. Silvers was a Law Clerk at the Delaware Court of Chancery for Chancellor William T.

Allen and Vice-Chancellor Bernard Balick. Mr. Silvers has previously worked in the Mergers and Acquisitions Department at Credit Suisse First Boston for the law firm of Cravath, Swaine & Moore; the Enforcement Division of the United States Securities and Exchange Commission in Washington, D.C.; and in the General Counsel's office at the International Brotherhood of Teamsters in Washington, D.C. Mr. Silvers has also been the Assistant Director of the Office of Corporate and Financial Affairs for the Amalgamated Clothing and Textile Workers Union and the Research Director for the Harvard Union of Clerical and Technical Workers, American Federation of State, County, and Municipal Employees (AFSCME). Mr. Silvers received his J.D. with honors from Harvard Law School and an M.B.A. with high honors from Harvard Business School, both in Cambridge, Massachusetts. Mr. Silvers is a graduate of Harvard College, summa cum laude, and has studied history at Kings College, Cambridge University, in England.

Jayne Elizabeth Zanglein is the J. Hadley Edgar Professor of Law at Texas Tech University School of Law in Lubbock, Texas. As an attorney, she has specialized in job-creating pension investments since the 1980s. She was a member of New York Governor Cuomo's Task Force on Pension Investments and Co-Chair of the American Bar Association Task Force on Social Investing. Professor Zanglein has written numerous articles on economically targeted investments, as well as a book written for the American Federation of Labor-Congress of Industrial Organizations (AFL-CIO): *Solely in Our Interest: Creating Maximum Benefits for Workers through Prudent Pension Fund Investments* (AFL-CIO, 1992). She currently coordinates the Investment Strategies for Employee Benefits Program at the George Meany Center in Silver Spring, Maryland.

INDEX

Page numbers followed by *f* indicate figures; numbers followed by *t* indicate tables.